What a fantastic tool to ensure school districts will be successful in increasing student performance and implementing academic improvement! The authors have used their understanding of the current issues in education today to provide districts with comprehensive guidelines that will guarantee success for schools involved in action research. In our district, this book will serve as road map and compass for our journey with Whole-Faculty Study Groups.

Cynthia Wendell
Superintendent
Holdrege Public Schools
Holdrege, NE

In an age of increasing accountability, it's more important than ever that schools focus on leadership and learning to become Professional Learning Communities (PLC). This book provides a practical guide and framework for using Whole Faculty Study Groups (WFSG) to help schools create the foundation of a PLC. Hawthorn School District has used the WFSG model in our journey to become a PLC for over four years, with some of our schools using WFSGs for nearly ten years.

Clauset, Lick, and Murphy get to the heart of continuous improvement and closing the knowing-doing gap with this powerful tool. I hope after reading this book you will be the catalyst in building your school's leadership capacity through collaborative teams . . . teams that engage in collective inquiry and take the necessary action to increase student achievement.

Susan Zook, Ed.D.
Associate Superintendent/Superintendent Elect
Hawthorn School District 73
Vernon Hills, IL

Using this resource will accelerate the transition from an adult-driven system to a student-driven system. The authors lay out a practical and effective framework for continuous improvement. And the many case studies provide meaningful word pictures of effective practices.

We've been using Whole-Faculty Study Groups (WFSGs) for the past seven years in our district, and it has proven to be an effective vehicle for job-embedded professional learning. We will employ this new resource to take us to the next level!

Anita Kissinger
Executive Director, Quality and Development
Springfield Public Schools
Springfield, MO

I recommend this book highly, for both aspiring and beginning principals and those with years of experience. It's a helpful guide for the newly-assigned principal who has inherited a veteran staff that appears unwilling to change. This book clearly shows the success that can result when a staff learns together. I could have used these supportive facts and ideas years ago when I went into the process blindly. This would have been a great resource.

Paul Young, Ph.D.
Executive Director
West After School Center
Lancaster, Ohio
Past President, National Association of
Elementary School Principals (NAESP)

SCHOOLWIDE ACTION RESEARCH

for

Professional Learning Communities

Improving Student Learning Through The Whole-Faculty Study Groups Approach

KARL H. CLAUSET • DALE W. LICK • CARLENE U. MURPHY

Foreword by Bert L'Homme

CORWIN PRESS
A SAGE Company
Thousand Oaks, CA 91320

For information:

Corwin Press
A SAGE Company
2455 Teller Road
Thousand Oaks, California 91320
www.corwinpress.com

SAGE Ltd.
1 Oliver's Yard
55 City Road
London EC1Y 1SP
United Kingdom

SAGE Pvt. Ltd.
B 1/I 1 Mohan Cooperative Industrial Area
Mathura Road, New Delhi 110 044
India

SAGE Asia-Pacific Pte. Ltd.
33 Pekin Street #02-01
Far East Square
Singapore 048763

Printed in the United States of America.

Library of Congress Cataloging-in-Publication Data

Clauset, Karl H.
Schoolwide action research for professional learning communities: improving student learning through the whole-faculty study groups approach/by Karl H. Clauset, Dale W. Lick, and Carlene U. Murphy.
      p. cm.
Includes bibliographical references and index.
ISBN 978-1-4129-5207-1 (cloth)
ISBN 978-1-4129-5208-8 (pbk.)
    1. Action research in education—United States. 2. School improvement programs—United States. I. Lick, Dale W. II. Murphy, Carlene U. III. Title.

LB1028.24.C54 2008
370.7'2—dc22   2008004888

This book is printed on acid-free paper.

08   09   10   11   12   10 9 8 7 6 5 4 3 2 1

Acquisitions Editor:	Dan Alpert
Editorial Assistant:	Tatiana Richards
Production Editor:	Veronica Stapleton
Copy Editor:	Tina Hardy
Typesetter:	C&M Digitals (P) Ltd.
Proofreader:	Joyce Li
Indexer:	Naomi Linzer
Cover Designer:	Scott Van Atta

Contents

List of Tables and Figures

Chapter 6

Chapter 7

Chapter 8

Resources

Foreword

Education reform is rampant these days. Everybody wants school improvement. Educators, parents, politicians, public—they want it, we want it, and all of us want it now. From the lowest performing to the highest ranking school districts, the focus is on increasing student achievement. That is as it should be, of course; even as we reach our goals, we set higher, shinier, greater goals for our students to reach. To reach these lofty goals we have a myriad of tools spread before us. How do we choose the right ones?

Three years ago Franklin County Schools (North Carolina) embarked on a school reform effort that has been no less than transformational. Our plan was not a haphazard choice or a lucky draw. We took careful stock of where we were, where we wanted to go, and the obstacles in our way.

Franklin County is a historically rural district with deep roots in the tobacco industry that is struggling with becoming a fast-growing suburban community. Our school system employs talented district- and school-level administrators as well as motivated, well-trained, and dedicated teachers. The school board is both insistent and supportive as we "ratchet up" student expectations. We want all our students to graduate with choices for their future and to be well prepared for their chosen paths: college, vocational training, and work.

Soon after I became superintendent of Franklin County Schools, I found I had a committed cadre of educational leaders among district staff and principals as eager and enthusiastic as I was to make the changes we needed. This core team was our starting point. We realized if meaningful reform was going to happen, it had to happen at the teacher level. In fact, it had to happen within small groups of teachers working within professional learning communities. We surveyed the field and set out on a path that led us to Whole-Faculty Study Groups® (WFSG) and Carlene Murphy.

In the summer of 2004, Dianne Carter, a dynamic curriculum administrator on my staff, attended a WFSG institute in Augusta, Georgia. She brought back a contagious enthusiasm and a strategy for school reform that starts with teachers. By early August we decided to invite Carlene to come to North Carolina and present a plan for us to introduce the WFSG model into our schools. She came and met with teachers, principals, and central office staff and gave us the tools to turn our school improvement goals into reality.

Imagine the impact when every teacher, principal, and central office administrator participates in a small group that focuses on increasing student achievement. Experienced educators know that good things happen when the main topic of conversation centers on student work and student achievement.

Implementing new programs can be accomplished the wrong way and the right way. Telling teachers they will meet twice each month and discuss student achievement is a surefire guarantee for failure. Too many veteran teachers have seen too many poorly conceived or badly executed "reform" plans to buy into empty models. On the other hand, arranging for teachers to meet together twice each month, giving them protocols for examining student work, and assisting them in selecting strategies, administering pretests and posttests, and analyzing tests results is a formula for real success.

Clauset, Lick, and Murphy's new book is both a chronicle of what happened in Franklin County and several other school systems that implemented Whole-Faculty Study Groups and a guide to help us improve the schoolwide action research process that is at the heart of WFSG. It describes the process from deciding to adopt professional learning communities through the stress and successes of implementing a new program. The strength of WFSG and this book leads your faculty beyond initial implementation to fine-tuning and long-term maintenance.

Educators know the surest way to destroy an initiative is to implement haphazardly and not provide ongoing training and oversight. This book accomplishes both by providing strategies for ensuring fidelity of implementation and vehicles for continuous training and program oversight.

The program described in this book is not mere reform—results are nothing less than transformational. Just like any new program there will be a strong cadre of teachers who get on board immediately, the next group will wait and see if the initial results are positive, and of course there will be a few who refuse to get on board at all. The process of follow-up and support described in this book acknowledges this dynamic and provides strategies for teachers, principals, and district staff at every stage of implementation and operation.

Educators are prone to selecting programs and strategies that promise great results over a short period of time. Experience and research indicate that quick academic gains are not sustained from year to year. WFSG are not a quick fix, but if implemented faithfully, the results sustained from year to year will be twofold: (1) improved teacher practice and (2) increased student achievement.

The WFSG System is based on the notion that teachers' practice, what teachers teach and how they teach, must improve to reach the academic goals set by state houses and the U.S. Congress. Teachers and administrators respect the WFSG approach because the process is rooted in small groups of caring, talented, and dedicated teachers working from a structured and predictable rubric.

If you choose to implement professional learning communities and specifically WFSG, get ready for a great adventure that will surely lead to achieving the single most important goal in education—increasing student achievement.

I would like to express my appreciation to Franklin County Schools' teachers, principals, and administrators who work tirelessly to ensure that all children achieve academically.

Bert L'Homme, PhD (University of Maryland)
Superintendent, Franklin County Schools
53 West River Road
Louisburg, NC 27495
bertlhomme@fcschools.net

In Memory of
Dianne Carter
1951–2008
Director of Elementary Education
Franklin County Schools
Louisburg, NC

Preface

This is a "how-to" book on developing professional learning communities and using schoolwide action research to improve teacher practice and enhance student learning.

Professional learning communities hold great promise for changing the face of traditional professional development practices. A key part of the professional learning communities that are discussed in this book is the concept of continuous professional development. Continuous professional development, in which teachers are given time to collaborate with colleagues and update knowledge and skills and are expected to assume much of the responsibility, with the assistance of their principal and district leaders, for their own professional growth and development, has been identified by teachers as a critical element in school reform (Office of Technology Assessment, U.S. Congress, 1995). The National Staff Development Council's (2001) Standards for Staff Development call for teachers to be working in learning communities and engaged in staff development that improves learning for all students.

The Whole-Faculty Study Group (WFSG) System is a professional learning communities design that has schoolwide action research as its central component. In conducting schoolwide action research, the whole school is a professional learning community as is each study group within the school. "Learning" is the key word and in the WFSG design, because students, teachers, and administrators, individually and collectively, are learning.

The WFSG system is one of the successful professional learning community designs for academic school improvement available today. When applied properly, it has resulted in significant student results. The WFSG System evolved from a need to increase student achievement by changing the norms of how teachers work together and how new teaching strategies become routine teaching practices. This work began in Augusta, Georgia, in 1987, when Carlene Murphy was director of staff development for the Richmond County School District. Murphy engaged Bruce Joyce and Beverly Showers to train staff in different models of teaching. The issues addressed in 1987 by Joyce, Showers, Murphy, and her district colleagues still concern educators today: How do we ensure that high-quality professional development leads to substantive changes in what teachers teach and how they teach and that these changes result in improved student learning?

When fully executed, the WFSG design or system contains several approaches to professional development: theory and knowledge development, action research, coaching and mentoring, lesson study, practicing, modeling, and demonstrating teaching and learning skills and strategies, and looking at student work. The component of the WFSG System that is magnified and examined in this book is action research, using data about student learning to determine what teachers will learn and do and to determine the effects of teacher actions in classrooms.

PURPOSE AND NEED

This book is the third volume published by Corwin Press about WFSG. Each book may be used as a "stand-alone" text.

The first book, now in its third edition, is *Whole-Faculty Study Groups: Creating Professional Learning Communities That Target Student Learning,* by Carlene U. Murphy and Dale W. Lick (2005). This book describes the WFSG System in detail and the research base undergirding WFSG. It provides detailed information on how to launch WFSG in a school with a step-by-step guide for schools to use. It also contains more than 100 pages of resource materials and examples for schools to use.

The second book is *The Whole-Faculty Study Groups Fieldbook: Improving Schools and Enhancing Student Learning* by Dale W. Lick and Carlene U. Murphy (2007). This book is primarily focused on firsthand experiences by teachers, principals, instructional specialists, district office staff, superintendents, and staff in other organizations with implementing the WFSG System. The book also includes an overview of the WFSG System and the action research cycle that study groups use.

The purpose of this third book is to pull out the successful schoolwide action research approach found in the WFSG System to provide a powerful new methodology for creating professional learning communities that improve teacher practice and student learning. This new schoolwide action research approach has the potential to help create, strengthen, and focus professional learning communities in schools and districts and deepen administrators', teachers', and students' understanding of and ability to use and support meaningful action research processes for improving schools and enhancing student learning. In this book, the many concepts and methods modeled in this action research approach will provide an array of new understandings and tools for implementing major and successful academic school improvement and increased student performance.

In particular, this action research book will demonstrate how the critical concepts in the process can be applied in a wide variety of school reform efforts; provide a broad array of relevant strategies, concepts, and activities; help readers bring ideas to life by illustrating how to use and apply them in their "real-world situations"; contain firsthand case studies that highlight the details of how concepts worked for a variety of activities and in different settings; and offer tips, strategies, and lessons learned on a wide range of pertinent approaches, processes, circumstances, problem areas, and concepts and ideas.

The case studies and examples in this book are drawn primarily from study groups in the elementary, middle, and high schools in the United States and Canada that Clauset and Murphy have worked with over the past five years. Just as there are more elementary schools than high schools, there are more examples of study group work in this book from elementary and middle schools than there are from high schools.

However, the small school movement, creating small high schools out of large high schools, has created a new opportunity—to create a new school with the WFSG System as an integral part of its design. The grade 7–12 Daniel Hale Williams Preparatory School of Medicine in Chicago is the first school created with WFSG as part of its design.

WHO SHOULD READ AND USE THIS BOOK?

The primary audience for this book are the key players involved in school reform and school improvement. This book provides them with concrete and practical suggestions for focusing professional learning communities in schools to improve teacher practice and student learning by using schoolwide action research. The most natural audiences and potential users of this book would be all who have been involved or are becoming involved with academic school change, for example, school systems and districts, individual schools, administrators, teachers, educational consultants, and higher education faculty and students. This action research book would be an especially valuable addition to every school and college library.

In addition, since this book provides a wide variety of experiences, examples, and illustrations of concepts and approaches common to most academic school reform and improvement efforts, it should be of particular value to anyone seriously interested in school improvement. Specifically, this book will be unique in its approach, broadly understandable, and relevant to those who want to lead, be involved in or support school improvement, and increase student performance levels now and in the foreseeable future.

In particular, teacher leaders and principals might use the book to deepen and strengthen their application of schoolwide action research; central office staff to understand what they need to do to support schools in their study group approaches; state department of education staff to support school and district efforts to engage in this work, as Louisiana has done; those in higher education to prepare teachers to do schoolwide action research and work synergistically in teams; policy makers to shape policies that support professional learning communities doing action research to improve practice and learning; union leaders and district leaders to negotiate contracts that enable and support this work rather than hinder it.

This book is especially applicable to those already utilizing, or planning to utilize, the WFSG System. However, it is equally applicable to those involved with other school-change approaches encompassing action research and professional learning communities for increasing student learning and improving teacher practice.

ORGANIZATION AND CONTENTS

The book has two sections. The first section introduces the concept of schoolwide action research in Chapter 1, describes the WFSG approach to schoolwide action research, and compares the WFSG approach to other action research approaches in Chapter 2. Chapter 3 explores the theoretical underpinnings for creating learning teams and learning communities, and compares the WFSG System with DuFour and Eaker's design (1998) for professional learning communities. While the primary focus of this book is on the explication of the WFSG approach to schoolwide action research, we feel it is important to the reader to show in Chapter 2 how the WFSG approach is similar to and different from other approaches to action research.

The second section, Chapters 4–9 and the Resources, is the "how-to" section for practitioners. It builds on the description of the WFSG System for school-wide action research in Chapters 1–3 to explore in depth the action research that study groups do (Chapter 4), its impact on changing teacher practice and student learning (Chapters 5 and 6), and how principals, district leaders, and external organizations support school staff and their study groups (Chapters 7 and 8). Chapter 9 builds on the other chapters in this section to explore challenges ahead for continuing to refine and strengthen the WFSG approach to school-wide action research. The Resources section provides supplementary materials that expand on material in Chapters 4–8.

The chapters in this book are organized around the following Guiding Questions:

Chapter 1

- What is schoolwide action research?

Chapter 2

- How does the WFSG approach to schoolwide action research compare with other approaches to action research?

Chapter 3

- Do schools implementing schoolwide action research function as professional learning communities and do their study groups function as learning teams?
- How do study groups become active learning teams and schools become professional learning communities to improve teacher practice and enhance student learning?

Chapter 4

- What are the steps in the schoolwide action research process, and what do study groups do at each step?
- Does the schoolwide action research process change depending on whether a school is elementary, middle, or high school?

Chapter 5

- How do study groups move from discussion to action that improves teacher practice?

Chapter 6

- Does schoolwide action research lead to improvements in student learning as measured by classroom, school, district, and state assessments?

Chapter 7

- How do principals and other school leaders support schoolwide action research?

Chapter 8

- **How do district leaders support schoolwide action research in district schools?**
- **What resources are available to help schools and districts do schoolwide action research?**

Chapter 9

- **What are the challenges for taking the WFSG approach to schoolwide action research to the next level?**

The following paragraphs briefly describe the contents of each chapter.

Chapter 1 discusses the meaning of schoolwide action research and its importance as a tool to help schools and districts improve and enhance student learning. It also introduces the reader to the essential elements and key success factors of the WFSG System.

Chapter 2 focuses on what the WFSG approach to schoolwide action research actually looks like and how it is similar to and different from other approaches to action research.

Chapter 3 develops a perspective for learning teams and learning communities by providing a greater understanding of the concepts of change, learning, and synergy and their implementation as part of the process to create professional learning communities in schools. The chapter also compares WFSG professional learning communities with DuFour and Eaker's (1998) design for professional learning communities.

Chapter 4 describes in detail the action research process that WFSG study groups use to increase their effectiveness as teachers and improve student learning.

Chapter 5 explains how the work of study groups in the WFSG System leads to improvements in teacher practice and why those improvements only occur if study groups of teachers go beyond "business as usual," beyond a superficial application of the action research process and minor tinkering in classrooms with what they teach and how they teach.

Chapter 6 shows how WFSG study groups address the "bottom line" for school-wide action research—improving student performance each year, every year, in the specific student-learning needs that the school's faculty has chosen to address in their study groups.

Chapter 7 explains how the principal and other school leaders are key to ensuring the success of schoolwide action research and the creation of professional learning communities, leading to improved teacher practices and increased student learning.

Chapter 8 builds on policy makers' recent realization that schools operate within districts and the district context and that district support is fundamental to the enhancement or inhibition of the efforts of principals and their faculty to engage in schoolwide action research to improve student learning. The chapter also describes the roles that external organizations are playing in supporting districts and schools in implementing a system for schoolwide action research.

Chapter 9 explores the challenges of taking schoolwide action research and support for this approach to the next level. In this chapter we explore sets of questions in four areas: understanding the WFSG System as a bundle of innovations, teachers' transfer and use of content and pedagogy from learning in professional development opportunities to skillful use in classrooms, providing support for study groups, and sustaining changes, such as WFSG, over time.

The book concludes with an epilogue by the creator of the WFSG System, Carlene U. Murphy, that offers her overarching thinking on the WFSG System for schoolwide action research, the building of professional learning communities, and the improvement of student learning and teacher practices.

We hope this book inspires you to engage in, or support, schoolwide action research which creates a collaborative culture that improves teacher practice and student learning.

Acknowledgments

First and foremost, we acknowledge the individuals in schools, districts, state departments of education, and other organizations in the United States and Canada engaged in the implementation of the WFSG System of schoolwide action research who have shared their ideas and artifacts with us as we developed this book. It is their work that has enabled us to refine our thinking about the WFSG System and illustrate this book with a rich array of examples.

Some of the people in the WFSG "family" whom we would like to acknowledge for their contributions to this book include the following:

- Franklin County Schools—Bert L'Homme, Eddie Ingram, Dianne Carter, Jewel Eason, Kim Ferrell, Rob Bendel, and the study groups from Royal Elementary, Laurel Mill Elementary, and Bunn Elementary, especially the Radical Readers.
- Springfield Public Schools—Anita Kissinger, Nancy Hopkins, Sheila Lovewell, Vicki Ricketts, Bret Range, Jonathan Apostol, Ron Snodgrass, and Lynne Miller.
- Gill-Montague Regional School District—Sue Gee and Jeffrey Kenney.
- Hawthorn School District 73—Sue Zook and John Ahlemeyer.
- Qualicum Beach Middle School—Don Boyd and Jessica Antosz.
- Western Harnett High School—Terry Hinson, Roberta Brown, and Denise King.
- Daniel Hale Williams Preparatory School of Medicine—Delores Bedar.
- Clarke Middle School—Ken Sherman.
- Louisiana Department of Education—Janet Langlois.
- Centers for Quality Teaching and Learning—Harold Brewer, Janice Johnson, Rachel Porter, and Pam Edwards.
- WFSG National Center—Terri Jenkins, Emily Weiskopf, and Lynn Baber.

The genesis of this book began with a chapter on action research that Karl Clauset wrote with Brenda Atwell from *ATLAS Learning Communities for the WFSG Fieldbook*, edited by Dale W. Lick and Carlene U. Murphy (2007). When the chapter was cut from the Fieldbook because of space limitations, the editors began conversations with Murphy, Lick, and Clauset about a third WFSG book on schoolwide action research.

We acknowledge our editors at Corwin Press, Rachel Livsey and Dan Alpert, for their initial encouragement of us to write this book and their guidance and support during the entire process, from idea to publication.

We thank our reviewers for taking time from their busy schedules to read our draft manuscript and to provide detailed and thoughtful feedback to us. We have incorporated many of their suggestions into the final version of the manuscript. Their thoughtful feedback has made this a better book. Our reviewers were as follows:

Yolanda Abel
Instructor, Johns Hopkins University
Baltimore, MD

Barb Keating
FW Howay Community School
New Westminster, BC, Canada

Marsha Speck
Professor, Educational Leadership/
Director of the Urban High School
Leadership Program
San Jose State University
San Jose, CA

Paul G. Young
Executive Director, West After School
Center
Lancaster, OH

About the Authors

Karl H. Clauset is Director of the National WFSG Center. He is an experienced school improvement coach and WFSG trainer. Since 1999 he has helped more than 50 elementary, middle, and high schools launch WFSG and has supported the schools through the implementation phase. He is also a senior consultant with Focus on Results and works with district offices in school systems to help them align and support reform efforts in schools. Previously, he worked as a site developer with ATLAS Learning Communities, a nationally recognized school reform program, and in standards-based reform and international education development at the Education Development Center.

In his earlier careers in education, he worked as a teacher and administrator at the Jakarta International School in Indonesia, and taught in secondary schools in Philadelphia, Zambia, and Tanzania. He received a national award from the Association for Supervision and Curriculum Development for the outstanding dissertation in supervision in 1983 for his doctoral dissertation on the dynamics of effective schooling. As a faculty member at the Boston University School of Education, he taught graduate courses in educational policy analysis, organizational analysis, and planning. Before moving to western Washington in 2003, he served as an elected school board member and board chair for six years in his Massachusetts community.

Dale W. Lick is a past president of Georgia Southern University, University of Maine, and Florida State University and is presently a university professor in the Learning Systems Institute at Florida State University. He teaches in the Department of Educational Leadership and Policy Studies and works on educational and organizational projects involving the WFSG System, school reform, school improvement, enhancement of student learning, transformational leadership, change creation, leading and managing change, learning teams, learning organizations, professional learning communities, distance learning, new learning systems (e.g., the HyLighter Learning, Assessment and Collaborative Document Preparation Systems), strategic planning, and visioning.

Included in over 50 national and international biographical listings, Dr. Lick is the author or coauthor of seven books and more than 90 professional articles and proceedings, and 285 original newspaper columns. Three of his recent books are *New Directions in Mentoring: Creating a Culture of Synergy* (with Carol A. Mullen), 1999;

Whole-Faculty Study Groups: Creating Professional Learning Communities That Target Student Learning (with Carlene U. Murphy), 2005; and *The Whole-Faculty Study Groups Fieldbook: Lessons Learned and Best Practices From Classrooms, Districts, and Schools* (coedited with Carlene U. Murphy), 2007.

Carlene U. Murphy is founder and executive director of the National WFSG Center and the principal developer of the WFSG System of professional development. In August 2007 she began her 50th year of work in public schools. She started her teaching career in 1957 as a fourth-grade teacher in her hometown of Augusta, Georgia, and retired from the district in 1993 as its director of staff development. During her 15 years as the district's chief staff developer, the district received many accolades, including the Award for Outstanding Achievement in Professional Development from the American Association of School Administrators and Georgia's Outstanding Staff Development Program Award for two consecutive years. She was awarded the National Staff Development Council's Contributions to Staff Development Award and served as the National Staff Development Council's chair of the annual national conference in Atlanta in 1986, president in 1988, and board member from 1984 to 1990.

After retiring from the Richmond County Schools, she has worked with schools throughout the United States implementing WFSG. She and her colleagues established the National WFSG Center in 2002, sponsoring the annual National WFSG Conference and WFSG Institutes and providing technical assistance to schools. She has written extensively about her work in *Educational Leadership* and *Journal of Staff Development* and has written, with Dale Lick, two other books about the WFSG System: *Whole-Faculty Study Groups: Creating Professional Learning Communities That Target Student Learning* (2005) and *The Whole-Faculty Study Groups Fieldbook: Lessons Learned and Best Practices from Classrooms, Districts, and Schools* (2007).

For our spouses
Julia B. Clauset
Marilyn K. Lick
Joseph A. Murphy
with grateful appreciation for their love, care, patience, support,
and encouragement for our efforts on this book

Introduction

1

Guiding Question

- **What is schoolwide action research?**

School improvement and increasing student achievement stand out as two of the most critical issues in education today. For real academic improvement in schools, the active and intimate involvement of teachers and administrators is essential. Teachers and administrators are the practitioners who must improve the school or it doesn't happen.

> The goal of teachers to be professional problem-solvers who are committed to improving both their own practice and student outcomes provides a powerful reason to practice action research.
>
> Geoffrey Mills (2007, p. 10)

In schools, the *action research* we are focused on in this book is practitioners working together to study and modify the teaching and learning systems to increase student learning, sustain the new learning level, and, as a result, improve the effectiveness of the school's staff.

Among many formal definitions of action research, we find two descriptive and helpful:

> Action research *is a disciplined process of inquiry conducted by and for those taking the action. The primary reason for engaging in action research is to assist the actor[s] in improving or refining his or her [their] actions.*
>
> Sagor (2000, p. 1)

> Action research *consists of planned, continuous, and systematic procedures for learning about your professional practice and for trying out alternative practices to improve outcomes.*
>
> Schmuck (2006, p. 29)

These are the general steps in an action research cycle: assess needs and establish baseline and target performance, research content and best practices and develop expertise, plan interventions, implement interventions and monitor, and look at student work and data and assess changes. Then practitioners evaluate student performance to decide whether to start a second action research cycle around the same student learning need or to start a new cycle focused on a different student learning need.

COLLABORATIVE ACTION RESEARCH

Action research can be done by individuals, *individual action research,* or by groups, *collaborative action research.* In this book, we deal with the latter, where the members of a group collaborate together to focus on a common concern or issue. Such a group is often called a "team," "study group," or a "professional learning community."

In collaborative action research, practitioners work together to become a team and develop synergy to inspire each other and gain new insight to, as Covey (1990, p. 264) says, "create a momentum toward more and more insight, learning and growth" relative to the issue they are addressing. We discuss in detail collaborative action research and the concepts of "teams," "synergy," "learning teams," and "professional learning communities" in Chapter 3.

SCHOOLWIDE ACTION RESEARCH

When a school staff decides that every teacher in the school will be involved in action research involving specific concerns, and action research efforts are coordinated across the school, the overall approach is referred to as *schoolwide action research.* Typically, administrators and teachers collectively determine priority concerns and study groups or teams are formed to focus on specific parts of these concerns.

Calhoun (1994, p. 11) describes three different purposes for schoolwide action research: improvement in equity for students so all students benefit, improvement in teaching so teaching practices improve in every classroom in a chosen area such as writing, and improvement in the school's ability to identify and solve problems which may relate to teaching and learning or other aspects of the school operations and culture.

In schoolwide action research, the faculty might decide that all teams will focus on improving one area of teaching and learning, such as improving the teaching of the writing process and students' writing performance, or they might decide that different groups will address different areas. For instance, one team might be focused on improving reading comprehension, while another team might take on using mathematics manipulatives to improve students' understanding of basic operations.

In this book, we concentrate specifically on collaborative action research in study groups and schoolwide action research across the school.

The following vignette describes how the staff of one school implemented schoolwide action research.

Schoolwide Action Research at Bunn Elementary School

At Bunn Elementary School, in Franklin County, North Carolina, the entire faculty is engaged in schoolwide action research to improve student learning.

Launching Schoolwide Action Research: At the beginning of the 2005–2006 school year, the entire faculty met to review data on student learning and develop a master list of student learning needs. After categorizing these needs, faculty members each identified a category of needs and specific student learning needs that they felt needed to be addressed during the school year for their students as they taught their grade-level curriculum. With these personal choices, faculty members then formed study groups of three to five members who wanted to work on the same category of student needs.

The following table shows the nine cross-grade, cross-content area groups that were formed and the student needs they addressed.

Radical Readers (Grades 3 & 4): • Recognize main idea • Identify author's purpose	Book Worms (Grades K & 2): • Identify and use rhyming words • Identify and create similes
Math Inspectors (Grades 1, 3, 4, & PE): • Demonstrate understanding of place value, greater and less than • Demonstrate mastery of basic math facts	Phoniacs (Grades PreK, K, ESL, & Speech/Language) • Discriminate rhyming vs. nonrhyming word pairs • Discriminate and identify beginning and ending sounds in real words
Math Investigators (Grades 1, 3, 4, & 5): • Use basic math facts in addition, subtraction, multiplication, and division • Extend and identify missing terms in algebraic patterns	Alpha (Grade 5, Spanish, Music, EC Resource): • Improve test-taking skills • Identify key words in a passage or question • Mark out incorrect answers • Circle unclear questions to return to later
Round Robins (Grades 2 & 5, CRT): • Write poems in correct sequence and form • Recall and retell facts from a story	Scribblers (Grades 1, 2, & 5): • Construct complete sentences • Use correct capitalization and punctuation
Green Science Sisters (Grade 2, AIG, EC Resource, Media, Art): • Understand key science concepts through hands-on engagement	

Note: K = kindergarten; PE = physical education; PreK = prekindergarten; ESL = English as a Second Language; EC Resource = Exceptional Children Resource; CRT = Curriculum Resource Teacher; AIG = Academically or Intellectually Gifted.

The Action Research Plan: The following week, individual study groups began hour-long weekly meetings. By the end of their third meeting, each group had developed an action plan to guide its work.

(Continued)

(Continued)

The groups also agreed to group norms to guide their work and rotation schedules for the weekly group leader and recorder and the group's representative to the first Instructional Council (i.e., the school's coordinating body for all study groups) meeting the following week, where the principal and study group representatives reviewed all of the school's study group action plans and gave constructive feedback. Each group's weekly log was posted next to the group's action plan on a bulletin board in the school entrance hall for all to see and the principal gave regular supportive and constructive written feedback to each group.

Action Research Cycle No. 1: Over the next two to four meetings, each group decided which of their specific student needs to address first, identified or developed a simple classroom assessment task to give to students to collect data on how well their students currently perform on the need, used a scoring rubric or checklist to assess student work, developed specific performance targets to achieve by the end of the semester in December, and updated their action plans with the baseline and target data. Groups shared their assessment tasks, rubrics, results, and targets at a second Instructional Council meeting.

Then groups began the "real" work—changing what they taught and how they taught to improve student learning in the specific need area each group chose to address first. During this period from October through December, groups followed cycles of "plan-act-reflect"—planning at their study group meetings what to do differently in class, acting in class to implement the lesson plans and strategies, reflecting in the next study group meeting on the effectiveness of the lesson plan or strategy and planning next steps.

Groups used teachers' guides, the Internet, the school's instructional specialist, and district content specialists as resources to help them identify research and best practices related to their student learning needs and updated their action plans with the new resources they identified. Groups regularly readministered the baseline assessment task to students and examined samples of student work to understand how the changes they were making in their classes were affecting student thinking and understanding. In November, representatives from all of the study groups met for a third Instructional Council meeting to share interventions and what they were learning about improving student learning.

As the semester drew to a close in December, each study group gave students an assessment task similar to the one used in September to determine whether their students met their targets. Groups reflected on the results and effectiveness of the strategies they used, decided whether to continue working as a group on the same learning need during the second semester or switch to another need, and updated their action plan with the actual results. After the holidays in January, groups shared their first semester results and effective strategies at a faculty meeting.

Action Research Cycle No. 2: The action research cycle began again in January. Groups that decided to continue working on the same student learning need used the actual December results as their baseline data for the second semester, set targets for May, updated their action plans, and started planning for new interventions to boost performance for students who still had not achieved proficiency.

Groups that decided to work on a different student need identified or developed a new classroom assessment task to give to students to collect data on how well their students currently performed on the need. They also developed a scoring rubric or checklist to assess student work, developed specific performance targets to be achieved by the end of the semester in May, and updated their action plans with the baseline and target data. All groups shared their second semester assessment tasks, rubrics, results, and targets at a fourth Instructional Council meeting in late January.

During February, March, and April, study groups continued to research, identify, and develop interventions to change what they taught and how they taught and to engage in the "plan-act-reflect" cycle around these interventions. They shared interventions and what they were learning about improving student learning at a fifth Instructional Council meeting in March.

In May, as the school year came to an end, each study group gave students an assessment task similar to the one used in December and January to determine whether their students met their targets. Each study group reflected on the results and the effectiveness of the strategies they used and updated their action plan with the actual results.

Year-End Reflection, Sharing, and Planning: Each group summarized their reflections on their work over the year and its impact on changing their teaching practices and student learning. They also completed a year-end survey on the Whole-Faculty Study Groups® (WFSG) process at Bunn Elementary. The principal created a booklet with each study group's reflections, results, and action plans to share with staff and with district leaders. This booklet documented study group successes and reinforced the link between study group work and successes in improving teaching and learning.

The school held a half-day celebration to honor and share the accomplishments of all study groups. At the celebration, faculty were told that WFSG would continue for the 2006–2007 school year, the list of schoolwide student learning needs would be updated based on 2005–2006 data, and in the 2006–2007 school year, study groups could continue to work together on the same or different student needs or dissolve and regroup.

Source: Used with permission from Jewel Eason, Bunn Elementary School.

WHOLE-FACULTY STUDY GROUPS

The approach to schoolwide action research used by the staff at Bunn Elementary School is the WFSG System developed by Carlene Murphy. The WFSG approach to schoolwide action research is the focus of this book. All of the illustrations and examples given in subsequent chapters come from schools that are using the WFSG System.

The WFSG System has its origins in a professional development and school improvement program for schools in the Richmond County, Augusta, Georgia, school district.

In January 1987, when Bruce Joyce and Beverly Showers came to Augusta to work with Carlene Murphy, the director of staff development, and her district colleagues, they established goals that educators everywhere struggle to achieve today. As stated by Joyce, Murphy, Showers, and Murphy (1989), "we wanted to learn how to redesign the workplace of teaching so that students would learn more" (p. 70). Over a four-year period, they examined the following:

- Culture of schools
- Process of innovation
- Ways teachers learn new teaching strategies
- Ways teachers transfer new skills into the classroom
- Models of teaching

The superintendent, John Strelec, had the courage to publicly support the goals with high expectations that everyone would work together to implement the school improvement design being developed. By designing the workplace so that teachers worked in small collaborative groups focusing on how they taught (models of teaching) and what they taught, at the end of four years of working with the whole faculty in three schools, Joyce, Murphy, and Showers were able to document the following:

1. Changes in the culture of schools

2. Implementation and sustained use of new teaching strategies

3. Higher levels of teacher accountability for what teachers had been trained to do

4. Increases in student learning as measured by teacher-made assessments and standardized measures

5. More students promoted on merit

6. Fewer student referrals to the office for disciplinary action

The work is chronicled in a series of articles and chapters in books (Joyce, B., Weil, M., & Showers, B., 1992; Joyce et al., 1989; Joyce, B., Murphy, C., Showers, B., & Murphy, J., 1989; Murphy, 1992, 1995; Murphy, J., Murphy, C., Joyce, & Showers, 1988; Showers, B., Murphy, C. & Joyce, B., 1996).

After Murphy's retirement from the district in 1993, she has spent the last 15 years expanding and refining the whole-faculty small group structure Joyce, Murphy, and Showers introduced to the Augusta schools. Because Joyce was not part of the development work after 1992, models of teaching was no longer a component of the design. In schools where she has worked since 1993, the faculty, in their study groups, identified the content and pedagogy they used to address student-learning needs. The challenge was, and still is, to help districts and schools define appropriate content and pedagogy for the teacher study groups to use.

During Murphy's work in San Diego, from 1993 to 1995, the first version of the WFSG Decision-Making Cycle was developed. It was in San Diego that she began calling the work, Whole-Faculty Study Groups (Murphy, 1995). The Decision-Making Cycle (DMC) was developed to lead faculties to what study groups would do; however, the quality and substance of study group work was left unresolved until we put more work into Step 6 on the DMC, what we now refer to as the action research cycle. This shift began around 2001 and is clearly reflected in the differences between the action plan and log formats in the second and third editions of Murphy and Lick (2001, 2005, respectively). The action plan and log formats in this book are different from those in the third edition. With each iteration, we have sought to make the action research process more explicit and more rigorous.

Joyce and Showers (1983) indicate that it takes as many as 20 trials before a user of a strategy gains executive control and appropriate use of the strategy. WFSG trainers have certainly practiced what they preach. Before sharing what they have learned from guiding faculties through the DMC and particularly the action research cycle in Step 6, they have practiced with many faculties.

The WFSG System is a standardized set of procedures that any working group could use to manage group dynamics and logistics. Most of the guidelines or procedures were initially developed for the Augusta schools, making the standardization of the guidelines a 20-year process. It is these procedures that define WFSG for those who have not implemented the system. Many nonusers seem to think that we are only interested in organizing faculties into study groups. We know that simply having all teachers in groups that meet with some regularity will accomplish little in terms of changing teacher behaviors. The process without substantive content has little value.

Those implementing the system know that the guidelines only provide a structure for working on the work of teaching and learning. The heart of the system and what drives the system is what groups do when they meet. If collaboration does not result in teachers becoming more skillful in how they teach and more knowledgeable of what they teach so all students will learn more, the time spent in meetings may become questionable. The action research cycle builds accountability into the WFSG System.

When study groups follow the action research cycle described in this book, members actually experience the components of an effective training design. The group can study the theory, practice using new materials and strategies when they meet, and observe each other doing demonstrations when they meet or in their classrooms. The gem in the cycle is the assessment of student work to determine effectiveness of new practices.

The WFSG System and these stages of refinement are described in the three editions of *Whole-Faculty Study Groups* books by Carlene U. Murphy and Dale W. Lick, published by Corwin Press in 1998, 2001, and 2005, and the *Whole-Faculty Study Groups Fieldbook: Lessons Learned and Best Practices From Classrooms, Districts, and Schools,* edited by Lick and Murphy, published in 2007 by Corwin Press. The WFSG System is stronger today because of the struggles and trials and errors we experienced along the way. We continue to learn and to make adjustments to the system.

The WFSG System is now being used in many schools and school districts in the United States and Canada, as the following examples show:

- Springfield Missouri Public Schools is using the WFSG System to create professional learning communities in most of its 51 schools. Many other districts around the country are currently implementing the WFSG System, such as the Franklin County Schools in North Carolina, Hawthorn School District 73 in Illinois, and the Gill-Montague Regional School District in Massachusetts.
- The Centers for Quality Teaching and Learning in North Carolina have incorporated the WFSG System into Capacity First, their comprehensive school reform design, and are implementing the WFSG System in schools in Virginia, North Carolina, and Georgia.
- Louisiana State Department of Education has incorporated the WFSG System into its statewide Learning-Intensive Networking Communities for Success (LINCS) program with 272 schools to elevate and sustain teacher and student content knowledge and performance.
- Since 1997, ATLAS Learning Communities, a nationally recognized school improvement program, has incorporated the WFSG System into its design. More than 100 ATLAS elementary, middle, and high schools nationwide have launched the WFSG System.
- The National Staff Development Council has designated the WFSG System as one of the exemplary programs for meeting its National Standards for Staff Development and has featured the WFSG System as one of the designs in its 2004 publication, *Powerful Designs for Professional Development.*
- The Video Journal of Education published in 2004 a video program titled *Whole-Faculty Study Groups: Collaboration Targeting Student Learning,* which shows the DMC and vignettes of study groups in action.
- Carlene Murphy established the WFSG National Center and its Web site in Augusta, Georgia, in 2002. The center hosts an annual three-day conference in February. It is designed to provide additional skills and strategies to administrators and teachers who are implementing the WFSG System. The center also offers training institutes in February and in the summer for school and district teams to learn how to launch the WFSG System and to enhance and support implementation, and provides technical assistance to schools and districts in implementing the WFSG System.

Here in Chapter 1, we briefly introduce the WFSG System for creating professional learning communities that improve student learning here because this improvement system illustrates collaborative action research and schoolwide action research and their application in schools. In Chapter 2, we describe how WFSG schoolwide action research compares with other approaches to action research. In Chapter 4, we focus on the action research work of individual study groups within the schoolwide action research system.

The WFSG System is a job-embedded, self-directed, student-driven approach to professional development. It is a professional development system designed to build communities of learners in which professionals continuously strive to improve schools and increase student learning. This is accomplished by practitioners: deepening their own knowledge and understanding of what is taught, reflecting on their practices, sharpening their skills, and taking joint responsibility for the students they teach (Lick & Murphy, 2007).

"Whole-faculty" means that every faculty member at the school is a member of a study group of three to five individuals focusing on data-driven student instructional needs and working collaboratively to increase their capacities to enable their students to reach higher levels of performance. The collective action research and synergy of the study groups advance teaching and learning for the whole school.

The essence of the WFSG System resides in the following two "grounding" questions:

- What do students need teachers to do so that teachers will have a deeper understanding of what they teach?
- What do students need teachers to do so that teachers will be more skillful in how they teach?

Whole-faculty study groups are focused on students. The overarching question that guides the WFSG System is as follows:

> ■ **What are our students learning and achieving as a result of what we are learning and doing in our study group? (Murphy & Lick, 2005, p. 2)**

The WFSG System is based on the following five guiding principles:

- Students are first.
- Everyone participates.
- Leadership is shared.
- Responsibility is equal.
- The work is public. (Lick & Murphy, 2007, p. 4)

The WFSG System is grounded in student instructional needs and is governed by a seven-step decision-making cycle schools follow each school year (see Figure 2.1). In Steps 1 through 4, the whole faculty meets to analyze student data, specify student needs that study groups will address, and form study groups. Steps 5 through 7 have study groups design action plans, implement cycles of action research, and evaluate their impact on student learning. This seven-step cycle is described more fully in Chapter 2; Step 6, Implement Cycles of Action Research, is presented in Chapter 4.

The goal of the WFSG System is to focus the entire school faculty on creating, implementing, and integrating effective teaching and learning practices into school programs that will result in increases in student learning. It is the collective synergy and action research generated from the study groups that propel the school faculty forward.

In our experience, students do not excel as middle school students because they had a great sixth-grade teacher. The more likely reason is because the students had outstanding learning opportunities as kindergarteners through fifth graders. The cumulative effect of good teaching over years of schooling produces students and graduates who do well and can be expected to continue as learners. When every teacher in a school is in a study group that targets student learning needs and effective teaching practices, an important range of schoolwide needs can be met.

Schools that have successfully implemented the WFSG approach have many differences in student age, level and ethnicity, location (e.g., rural vs. urban), socioeconomic circumstances, and size. Even with the many demographic differences in schools, these factors do not make significant differences in how adults in schools work together in study groups.

Where properly implemented, the WFSG System has been unusually successful in facilitating schoolwide change and enhancing student learning (see, e.g., Joyce et al., 1989; Lick & Murphy, 2007; Murphy, 1992, 1995; Murphy & Lick, 1998, 2001, 2005). The driving force in the WFSG process is the self-directed, synergistic study groups effectively using action research (see Lick, 1999a, 2000, 2006). Such study group teams creatively do the following:

1. Produce learning communities that set common goals, support group interdependence, empower participants, and foster active participation

2. Plan and learn together

3. Engage broad principles of education that modify perspectives, policies, and practices

4. Construct subject-matter knowledge

5. Immerse everyone in sustained work with ideas, materials, and colleagues

6. Cultivate action researchers, producing, evaluating, and applying relevant research

7. Struggle with fundamental questions of what teachers and students must learn, know, and apply (Lick & Murphy, 2007, pp. 7–8)

The overarching question that guides study groups is this: What is happening differently in the classroom as a result of what we are doing and learning in study groups? With that vision, "study groups are motivated, work harder, and take responsibility for the successful implementation of required processes and procedures" (Murphy & Lick, 1998, p. 18). The benefits include the following:

- Improvement in the student needs areas that study groups target
- Culture shifts from isolation to collaboration

- Data being prominent in making instructional decisions
- Principals who are more instructionally focused
- New teachers who are in study groups surrounded by support
- Teachers seeing themselves as action researchers
- New instructional initiatives being implemented sooner and more thoroughly
- Multiple initiatives that are more coherent and integrated for maximum effects
- All teachers being viewed as leaders
- Behavioral norms for faculty becoming standard
- Looking at student work in collaborative settings becoming the norm
- Teachers taking full responsibility for students represented in a study group (Lick & Murphy, 2007, p. 7)

The WFSG System, centered around collaborative study groups and action research, is, in fact, a massive change management process. It is one of the most practical and effective change processes presently available in the literature.

In particular, application of the WFSG System dramatically increases the following:

1. *Focus on imperative changes,* as determined by school personnel

2. *Change of sponsorship effectiveness,* both project and schoolwide

3. *Preparation of change agents,* including the principal, faculty, and others

4. *Commitment of targets (those who must change) and the reduction of resistance*

5. *Positive advocacy,* including that of the school board, superintendent, principal, faculty, students, parents, and others from the general community

6. *Individual, group, and school resilience,* enhancing stakeholders' change-adaptability

7. *Knowledge of change and change principles* for stakeholders

8. *Organized processes for transition,* including integrated, cocreative learning experiences that are teacher and student centered, experimental and research oriented, reflective, supportive, and inspiring

9. *Group synergy and learning team development,* setting new school operational and relationship norms for action research and improving learning systems

10. *School and educational culture modification,* allowing a critical reexamination of basic assumptions, beliefs, and behaviors, and required learning systems and practices (Lick & Murphy, 2007, p. 8)

The WFSG System, through the aforementioned 10 elements for leading and managing change, generates a collective and inspiring vision and creates a high level of synergy and effective action research, allowing substantive learning, change, and continuous improvement to become the norm in the school workplace and culture.

In Chapter 2, we deepen our discussion of schoolwide action research and explain, in some detail, how it differs from other approaches to action research.

A Schoolwide Approach to Action Research

Guiding Question

■ How does the WFSG approach to schoolwide action research compare with other approaches to action research?

While the primary focus of this book is on the explication of the Whole-Faculty Study Groups (WFSG) approach to schoolwide action research, we feel it is important to the reader to know how the WFSG approach is similar to and different from other approaches to action research. In this chapter, we build on the description in Chapter 1 of schoolwide action research to explain the WFSG approach to schoolwide action research in more detail and then to show similarities and differences with other approaches with regard to the (1) purpose or focus of the action research and how the focus is determined, (2) participants in the action research process, (3) steps in the action research process, and (4) expected results and products.

The fact that practitioners can and do have different approaches for action research is evident throughout the action research literature.

The earliest action research approaches in education, which date back to work in the 1940s and early 1950s of Alice Miel and Stephen Corey at the Horace-Mann-Lincoln Institute of School Experimentation at Columbia University (Schmuck, 2006), focused on process. Miel focused on using action research approaches "to help elementary school teachers use cooperative learning procedures in their classrooms" (p. 146), while Corey used action research to improve school practices, such as determining the most effective method for forming curriculum committees in high schools.

In preparation for writing this book, we did an extensive review of the recent literature on action research (Calhoun, 1994, 2002; Caro-Bruce, 2004; Sagor, 2000, 2005; Schmuck, 2006), teacher research (Cochran-Smith & Lytle, 1995; Dana & Yendol-Silva, 2003; Hopkins, 2002; Martin-Kniep, 2004), and practitioner research (Anderson, Herr, & Nihlen, 1994; Robinson & Lai, 2006) to understand the similarities and differences between Murphy and Lick's WFSG approach to schoolwide action research and other authors' approaches. Other authors, such as Anderson et al. (1994), Cochran-Smith and Lytle (1995), and Schmuck (2006), provide chapters on the history of each of these research traditions.

The following pages are organized into four sections, one for the WFSG approach and three for the approaches to action research described in the writings of Richard Sagor, Cathy Caro-Bruce, and Emily Calhoun. We selected these three authors for comparison with the WFSG approach because they represented the range of writings about action research, teacher research, and practitioner research.

Within each section, we describe for each approach, the focus or purpose of action research, action research participants, the action research process—steps and timeline, and action research products and results. At the end of the chapter, we present summary tables that compare side-by-side the four approaches to action research.

Richard Sagor has been writing about action research since 1992 when he published a book on collaborative action research for the Association for Supervision and Curriculum Development. We use material from his 2005 book, *The Action Research Guidebook: A Four-Step Process for Educators and School Teams*. We selected Sagor for comparison with the WFSG approach because he, like Schmuck and Mills, has written extensively about action research.

Cathy Caro-Bruce has directed a classroom action research program for the Madison Metropolitan School District in Wisconsin for more than 12 years and wrote *Action Research: Facilitator's Handbook* (2000) for the National Staff Development Council. In this chapter we refer to her recent chapter on action research (Caro-Bruce, 2004) in *Powerful Designs for Professional Learning*. We selected Caro-Bruce for comparison with the WFSG approach because her work has focused on teacher and practitioner research and shares many similarities with the research cycles described by Robinson and Lai for practitioner research and Dana and Yendol-Silva for teacher research.

Emily Calhoun wrote *How to Use Action Research in the Self-Renewing School* (Calhoun, 1994) based on her work with the Georgia League of Professional Schools and the Ames, Iowa, Community Schools. Calhoun focuses her writing on schoolwide action research. We selected Calhoun for comparison with the WFSG approach because she and Murphy and Lick are the only published authors on schoolwide action research.

WFSG SCHOOLWIDE ACTION RESEARCH

The Purpose of Action Research

As the vignette in Chapter 1 suggests, the purpose of the WFSG schoolwide action research approach for classroom teachers is on addressing student academic learning needs in classrooms with their current students by changing what they teach and how they teach. The student learning needs chosen by the nine Bunn Elementary study groups were those deemed the most important at the beginning of the 2005 to 2006 school year. Each of the Bunn Elementary study groups set improvement targets from October to December/January and January to May.

Often, the needs a school identifies are specific ones that address the school's academic learning goals in the school improvement plan. At Bunn Elementary, the top three goals in the school's 2005–2008 School Improvement Plan were improving student achievement in reading, writing, and mathematics.

A school creates a list of needs by examining quantitative and qualitative data on student learning. Bunn Elementary used disaggregated state and district data in reading, writing, and mathematics and teacher experience with students to identify student learning needs and create a master list of student needs.

To summarize, the focus of WFSG schoolwide action research approach is on the following:

- Student academic learning needs in classrooms with current students
- Specific needs that address the school's academic learning goals in the school improvement plan
- Understanding the past, why current problems and gaps exist, to improve current performance this year
- Student needs that practitioner researchers have the power to ameliorate
- Short-term changes to improve performance in classrooms by teachers and students
- Examining quantitative and qualitative data on student learning

Action Research Participants

In the WFSG approach to schoolwide action research, the whole faculty is involved in study groups engaged in action research. Murphy and Lick (2005) explain the following:

> By whole faculty, we mean all classroom teachers, all resource teachers, all special area teachers, librarians, counselors, and anyone else holding professional certification. Usually administrators will form a study group of administrators within the school or will be in a study group with administrators across the district. Some of the schools that have teaching assistants will include the assistants in the study groups with the professionally certificated personnel; most, however, will have study groups with only teaching assistants. In many schools, nonteaching personnel form study groups that focus on the role they have in supporting instruction. (pp. 11–12)

The decision about how nonteaching staff will participate in schoolwide action research is made before the groups are formed. At Bunn Elementary, the school's Leadership Team decided that nonteaching personnel, such as the media specialist and the counselor, would participate in study groups with classroom teachers. Since the entire district was implementing the WFSG System, the principal belonged to a study group with principals from other schools.

In WFSG schools, all certificated personnel participate in study groups. Working in study groups is part of a staff member's professional responsibilities. "Opting out" is not an option.

The Action Research Process—Steps and Timelines

Steps

All WFSG schools follow a seven-step Decision-Making Cycle (DMC) that guides the schoolwide action research (Murphy & Lick, 2005). The whole faculty completes the first part of the DMC together. Individual study groups each complete the second part of the DMC.

The Whole Faculty

Step 1: Analyze schoolwide student learning data

Step 2: Identify schoolwide student learning needs

Step 3: Categorize student learning needs

Step 4: Write individual action plans and form study groups around common student needs

Each Study Group

Step 5: Designs a study group action plan

Step 6: Implements cycles of collaborative action research

Each Study Group and the Whole Faculty

Step 7: Assesses the impact of study groups on student learning

Working independently, each study group implements cycles of collaborative action research (Step 6) by engaging in the following tasks:

- Analyze student needs to decide what to focus on, establish baseline performance, and set targets
- Identify content and best practices and develop expertise
- Plan interventions and data collection
- Implement interventions and decide whether specific interventions work
- Look at student work, assess changes, and decide the next step
- Monitor student progress and make midcourse corrections
- Assess end of the year results and plan for next year

Chapter 4 describes the study group's collaborative action research steps in greater detail.

As shown in Figure 2.1, context is an important consideration in implementing the WFSG DMC in schools. The school culture may shape how the Focus Team prepares for and leads the school faculty through Steps 1 to 4. The uniqueness of the school's students and their learning needs and the faculty's School Improvement Plan will shape the student learning data used in Step 1. Calendar and schedule options will influence how study groups are formed in Step 4. Prior experience with formative assessments and collaborative problem solving may influence how study groups engage in action research in Step 6.

Figure 2.1   The WFSG Decision-Making Cycle

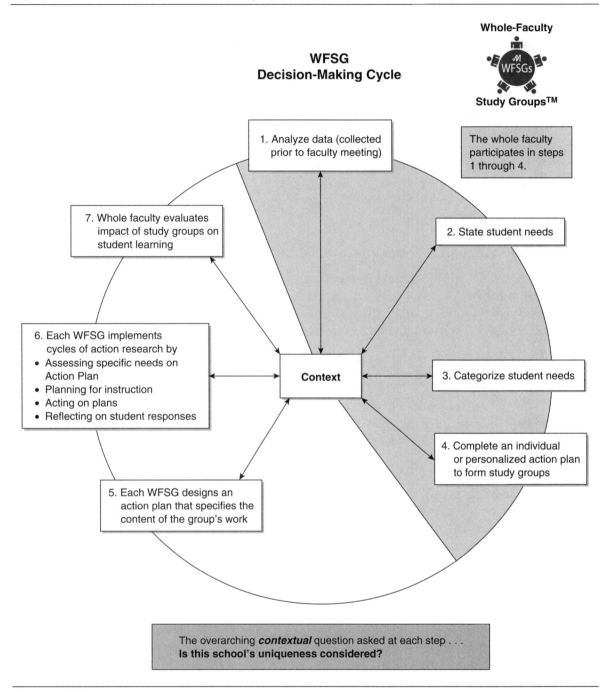

Timeline

Study groups are usually formed in the first two months of the school year as the staff together goes through Steps 1–4 of the WFSG DMC. Steps 1–4 take about three hours to complete. A detailed guide to the DMC is provided in Chapter 7 and Resource B in Murphy and Lick's 2005 edition of *Whole-Faculty Study Groups*.

Each study group is expected to stay together throughout the school year and meet weekly or biweekly throughout the school year during contract time. Schools are expected to provide time for WFSG study groups to meet. Some schools have all study groups meet at the same time, but most schools don't require this. In Chapter 7 we describe some of the different strategies schools have used to find time. Murphy and Lick (2005) provide 22 illustrations of ways schools have found to provide time for study groups to meet (pp. 54–59).

Study groups engage in several cycles of collaborative action research during the school year, addressing one or more student academic learning needs. Study groups are encouraged to spend most of their time in testing the effectiveness of interventions for improving student learning, get into the action research fairly quickly, reflect on what they are learning throughout the year, and conduct a year-end formal self-assessment using WFSG protocols.

Action Research Products and Results

All study groups create two products: a study group action plan that is updated throughout the school year and a study group log for every meeting. In addition, many groups also create interim reports and a final report. These products are described in the paragraphs that follow.

Study Group Action Plan

Each study group creates an action plan within the first three meetings, then revises and updates the plan throughout the year. The WFSG action plan includes the category of student needs the group is addressing, such as reading, the specific student learning needs it plans to address, the essential question that guides its work, the actions or action research steps the group will take when it meets, the resources the group will use, its norms for collaborative group work, and its data sources or assessment tools for collecting quantitative and qualitative data about student learning relative to each need it addresses. The action plan also has space for the group to summarize, for several cycles of action research during the school year, the baseline data on student learning that is collected, its targets for improving performance, and actual results. WFSG schools post hard copies of action plans for review by staff, students, and parents. Many schools are now also posting action plans on Web sites.

The WFSG action plan template presented in Figures 2.2 and 2.3 is different from the template and illustrations of action plans in Murphy and Lick (2005, pp. 226–228, 238, 275, 298–299, 312, 316). The primary changes are in asking study groups to list the state or district standard that corresponds to their selected student needs and specifying the steps in the action research process.

We have presented examples of actual study group action plans from study groups in Chapter 5, Figure 5.3, and Chapter 7, Figure 7.1. The example in Figure 7.1 also includes the principal's feedback to the study group members on their action plan.

Figure 2.2   WFSG Study Group Action Plan, Page 1

Whole-Faculty
WFSGs
Study Groups™

WFSG Action Plan for Group # or Name_____

School: _____   Date: _____

Group Members: _____

What is the general category of student needs the group will address?

State the <u>specific skill</u> within the general category the group will target.		Check and list the specific actions the group will take when the study group meets.

Students need to:	*Standard(s)*	**We will:**
		☐ Diagnose students' current levels of performance (relative to need)
		☐ Develop assessment tools
		☐ Identify strategies/materials to address need
		☐ Plan lessons for how each member will use the strategy/material
		☐ Develop/design materials to address need
		☐ Demonstrate/practice strategies members have used or will use
		☐ Articulate strategies we use
		☐ Examine samples of student work for evidence of student understanding
		☐ Assess results of using strategies in our classrooms
		☐ Other:
Beside each student need, indicate the STATE STANDARD(s) that will be addressed when members target the need. Only give the code or number of the Standard.		

ESSENTIAL QUESTION that will guide the group's work:

Our resources are:	**Our norms are:**
At least one of the following resources will be used <u>during</u> study group meetings.	
	**
	Complete chart(s) on Page 2 to indicate how study group work will be assessed.

Figure 2.3   WFSG Study Group Action Plan, Page 2

Whole-Faculty
Study Groups™

WFSG Action Plan for Group # or Name

School: _____ Date: _____

Group Members: _____

State specific student need that is being targeted — *Students need to:*	**Data Sources:** What type of pre/post assessments will members give to document current performance level?	**Baseline:** What percentage of students meet, approach, or are far below performance standards **when work begins?** _____ (DATE)	**Target:** What do members predict will be the percentage at each performance level **after interventions?** _____ (DATE)	**Actual:** What percentage of students meet, approach, or are far below performance standards **after interventions?** _____ (DATE)

State specific student need that is being targeted — *Students need to:*	**Data Sources:** What type of pre/post assessments will members give to document current performance level?	**Baseline:** What percentage of students meet, approach, or are far below performance standards **when work begins?** _____ (DATE)	**Target:** What do members predict will be the percentage at each performance level **after interventions?** _____ (DATE)	**Actual:** What percentage of students meet, approach, or are far below performance standards **after interventions?** _____ (DATE)

Complete a chart every 9 to 12 weeks to track student effects of study group work.

Column 1: List the SPECIFIC student needs currently being addressed by the study group.

Column 2: Indicate the types of assessments that will be used by members to determine or diagnose the current status of the student need. The data may be derived from assessments designed by teachers, textbook publishers, and/or testing agencies.

Columns 3, 4, & 5: Give the percentage of students in each member's classes that meet different performance levels. For example: 25% meet expectations, 30% almost meet, and 45% struggling or far below. Performance levels are defined by study group members. The same rubric or other rating system is used by all members.

Study Group Logs

Each study group completes a study group log during or immediately after each meeting. These logs are one form of interim reports on the study group's work. The study group log asks groups to indicate the need they addressed; the action research step they are working on; their findings, insights, or decisions from their work; whether they brought student work to the meeting to examine together; and what resources they used. The form also has space for each member of the group to indicate, since the last meeting, the specific instructional strategies members used in their classrooms that were the focus of the last meeting and the student results. At the bottom of the form, groups are asked to describe what members have agreed to do in their classrooms prior to the next meeting; indicate whether the group is ready to share a proven strategy with the whole faculty; list any questions, concerns, or comments for the principal or other administrator who regularly reads their logs and provides feedback; and specify the focus and materials needed for the next study group meeting. WFSG schools post hard copies of logs for review by staff, students, and parents. Many schools are now also posting logs on Web sites.

The WFSG log template presented in Figure 2.4 is different from the template and illustrations of logs in Murphy and Lick (2005, pp. 229–230, 276–282, 300–320). The changes make it easier for study group members to provide more detailed information about their meeting. These changes include asking study groups to indicate the student need and the action research step addressed, whether student work was examined, the resources used in the meeting, and the group's readiness to share a proven strategy. In addition, the revised log template asks each group member to describe the strategy being used in classes with students and the observed results.

Each study group member keeps a binder with the study group's action plan, logs, resources, assessment tools, artifacts, and data the group uses during the year.

We have presented an example of an actual log from a study group in Chapter 7, Figure 7.2. This example also includes the principal's feedback to study group members on their log.

Interim Reports

The Instructional Council comprises a representative (rotating) from each study group, the principal, and one or two involved members of the faculty. Its primary purpose is to communicate among study groups and deliver pertinent information to each one. Study groups share progress reports, tools, and artifacts at Instructional Council meetings every 4–6 weeks with representatives from different study groups. The Bunn Elementary vignette at the beginning of Chapter 1 mentioned five Instructional Council meetings.

Final Report

For the year-end evaluation in the WFSG System, each study group updates its action plan, describes changes in student learning and teacher practices resulting from the group's work, and assesses how well the WFSG process guidelines were followed. (See Resource D for examples.) Most WFSG schools hold a year-end sharing and celebration session for study groups to present their work.

Many WFSG schools also survey staff about their experiences in study groups and about their recommendations for improving the WFSG System, including the

Figure 2.4   WFSG Study Group Log

Whole-Faculty Study Groups™	**WFSG Log for Group # or Name** _____ School: _____ Log #: _____ Date: _____ Leader: _____ Members Present: _____

What specific student learning need did the group target today?

Check the steps on the WFSG action research cycle that best describe what the group did today. In Column 2, elaborate on items checked (key findings, decisions, insights).

_____ Diagnosed students' current levels of performance (relative to need)	
_____ Developed assessment tools	
_____ Identified strategies/materials to address need	
_____ Planned lesson(s) for how each member will use strategy/material	
_____ Developed/designed materials to address need	
_____ Demonstrated/practiced strategies members have used or will use	
_____ Articulated strategies used last week	
_____ Examined samples of student work for evidence of student understanding	
_____ Assessed results of using strategies in our classrooms	
_____ Other	

Did the group examine student work today? __ If yes, who brought? __
What resources/materials did members use during the meeting today?

Since the last meeting, describe the specific instructional strategies members used in their classrooms that were the focus of last meeting.

MEMBER:	*STRATEGY:*	*STUDENT RESULTS:*

What have members agreed to do in their classrooms prior to the next meeting?

Is the group ready to share a proven strategy with the whole faculty?	**Questions, Concerns, Comments:**

NEXT MEETING: Date _____ Time _____ Location _____ Leader _____ Recorder _____

Materials needed: _____

Focus: _____

data used to identify student needs, the methods for forming study groups, the time available for study group meetings, the feedback and support provided by the principal and other administrators, the opportunities for cross-group sharing, and the resources and professional development for study groups.

Timelines for Products

WFSG study group products are created at different times during the school year, such as the following:

- Action plan—initial draft developed within the first three study group meetings, and updated throughout the year as needed and as new data are collected
- Meeting logs—weekly or biweekly
- Interim reports—at Instructional Council meetings every 4–6 weeks
- Interim progress data on changes in student learning—every 4–9 weeks, often corresponding to grading periods
- Typical action research cycle—6–12 weeks, with 2–4 cycles per year
- Summative evaluation of changes in student learning and teacher practice—end of school year
- Summative presentation of results, reflections, and recommendations—end of school year
- Survey feedback on the WFSG System—end of school year

Results

Lick and Murphy (2007, p. 7) report the following benefits from WFSG schoolwide action research:

- Improvements in the student needs areas that study groups target
- Culture shifts from isolation to collaboration
- Prominent use of data when making instructional decisions
- Principals who are more instructionally focused
- New teachers who are in study groups surrounded by support
- Teachers who see themselves as action researchers
- New instructional initiatives that are implemented sooner and more thoroughly
- Multiple initiatives that are more coherent and integrated for maximum effects
- All teachers are viewed as leaders
- Behavioral norms for faculty become standard
- The process of looking at student work in collaborative settings becomes the norm
- Teachers take full responsibility for students represented in a study group

Also, Chapters 5 and 6 in this book focus specifically on using schoolwide action research for changes in teacher practice and student learning.

Schools implementing WFSG schoolwide action research see many of the results described earlier in the first year of implementation with improved results in subsequent years of implementation.

SAGOR'S ACTION RESEARCH APPROACH

The Purpose of Action Research

Richard Sagor (2005, p. 11) describes three focuses for action research in schools, addressing questions, problems, or concerns about the following:

- Student performance (academic performance, behavior, and attitudes)
- Process (teaching practice or school procedures)
- Program (curriculum or offerings)

Action Research Participants

Sagor (2005) primarily describes action research in terms of individuals and small groups engaged in action research. Sagor discusses action research by school teams.

The Action Research Process—Steps and Timelines

Sagor (2005) defines two categories of action research: *descriptive action research* and *quasi-experimental action research* (p. 6).

The focus of descriptive action research is on determining what is currently occurring, developing a deeper understanding of why things operate as they do (what Sagor calls developing a theory of action), and making recommendations for future improvements. Practitioners collect and analyze data on the way things currently occur. Action comes after the research.

Quasi-experimental action research focuses on testing a hypothesis or a new theory of action during the action research process. Practitioners collect and analyze data on the implementation and impact of the actions taken. Action is the focus of the research.

Sagor (2005) defines a four-stage action research process (p. 5) for both types of action research:

1. Clarifying vision and targets
   - Identify a focus
   - Select achievement targets
   - Establish assessment criteria

2. Articulating theory
   - Develop a theory of action

3. Implementing action and collecting data
   - Determine the research question
   - Create a data collection plan
   - Take action

4. Reflecting on the data and planning informed action
   - Analyze data
   - Revise the theory of action
   - Plan future action

The key step in Sagor's approach is Step 2—articulating theories. Sagor emphasizes building theories of action in words and diagrams to lay out the causal links that drive behavior before collecting data in the descriptive research and before taking action in the quasi-experimental research.

The primary difference between descriptive and quasi-experimental action research lies in the execution of Steps 2 and 3 (Sagor, 2005, p. 9). In descriptive research, the focus is on building a theory of action around current practice and collecting data about current practices. The action in Step 3 is collecting data about current practices.

In quasi-experimental research, the focus is on building a new theory of action to support changes in practice and then collecting data about the implementation and impact of the new practices. The action in Step 3 is trying out the new practices derived from the new theory of action.

The action research cycle that individual WFSG study groups follow is similar to Sagor's quasi-experimental action research. Each study group decides which student learning needs to address, sets targets, and develops assessment criteria for collecting baseline data. The group analyzes baseline data and develops "theories of action" about the types of interventions that need to be made in classrooms to improve student learning. The group then plans how to implement the selected interventions, collect data about the interventions, and take action. The data is then analyzed to determine the effectiveness of the interventions and the next steps are planned.

Sagor does not present a timeline for action research but the steps he articulates could be accomplished over a school year.

Action Research Products and Results

Research Plan

Sagor (2005) does not include the development of a research plan as a formal step in the action research process he describes. However, he does emphasize the importance of clarifying up front the nature of the research, the research questions and theories of action to investigate, and methods for data collection and analysis.

Interim Reports

Sagor (2005) recommends using spreadsheets (p. 105) to collect data during the research process and keeping a researcher's journal (p. 108) to record observations, reflections, and changes in approach or actions based on context changes. During the data analysis phase, Sagor encourages researchers to summarize the findings, draw tentative conclusions, and share emerging findings with others (pp. 129–130, 140).

Final Report, Presentation, or Portfolio

Sagor (2005) recommends that researchers revisit and revise their theory of action based on the data they have collected and assess their findings for their relative importance for improving performance. This leads to the generation of action alternatives and assessing their relative efficacy (pp. 148–150).

He (Sagor, 2005, pp. 156–159) suggests that the type of action research report prepared depends on the audience, purpose, and level of detail. He notes that some districts request full reports while others ask for abstracts. The five areas a research report should cover include an explanation of the context and problem, the theoretical perspective, the research design, the analysis of data, and action planning (Sagor, 2005, p. 162).

Results

Sagor (2005) affirms that the overarching goal of action research is "universal student success" (p. 8). He notes that descriptive and quasi-experimental action research yield different results with descriptive research focused more on understanding and quasi-experimental research focused on test action hypotheses (p. 7).

CARO-BRUCE'S ACTION RESEARCH APPROACH

The Purpose of Action Research

Cathy Caro-Bruce, who has supported action research in the Madison, Wisconsin, school district for many years, identifies teacher action research questions for different purposes, such as to improve practice, better understand a particular aspect of practice, better understand one's practice in general, promote greater equity, and influence the social conditions of practice (Caro-Bruce, 2004, p. 57). These purposes relate to Sagor's process category.

Action Research Participants

Caro-Bruce (2004) primarily describes action research in terms of individuals and small groups engaged in the process. She also discusses both within school and cross-school teams. Caro-Bruce does mention that some districts have implemented schoolwide action research (p. 60).

The Action Research Process—Steps and Timelines

Caro-Bruce (2004) proposes a seven-step action research process:

1. Decide whether to do action research as an individual or in a group.

2. Find a focus.

3. Develop a plan for doing action research.

4. Collect data.

5. Analyze the data.

6. Write about the work.

7. Plan for future action.

Whether action occurs during the action research process or after depends on the focus. If the focus of the action research is on improving practice, then the practitioners might be trying out new practices in classes and collecting and analyzing data about the impact of these practices.

Caro-Bruce (2004) emphasizes the importance of Step 6, writing about the work. "Writing pushes the researcher to a new level of understanding as they have to communicate what they have learned" (p. 58). Writing also allows researchers to share their work with others.

In the Madison Metropolitan School District in Madison, Wisconsin, where Caro-Bruce coordinates action research, and in the Fairfax County Public Schools (2006), one cycle of action research encompasses an entire school year. The focus of the action research is usually not on immediate short-term changes during the current school year except when changes are part of the research design.

Action Research Products and Results

Research Plan

Caro-Bruce (2004, p. 57) includes the development of an action plan as Step 3 in the action research process and expects that teacher researchers will update and revise the plan as the work progresses. She provides a simpler template with research topic, research questions, and action steps. For each action step, she asks researchers to indicate who will do the step, the person responsible for the plan, and what resources or support are available.

Interim Reports

No interim reports are recommended but Caro-Bruce (2004) suggests sharing work during the data collection and analysis phases to get feedback from others (p. 58).

Final Report, Presentation, or Portfolio

Caro-Bruce (2004) suggests two final reports—a report on the action research and a plan for action. She suggests that the report (p. 59) include a description of the problem or question addressed, the context, the actions the researcher took to learn about the topic, an explanation of research and data collection methods, a literature review, the data analysis, and recommendations. The second document—a plan for action (p. 59 and Handout No. 5 on CD)—builds on what the researcher has learned from the research and the conclusions formed. It identifies additional questions arising from the research, possible actions, people interested in the research, and strategies for engaging them. The Madison Metropolitan School District in Madison, Wisconsin, compiles annual anthologies with abstracts of the year's action research projects (Madison Metropolitan School District, 2006).

Results

The results depend on the focus of action research. Caro-Bruce (2004) states that action research may lead to individual progress, student progress, knowledge production, social change, and personal meaning (pp. 55–56).

Using Caro-Bruce's characterization of the different purposes for action research, results from action research might include the following:

- To improve practice
  o Impact on student learning from testing new practices and follow-up recommendations
  o Recommendations for improvements based on analysis of current implementation

- To better understand a particular aspect of practice
  - o Better understanding of the strengths and limitations of the effective application of the practice
  - o Recommendations for improvements based on analysis of current implementation
- To better understand one's practice in general
  - o Better understanding of the nature, origins, and implications of one's practice
  - o Recommendations for improvements
- To promote greater equity
  - o Description and analysis of current inequities
  - o Recommendations for change
- To influence the social conditions of practice
  - o Better understanding of the impact and influence of practice on social conditions
  - o Recommendations for change

CALHOUN'S SCHOOLWIDE ACTION RESEARCH APPROACH

The Purpose of Action Research

Calhoun (1994), building on her work with the Georgia League of Professional Schools and community schools in Ames, Iowa, describes three different purposes for schoolwide action research: improving equity for students so all students benefit from improved instruction, improving curriculum and teaching so teaching improves in every classroom in a chosen area such as writing, and improving the school's ability to identify and solve problems which may relate to teaching and learning or other aspects of the school operations and culture.

A key difference between the WFSG approach to schoolwide action research and other approaches to action research is that the WFSG approach has an exclusive focus on enhancing student performance, and by so doing, improving schools.

Action Research Participants

Calhoun involves the entire faculty in schoolwide action research. She recommends a facilitation team to develop a plan and timeline for the research and to lead the process, data collection by faculty study groups, a task force or leadership team, and action research by faculty study groups or liaison groups.

The Action Research Process—Steps and Timelines

Calhoun uses a five-step cycle for schoolwide action research:

1. Select an area of focus for the study.

2. Collect data.

3. Organize data.

4. Analyze and interpret data.

5. Take action.

She notes that work at each step often leads groups back to earlier steps to redefine the area of focus, collect more data, reorganize data, and reinterpret data.

Calhoun (1994, pp. 96, 97) provides an example of a yearlong timeline for schoolwide action research from an elementary school in Iowa that is similar to the WFSG timeline. In September and October, the building leadership team decided on an area of focus, expository writing, identified through the literature the key attributes of expository writing, and developed a plan for the year. In October and November, they developed a common assessment task and scoring system for expository writing, developed a data collection process, and study teams collected schoolwide baseline writing samples. In November, study teams analyzed the data from their students, identified specific areas for improvement, investigated instructional strategies to use, and developed classroom action plans to implement from December through May. From December through May, individual teachers implemented their classroom action plans with support from their study teams. Teachers collected and analyzed writing samples and shared results, conferred with students, modified their action plans based on results, and worked with their study teams to discuss results and share and develop lessons. In April and May, all staff collected final writing samples from students, and study teams analyzed the data and reported their findings. In May, the building leadership team synthesized the study team findings and prepared a report to the district. Faculty and students celebrated the improvements in writing in May and the faculty met to identify a goal and plan for the following school year.

Both the action research cycle described by Calhoun and the WFSG DMC occur over an entire school year with study teams or study groups engaged in their own cycles of action research within the larger cycle. Both begin with the faculty together deciding on a focus and coming together at the end of the year to review results and celebrate successes. Both expect study teams or groups to use research to define the attributes of the needs they are addressing, use data from their students to identify the specific areas to address, and do research and use effective instructional strategies.

There are also differences between the two cycles. In the Calhoun schoolwide action research example, the faculty decided to focus on a single area, expository writing. In the WFSG System, schools may choose to focus on a single area, like writing, or they may choose to allow study groups to work on different student needs. A second difference lies in the initial and final data collection. In the Calhoun example, a common assessment task and scoring guide was developed for all study teams to use. In the WFSG System, each study group develops its own task and scoring guide. A third difference is in the plans individual study teams or groups develop. In Calhoun's example of schoolwide action research, each teacher on the team develops a personal-classroom action plan with improvement targets for the students taught by the teacher. Teachers get input and feedback from the rest of the study team. In the WFSG System, each study group develops a group action plan but members of the study group set individual student improvement targets and then create composite group targets.

Action Research Products and Results

Research Plan

Calhoun (1994) describes three types of planning documents for schoolwide action research. The first is a general timeline for the different stages in the action research cycle, similar to the description we referenced in the preceding section on action research timelines. The second type of planning document is the schoolwide action plan that the faculty, working in study groups or teams, develops after collecting and analyzing baseline data and reviewing relevant research for information on underlying causes and effective interventions. The third type of planning document is an individual teacher classroom action plan in which teachers define the specific areas to be addressed in their classrooms, the interventions they will use, how they will collect data to monitor student progress, how the interventions are actually implemented, and what results they expect. Calhoun (1994, p. 95) describes the schoolwide plan and the classroom teacher plans as "living plans" that faculty will use to guide implementation and modify as needed during the action step, Step 5.

In the WFSG System for schoolwide action research, the equivalent of the Calhoun's schoolwide timeline and schoolwide action plan is encompassed in the WFSG DMC, the school's timeline for the steps, the master list of student learning needs developed in Step 2, and the list of study groups formed in Step 4 and the needs they will address. The individual WFSG study group action plans are equivalent to Calhoun's classroom action plans and represent each group's research plan.

Interim Reports

Interim reports in the context of Calhoun's approach to schoolwide action research would include analyses and interpretations of materials in the professional literature that relate to the research target, analyses of data collected, progress reports, updates to the schoolwide action plan, and individual action plans (pp. 86–88, 109).

Final Report, Presentation, or Portfolio

Calhoun (1994) recommends that the facilitation team or task force guiding the schoolwide action research prepare a final report that includes the schoolwide action plan, innovations used, data on actual implementation of innovations, results on student learning, analyses of the data, and conclusions and recommendations. In WFSG schoolwide action research, schools schedule a study group celebration and sharing event at the end of each school year and develop strategies for moving effective practices from individual study groups to the whole faculty by incorporating these practices into the school's annual improvement plan.

Results

In Calhoun's description (1994) of schoolwide action research, results in changes of student learning occur during the action step of her action research cycle, just as they do in Step 6 of the WFSG DMC.

A SUMMARY COMPARISON OF DIFFERENT ACTION RESEARCH APPROACHES

The Purposes of Action Research

Different authors have stated different purposes for action research. Table 2.1 summarizes the purposes of action research as seen by the WFSG approach, and Sagor, Caro-Bruce, and Calhoun.

Participants in Action Research

Most approaches to action research describe practitioners working as individuals or in small groups. Table 2.2 summarizes participants in action research as seen by the WFSG approach , and Sagor, Caro-Bruce, and Calhoun.

Table 2.1   The Purposes of Action Research

Whole-Faculty Study Groups	Action Research—Sagor (2005)	Action Research—Caro-Bruce (2004)	Schoolwide Action Research—Calhoun (1994)
• Address schoolwide student academic learning needs in classrooms for teachers' current students by changing what is taught and how it is taught.	• Improve student performance (academic performance, behavior, and attitudes) • Improve processes (teaching practice or school procedures) • Improve programs (curriculum or offerings).	• Improve practice • Understand a particular aspect of one's practice • Understand one's practice in general • Promote greater equity • Influence the social conditions of practice.	• Improve equity for students • Improve curriculum and teaching in every classroom in a chosen area such as writing • Improve the school's ability to identify and solve problems.

Table 2.2   Participants in Action Research

Whole-Faculty Study Groups	Action Research—Sagor (2005)	Action Research—Caro-Bruce (2004)	Schoolwide Action Research—Calhoun (1994)
Whole faculty participates Study groups of 3–5 members from all certificated staff Aides and para- professionals–optional Administrators also form study groups	Individuals or school teams	Primarily individuals or small groups working with one school or across schools Caro-Bruce does mention schoolwide action research where the entire staff studies a school issue or problem of interest to everyone	Entire faculty participates Structures include: • A facilitation team to develop a plan and timeline for the research and to lead the process • Data collection by faculty study groups, a task force, or the facilitation team • Action research by faculty study groups or liaison groups

Action Research Process Steps and Timeline

There are similarities and differences among the process steps and timelines for action research. Table 2.3 summarizes process steps and a timeline in action research as seen by the WFSG approach, and Sagor, Caro-Bruce, and Calhoun.

Action Research Products and Results

Research Plan

All approaches to action research recommend up-front planning, but they differ on the nature of the planning. Table 2.4 summarizes research plans in action research as seen by the WFSG approach, and Sagor, Caro-Bruce, and Calhoun.

Table 2.3   Action Research Process Steps and Timeline

Whole-Faculty Study Groups	Action Research— Sagor (2005)	Action Research— Caro-Bruce (2004)	Schoolwide Action Research— Calhoun (1994)
Step 1: Analyze student learning data.	Step 1: Clarify vision and targets. • Identify a focus. • Select achievement targets. • Establish assessment criteria.	Step 1: Decide whether to do action research as an individual or in a group.	Step 1: Select an area of focus for the study.
Step 2: Identify schoolwide student learning needs.		Step 2: Find a focus.	Step 2: Collect data.
Step 3: Categorize student needs.		Step 3: Develop a plan for doing action research.	Step 3: Organize data.
Step 4: Form study groups.	Step 2: Articulate theory.	Step 4: Collect data.	Step 4: Analyze and interpret data.
Steps 1–4: 2 1/2 hours at beginning of the school year.	Step 3: Implement action and collect data. • Determine research question. • Create a data collection plan. • Take action.	Step 5: Analyze the data.	Step 5: Take action.
Step 5: Create study group action plan *(2 meetings - draft).*		Step 6: Write about the work.	*Timeline: Steps implemented over a school year.*
Step 6: Implement cycles of action research *(October – May).*		Step 7: Plan for future action.	
Step 7: Assess the impact of study groups on student learning.	Step 4: Reflect on the data and plan informed action. • Analyze data. • Revise theory of action. • Plan future action.	*Timeline: In the Madison, WI, district, one cycle of action research encompasses a school year. Changes occur during the current school year if they are part of the research design.*	
During and at the end of the year.	*Timeline: Over a school year.*		

Table 2.4   Research Plans for Action Research

Whole-Faculty Study Groups	Action Research— Sagor (2005)	Action Research— Caro-Bruce (2004)	Schoolwide Action Research—Calhoun (1994)
Study Group Action Plan–one per study group, created in the first two study group meetings, and updated during the year. The action plan includes the group's essential question and student learning needs, study group activities, resources, norms, classroom assessment tools for assessing student learning, and baseline data, targets, and actual results for each student need addressed.	Sagor does not include the development of a research plan as a formal step in the action research process he describes. However, he does emphasize the importance of clarifying up-front the nature of the research, the research questions and theories of action to investigate, and methods for data collection and analysis.	An action plan with research topic, research questions, and action steps. For each action step, Caro-Bruce asks researchers to indicate who will do the step, the person responsible for the plan, and what resources or support are available.	A general timeline for the different stages in the action research cycle. The schoolwide action plan (updated throughout the year). Individual teacher classroom action plans (updated throughout the year).

Interim Reports

While all approaches to action research expect practitioners to document their action research work, there are differences in the extent to which interim reports are prepared and shared. Table 2.5 summarizes interim reports in action research as seen by the WFSG approach, and Sagor, Caro-Bruce, and Calhoun.

Final Report, Presentation, or Portfolio

All approaches to action research recommend some level of final reporting on the action research, but they differ on the nature of the reporting. Table 2.6 summarizes final reports in action research as seen by the WFSG approach, and Sagor, Caro-Bruce, and Calhoun.

Results

The purpose for the action research determines the nature of the results to be expected. Table 2.7 summarizes the expected results in action research as seen by the WFSG approach, and Sagor, Caro-Bruce, and Calhoun.

Table 2.5   Action Research Interim Reports

Whole-Faculty Study Groups	Action Research— Sagor (2005)	Action Research— Caro-Bruce (2004)	Schoolwide Action Research—Calhoun (1994)
Study Group Logs – one for each meeting from each study group. The log asks groups to (1) indicate the student need and the action research step addressed, whether student work was examined, resources used, and readiness to share a proven strategy; (2) describe key findings, insights, and decisions, strategies used in classes with students and the results; and (3) indicate plans for the next meeting and list questions, comments, or concerns. Other reports – verbal or written reports on current work for cross-group sharing every 4–6 weeks.	Sagor recommends using spreadsheets to collect data during the research process and keeping a researcher's journal to record observations, reflections, and changes in approach or actions based on context changes. During the data analysis phase, Sagor encourages researchers to summarize the findings, draw tentative conclusions, and share emerging findings with others.	No interim reports are recommended but Caro-Bruce suggests sharing work during the data collection and analysis phases to get feedback from others.	Interim reports in the context of Calhoun's approach to schoolwide action research would include analyses and interpretations of materials in the professional literature that relate to the research target, analyses of data collected, and progress reports, updates to the schoolwide action plan and individual action plans.

CONCLUSIONS

The approaches to action research described earlier share some common elements with each other and with the WFSG approach to schoolwide action research. They are cyclical in nature. They seek to understand both what happens and why. They require planning before acting. They emphasize the analysis of and reflection on quantitative and qualitative data. They are guided by a desire to understand and improve.

Table 2.6   Action Research Final Reports

Whole-Faculty Study Groups	Action Research—Sagor (2005)	Action Research—Caro-Bruce (2004)	Schoolwide Action Research—Calhoun (1994)
Each study group updates its action plan, describes changes in student learning and teacher practices resulting from the group's work, and assesses how well they followed the WFSG process guidelines–May/June. Many WFSG schools also survey staff about their experiences in study groups and about their recommendations for improving the WFSG System.	Sagor suggests that the type of action research report prepared depends on the audience, purpose, and level of detail. He notes that some districts request full reports while others ask for abstracts. The five areas a research report should cover include an explanation of the context and problem, the theoretical perspective, the research design, the analysis of data, and action planning.	Caro-Bruce suggests a report on the research and a plan for action. The report might include a description of the problem, the context, actions taken to learn about the topic, an explanation of research and data collection methods, a literature review, data analysis, and recommendations. The plan for action identifies additional questions arising from the research, possible actions, people interested in the research, and strategies for engaging them.	Calhoun recommends that the facilitation team or task force guiding the schoolwide action research prepare a final report that includes the schoolwide action plan, innovations used, data on actual implementation of innovations, results on student learning, analyses of the data, and conclusions and recommendations. New or revised schoolwide action plans for the following year are also a form of final report.

Based on a review of the action research literature, we see the following differences between the WFSG approach to schoolwide action research and action research in other typical published works:

- *WFSG action research is schoolwide collaborative action research with all certificated staff.*

  While many authors mention collaborative action research (with small groups) and some mention schoolwide initiatives, only Calhoun (1994) has a model for doing it. The WFSG approach is similar to the Calhoun model.

- *WFSG action research only focuses on improving student academic performance.*

  Most other action research resources discuss using action research for a variety of purposes and rarely use improving student academic performance in examples. Calhoun (1994) explicitly targets improving student achievement as one of three purposes for implementing schoolwide action research. Teacher WFSG study groups are expected to improve student academic performance, while nonteacher WFSGs may focus on changing student attitudes and behaviors rather than academic performance. WFSG study groups do not address action research questions related to changing curriculum or programs.

Table 2.7 Action Research Results

Whole-Faculty Study Groups	Action Research— Sagor (2005)	Action Research— Caro-Bruce (2004)	Schoolwide Action Research—Calhoun (1994)
• Greater teacher collaboration. • Gains in student learning • Changes in teacher practices and in content taught • Greater schoolwide understanding of the action research process and the use of formative assessments with students • More broad implementation of study groups' changes in teaching and learning	Sagor affirms that the overarching goal of action research is "universal student success." He notes that descriptive and quasi-experimental action research yield different results with descriptive research focused more on understanding and quasi-experimental research focused on test action hypotheses	The results depend on the focus of action research Caro-Bruce states that action research may lead to the following: • Individual progress • Student progress • Knowledge production. • Social change • Personal meaning	Calhoun sees three results from engaging in cycles of schoolwide action research: • Improvement of the organization as a problem-solving entity • Improvement in equity for students so all students benefit • Specific improvements related to the content of the inquiries, such as improvement in teaching the writing process

- *WFSG action research expects results, changes in teacher practice and student performance, during the action research cycle, not after.*

  WFSG study groups are expected to change what they teach and how they teach during the action research cycle, not afterward—as some of the other action research approaches suggest. Calhoun (1994) provides examples of action in classrooms as part of a schoolwide action research cycle when schools have chosen to focus their research on improving teaching and learning.

- *WFSG action research expects study groups to go through several action research cycles within one school year.*

  While most authors do not include timelines in their descriptions of action research projects, the examples all seem to describe one action research cycle stretching over an entire year. However, Calhoun (1994) indicates that teacher study teams often engage in "mini" action research cycles as they implement their classroom action plans within the action phase of their action research cycle.

- *During an action research cycle, other approaches to action research emphasize more time upfront in designing research and building "theories of action" and more time after field research in writing up the results than does the WFSG approach.*

  Sagor (2005) emphasizes building theories of action to understand why problems exist. This is similar to root cause analysis in understanding gaps in student performance data (Preuss, 2003). Calhoun (1994) provides an example of a school faculty beginning to collect baseline data early in the school year so that a formal schoolwide research plan can be developed by November or December. Then, study teams implement classroom action plans from December through May. She encourages schools to try out innovations sooner than later to help build interest and momentum.

  The WFSG approach encourages study groups to move fairly quickly into trying out new content and pedagogy. The WFSG System asks study groups to look for underlying causes as they examine the baseline data they collect on student performance relative to the need, focusing on causes within their control to ameliorate. Rather than requiring formal research reports, the WFSG approach uses Instructional Council meetings, study group logs, updated action plans, and year-end sharing as ways to communicate results.

- *Action research texts have useful information and tools about the action research process that might benefit WFSG study groups—to help them deepen their work.*

  As noted earlier in this chapter, Sagor (2005) stresses the importance of constructing and testing theories of action. His book provides a step-by-step guide to constructing these theories. He also offers chapters on data collection and analysis.

  Mills (2007) has useful chapters on data collection, data analysis, and interpretation. He reviews observations, interviews, surveys, document and artifact analyses, and quantitative analyses of tests and rating scales of attitudes, agreement, and differences. Robinson and Lai (2006) have chapters on data collection, including interviews, questionnaires, and observations and other data collection methods, and data analysis, with guidelines and examples.

Observing students in classrooms is an important way to gather data about the effectiveness of teaching interventions designed to improve student learning. Hopkins (2002) presents four different methods of classroom observation: open, focused, structured, and systematic. He describes each method and provides examples. Open observation involves recording what transpires in the classroom as accurately as possible for later analysis and interpretation. Focused observation limits classroom observation to a particular area of concern, like questioning. Structured observation is focused observation that uses tally sheets or diagrams to determine which aspects of a practice are observed and who is involved. Systematic observation is focused, structured, and goes a step further to categorize or interpret the observations.

In Chapter 3, the topics of "creating change," "learning teams," and "professional learning communities" are introduced. This is followed by a comprehensive discussion of "schools, through schoolwide action research, becoming professional learning communities" and "study groups becoming learning teams," and how learning teams and professional learning communities function to improve teacher practice and enhance student learning.

3

Creating Learning Teams and Professional Learning Communities

Guiding Questions

- Do schools implementing schoolwide action research function as professional learning communities and do their study groups function as learning teams?

- How do study groups become actual learning teams and schools become professional learning communities to improve teacher practice and enhance student learning?

Our research and experiences (Murphy & Lick, 2005) over the last 20 years have shown that the processes for school improvement and student performance enhancement are most successful when the school's study groups become genuine learning teams and the school becomes an actual professional learning community.

The typical answer to the first question is "of course." Too frequently, though, study groups and schools function in ways that are contrary to learning teams and professional learning communities and operate far from these goals. This chapter explains and illustrates what teachers and administrators should understand to turn study groups into learning teams and schools into professional learning communities.

CHANGE AND LEARNING

It is change, continuing change, inevitable change, that is the dominant factor in society today.

Isaac Asimov (1978, p. xii)

When we talk about improving the effectiveness of schools and increasing student achievement, we are discussing major change, which is difficult to bring about and sustain.

Why do the majority of our significant school change initiatives seem to fail or be only partially successful? Typically, leaders and others involved would find the following (Lick & Kaufman, 2000, pp. 25–26):

- Those involved had not fundamentally reframed their own thinking relative to major changes in the school.
- They implemented a strategic planning approach in the school that was incomplete and inadequate for the major changes that were required.
- They failed to prepare their school for the important transformations that significant change requires.
- They did not provide or implement a detailed, disciplined transition plan for the school. Such a plan would include appropriate incentives and approaches for transitioning people, processes, and, most importantly, the culture from the old way of doing things to the new one.

Schools and faculty members typically have chosen, consciously or by default, to resist, ignore, or sidestep the realities and impact of change. They often turn to change management in the hope that once a change is upon them, they can manage or control the change and its effects. But, change management is reactive and this reactive approach frequently prevents one from defining useful change before being overtaken by other oncoming changes.

Change Creation

Instead of being just reactive, the school's administration, and the faculty must become proactive and define and then "join" change, embrace it as a partner, and use it creatively to advance the school's vision, mission, and goals and those of society. Management guru Peter Drucker (1985, p. 34) advises that since you can't predict the future, you must create it.

The number one issue facing schools today is the urgent requirement to design, implement, lead, and manage intentional, meaningful, planned change—change creation.

Change creation (Lick & Kaufman, 2000) is the process whereby a school and its leaders and faculty do the following:

- Take genuine responsibility for leading change; effectively define and plan for the desired change

- Comprehensively prepare the school for the planned change and modify aspects of the existing culture that inhibit creative approaches and effectiveness
- Develop and implement a change approach that capably transitions its people, processes, and culture from the existing ways of doing things to the new, more effective ones and includes replacing familiar processes and technologies with new ones that stretch our capabilities for greater educational quality and productivity (Lick & Kaufman, 2000)

These changes will be difficult and take us out of our comfort zones, but they are essential to our future educational success.

Learning and Change

Our research over the years has shown that *learning* is fundamental to change creation efforts in schools. While traditional definitions of learning are most often used, such as "a knowledge acquired by study, experience, or being taught," we propose a deeper meaning for learning for change creation in what might be called "capacity" or "action" learning.

Learning is defined as developing the capacity (i.e., willingness and ability), relative to the specific change under consideration, for effective action. "Effective action" is in relation to the totality of change being enacted. "Ability" includes information, knowledge, skill, experience, and understanding that would enhance effective action relative to the change. Capacity for effective action requires both willingness and ability. If either willingness or ability is lessened, capacity will be reduced. School staff often have the ability to bring about the desired changes, but not the willingness. In such cases, the change generally fails.

Learning, as defined earlier, involves a "fundamental shift or movement of the mind," as learning organization expert Peter Senge (1990) relates:

> Through learning we re-create ourselves. Through learning we become able to do something we never were able to do. Through learning we re-perceive the world and our relationship to it. Through learning we extend our capacity to create, to be part of the generative process of life. There is within each of us a deep hunger for this type of learning. (pp. 13–14)

This kind of learning is essential for effective change creation in schools.

The Universal Change Principle

Unfamiliar major changes almost always generate fear and anxiety in people, often requiring them to radically shift their thinking, feelings, beliefs, and behaviors. Consequently, the more individuals understand and accept about a change, the more comfortable and committed they tend to become to it. Such understanding gives people a sense of control over the change or a greater ability to anticipate relative to the change, contributing to their sense of comfort and security and lessening their resistance to the change (Conner, 1993).

These ideas and learning, as defined earlier, are the foundation for the seemingly simple but powerful overarching principle for change creation, the Universal Change Principle (Lick, 1999b, 2000), which is defined as follows: *Learning must precede change.*

When one attempts to bring about change in a school or similar setting, the Universal Change Principle is directly or indirectly applicable to essentially all change-related initiatives. The following illustrates the Universal Change Principle in schools.

Instead of just throwing money and computers at the faculty, the school responded to its new technology requirements with a training program on how, when, and why to use computers and computer support. Now, a few weeks later, those lessons seem to be paying off, faculty members are positively involved, things are running effectively, and performance has improved.

The application of this principle does not guarantee that resistance to change will be eliminated and that a desired change will be accomplished, but its proper application does significantly improve the chances for change success.

Notice that the principle implies no surprises, since it requires that learning must precede any change. For major educational initiatives, often there must be significant "learning" preceding change, such as several planned, multidimensional, many-level iterations of appropriate learning over a substantial time period (e.g., a staircase process with new learning at each step to move people from bottom to top in learning acquired).

The likelihood of people reacting favorably to change and assisting with it will be enhanced greatly if time is taken to provide for learning and understanding about the change. Simply put, school improvement requires change, and significant change in a school requires substantial learning by personnel and collaborative learning across the school.

The remaining sections of this chapter discuss the important transformational concepts of *learning teams* and *professional learning communities* in schools, which play a key role in helping to bring about change creation.

LEARNING TEAMS

The concept of a learning team has been defined in a wide range of ways and in many types of organizations and settings. In this chapter, we define learning team (Lick, 2006) in a way that goes well beyond most definitions in the literature. This definition is based on change creation and the Universal Change Principle, as discussed earlier, and consistent with the formal definition of *team learning* found in Senge (1990, p. 236).

A learning team is a group that develops and aligns its capacity (i.e., willingness and ability) as a team to create the results its members desire to achieve (Lick, 2006).

Align means to bring in line with other appropriate and relevant factors and characteristics in and related to the school. Alignment represents importantly dealing with a complex system of relationships for the school.

Learning Team Capacities

Learning teams in schools, as defined earlier, have the potential capacity to

- Learn and recreate themselves
- Set and focus on challenging new goals
- Have a spirit of inquiry and an action research capability

- Be self-directed and reflective
- Dialogue and think insightfully together about complex issues
- Take innovative, coordinated action
- Do things that they were never able to do before
- Invent together and experiment with their inventions
- Evaluate progress on issues and effectiveness of ideas
- Reperceive their school, its programs, personnel and groups, and their interrelationship
- Extend their capacity to create and be part of a major generative process in the school's operations and processes, productivity and effectiveness, and life and activities

Teams and Team Failure

Most teams are not learning teams. Unfortunately, research suggests that failure rates for teams and team implementations are high, ranging from 50% to 90% (Beyerlein, 2003, p. 4). Beyerlein's research (1997a, 1997b) provides some key causes of team failure in schools:

- Team implementation in schools is imported from elsewhere and not adapted and tailored to the specific needs of the school environment.
- Teams are introduced in schools more as a fad rather than as a serious means for improved performance.
- Teams in schools are adrift as isolated islands of structural change, not linked with other teams and appropriate resources and support.
- Teams in schools are not institutionalized in a team-based system, but left to depend on a single effective champion.
- Team processes in schools are not institutionalized so as to gain the full buy-in of the organization's leadership.
- Team preparation and support in schools are inadequate.
- Teams in schools are not provided adequate time for developing teamwork and the new norms that support it.
- Organizational leadership in schools is not prepared with the new manifestations for teamwork, such as supervisors transitioning into team coaches and team members taking leadership responsibilities.
- Teams are not planned to the ebb and flow of the academic year.

In all of the aforementioned areas of failure for teams in schools, the change creation process and the Universal Change Principal were less than adequately implemented.

Synergistic Teams and Relationships

Learning teams demonstrate synergistic teamwork. *Teamwork* is the ability of people to work together in a genuinely cooperative manner (i.e., interdependently) toward a common vision. Teamwork means joint work and joint responsibility. Teamwork is a vehicle that allows common people to attain uncommon results. Genuine teamwork is called *synergy* (Conner, 1993). Synergy occurs when the teamwork of a group allows it to get the maximum results from the available resources.

In a synergistic group, the members of a team work together to produce a total result that is greater than the sum of the efforts of the individual members. People energize and inspire each other, and the diversity of ideas and openness to them provide the basis for new creative ideas and approaches (Murphy & Lick, 2005, p. 165).

One important aspect of synergistic teamwork is *comentoring*. Comentoring (Lick, 1999a, 2000) means members of the group all agree to mentor each other. Peer coaching, where every member agrees to be a peer coach in the group, is one form of comentoring. In effective comentoring groups, each member acts as a sponsor, advocate, or guide. Members teach, advise, trust, critique, and support others to express, pursue, and finalize goals (Vanzant, 1980). They are also, in general, competent, supportive, sharing, unexploitative, positive, and involved (Cronan-Hillix, Gensheimer, Cronan-Hillix, William, & Davidson, 1986). Ideally, in a comentoring situation, "each member of a group offers support and encouragement to everyone else which expands individual and group understanding, improving the group's effectiveness and productivity" (Lick, 1999a, p. 209).

A comentoring group in schools, for example, might be a study group that explores a learning area together and whose members assist one another in expanding each other's capacity for understanding and creativity relative to the learning area. Synergy and comentoring can be meaningfully combined in groups in schools, as synergistic comentoring groups, to generate unusually effective and productive teamwork, as discussed in the next few sections.

Synergy Prerequisites

Change expert Conner (1993) explains that synergy is the "soul of a successful change project" (p. 188). His research found that the key requirements for a group to have synergistic capacity were *willingness*, arising from the sharing of common goals and interdependence (i.e., mutual dependence and genuine cooperation), and *ability*, growing from member and group empowerment and participative involvement. These are the same two critical components in the definition of learning presented earlier in this chapter.

Here are the four prerequisites for synergistic teams in schools:

1. Common Goals: Seek, create, and continue to focus on clear common goals for the group.

2. Interdependence: Operate interdependently in the group in a genuinely cooperative and mutually dependent fashion.

3. Empowerment: Function in the group so as to empower all members. People are empowered when they feel that they have something of value to contribute and that it may have a bearing on the final outcome.

4. Participative Involvement: Provide participative involvement where members are expected, encouraged, and free to openly and fully share their skills, knowledge, and ideas in a balanced approach in the group.

Synergistic relationships in schools are both powerful and productive. However, most groups don't naturally function synergistically; they either don't understand the requirements of synergy or don't choose to apply them very well.

Synergy Process

What is the process for creating the aforementioned prerequisites and synergistic teams? Conner's research (1993; see also Murphy & Lick, 2005) gives us an effective four-step process for building synergy in groups in schools:

1. Interaction: Group members must interact with one another and reciprocate. Required elements are effective communication, active listening, and the creation of trust and credibility; major diminishing factors are confusion, misunderstandings, and alienation.

2. Appreciative Understanding: Group members must understand why others see things differently than they do and work to appreciate the differences. Required elements are to create an open climate, delay negative judgment, empathize with others, and value diversity.

3. Integration: Group members must consider all input from the group, evaluate its value and usability, and collaboratively pull together appropriate ideas and perspectives to generate the best available solutions or outcomes. Required elements are to tolerate the ambiguity of the discussions and be persistent, flexible, creative, and selective as you work toward the best solutions or outcomes.

4. Implementation: Together as a unit, the group must implement the desired solution and introduce the various parts of the desired outcomes effectively in the school. Required elements are to strategize and develop an implementation plan; monitor, reinforce, and remain team-focused during the implementation process; and update and modify the implementation as needed to reach the desired outcomes.

The elements described earlier in the "prerequisites for synergy" and "synergy process" are the required *norms* for a group to become a synergistic team. Figure 3.1 lists the norms for synergistic teams.

Figure 3.1   Norms for Synergistic Teams

- Help create and focus on common goals
- Operate interdependently
- Work to empower members
- Share fully in discussions and encourage others to do likewise
- Communicate effectively and actively listen to others
- Help create trust in the group and credibility for members
- Work to create an open climate
- Delay negative judgments
- Empathize with others
- Value diversity
- Tolerate ambiguity in discussions but remain persistent and flexible
- Be creative and selective in formulating outcomes
- Help develop a team implementation plan and regularly monitor, adjust, and update the plan
- Remain team focused throughout the full implementation of the plan

The more closely members follow these norms, the more effectively their group will function as a genuine team. Groups can, at an initial meeting when norms are discussed, discuss the concept of synergy and the illustrative synergy norms presented in Figure 3.1. After the synergy norms have been selected, the group should develop an agreement that the group, individually and collectively, will strive to fulfill the synergy norms and function as a genuine team. If someone violates a synergy norm, this should be diplomatically called to the individual's attention, as appropriate, either in the meeting or immediately after it.

Synergy Checklist

As groups in schools collaborate to build teams, they should stop from time to time to monitor whether the group is continuing to function synergistically or, if not, to determine which synergy norm areas require additional attention. A synergy checklist containing the synergy norms (Lick, 1999a, pp. 42–43; Murphy & Lick, 2005, p. 174) is presented in Figure 3.2. This provides a practical checklist for assessing where the synergy norms are and are not satisfied. When the norms are present, they add to the synergy of the group and its capacity for effective action, and when they are not present, the synergy and effective action of the group is lessened.

A Synergy Example—Team-Building Efforts in the Tigerville School District

Turning study groups into learning teams is often easier said than done. Some groups find it easier than other groups, even within the same school district, as highlighted in the following example.

Team Building in Tigerville

This Whole-Faculty Study Groups (WFSG) case study by Koenigs (2004, 2007) took place in the Tigerville (a pseudonym) school district in a small rural community in central Kansas. The school district consisted of a primary, intermediate, middle, and high school.

Sharing was probably the most popular activity in study groups according to the teachers in Tigerville. The most common activities were sharing ideas; discussing instructional practices, lesson plans, strategies and student work, books and educational articles, and personal work experiences; aligning curriculum to state standards; creating products and projects; and researching best practices. For some teachers, study groups seemed almost a cathartic experience: "We did a lot of unwinding together, a lot of group building, team building," one teacher recalled.

In Tigerville, the strong cultural norms of each school faculty played a key role in collaboration and changes in teachers' practices. Elementary teachers continued to try new strategies and shared these with each other, because their culture of risk taking and collaborative sharing already existed at their level prior to the introduction of study groups. Additionally, it seemed that elementary teachers felt "pressure" to try new things if they heard others in their study group talk about using new strategies. This kind of team norm supported changes in practices rather than inhibit them. Middle school teachers also had a culture of working together in teams, so working collaboratively and trying new strategies was not as much of a stretch for them.

The culture of the high school, however, was not accustomed to collaboration and sharing prior to study groups. The high school culture was challenged and stretched by study groups, which reflected on members' practices and perceptions and, consequently, collaborative team building was, at times, new, uncomfortable, and difficult for them.

Figure 3.2 A Synergy Checklist for Study Groups

Whole-Faculty

Checklist for WFSG Study Group Synergy

Study Groups™

Study Group: _____ **Date:** _____

Directions: As a group, rate your study group using the following symbols:

* = We're there!   > = We're developing!   < = We're struggling!

Common Goals

_____ Has your group discussed, agreed upon, and written a clearly and precisely stated goal or goals for your work?

Interdependence

_____ Has the interaction and sharing of your group been interdependent (i.e., mutually dependent and genuinely cooperative)?

Empowerment

_____ Does each member feel that what he or she has to offer is important and may have an effect on the outcome of decisions?

Participative Involvement

_____ Do the members of your group feel that they can and do openly and freely participate in the discussions and activities of the group?

Interaction

_____ Do the members of your group, individually and collectively, communicate effectively and actively listen to each other?

_____ Has a sense of trust and credibility been created in the group?

Appreciative Understanding

_____ Do the members of your group show appreciative understanding to each other and their ideas?

_____ Does your group have an open climate? Does it value diversity, delay negative judgment, and empathize with others' ideas?

Integration

_____ Do your group members show persistence in their deliberations and tolerate ambiguity as your group works to consider input and pull it together to generate the best decision or outcome?

_____ Are members flexible, creative, and selective as they consider the issues and transition toward their final result?

Implementation

_____ Does your group create a plan for the implementation that sets its direction, manages the resources, and determines priorities?

_____ Does your group ensure that the various steps are completed, appropriate behavior and progress are monitored and sustained, the process remains team focused, and there are continual updates of the action plan?

Building Learning Teams

Effective learning teams in schools are difficult to create and sustain. That is why the successes of school change and learning teams are so problematical and school change fails so frequently. Consequently, actions toward the development of effective learning teams in schools have to be intentional and represent clearly defined commitments of the school. However, when this is done properly and well, the payoffs can be significant and can move the school to new levels of creativity, learning, change, and success.

Building on the earlier discussions, we now provide a practical design process for creating learning teams as an important part of generating change and new school learning. We illustrate each step with selections in italics from the Bunn Elementary School vignette from Chapter 1 and the vignette from the Bunn Elementary Radical Readers Study Group Vignette in Chapter 5.

Foundational Phase

1. Build group synergy: This represents the most important part of the process. Without it, the group is just not a genuine team and will fall short of its maximum potential. This is the foundation for being self-directed, setting and focusing on challenging new goals, having collaboration and reflection, and dialoguing and thinking insightfully together about complex issues in the school.

   After individual study groups had been selected, they began hour-long weekly meetings. By the end of their third week, each group had developed an action plan to guide their work. The groups also agreed to group norms to guide their work together.

2. Foster comentoring in the group: In comentoring groups, each member offers support and encouragement to everyone else, which expands individual and group thinking, understanding and learning, and thereby improving the group's effectiveness and productivity.

   The Radical Readers study group at Bunn Elementary worked on cause and effect during the fall semester. Teachers discussed strategies used within individual classrooms. They found that using everyday examples tend to work better to explain cause and effect than using a textbook to teach. One member brought in a list of books to accompany lessons using cause and effect. Another member, whose class had the lowest average on the pretest, brought in his posttest results, which showed a vast improvement. He incorporated test-taking strategies along with the cause and effect strategies all members had been using. One strategy he used was to (have students) read the questions before they read the passage. The whole group decided to use his strategy within their individual classrooms and continued to incorporate the charts and various graphic organizers.

Plan-Act-Reflect Phase

3. Utilize learning resources: The group utilizes a wide variety of learning resources, including research and literature, internal and external expertise, related experiences, relevant learning models, and professional development. As the learning team process unfolds, discovering, generating, and using appropriate learning resources provide an enhanced basis and higher plateau

for increased learning and potential for new creative solutions and outcomes in the school.

After creating draft action plans, each group decided which of their specific student needs to address first, identified or developed a simple classroom assessment task to give to students to collect data on how well their students currently perform on the need, used a scoring rubric or checklist to assess student work, developed specific performance targets to achieve by the end of the semester, and updated their action plans with the baseline and target data.

Groups used teachers guides, the Internet, the school's instructional specialist, and district content specialists as resources to help them identify research and best practices related to their student learning needs and updated their action plans with the new resources they identified.

4. Integrate knowledge and create potential solutions: The group pulls together all of the relevant information and knowledge available to it. These resources are then integrated synergistically and creatively into one or more potential solutions or desired outcomes. This allows the group to take innovative and coordinated actions, through a spirit of inquiry and an action research process (i.e., disciplined inquiry that leads to changes in practice and performance), toward inventing together and then experimenting with its creations. Further, from this process, the group not only gains new knowledge and learning, but can recreate itself and do things that it was never able to do before.

Then groups began the "real" work—changing what they taught and how they taught to improve student learning in the specific need area each group chose to address first. During the next three-month period, groups followed cycles of "plan-act-reflect"— planning at their study group meetings what to do differently in class, acting in class to implement the lesson plans and strategies, reflecting in the next study group meeting on the effectiveness of the lesson plan or strategy and planning next steps.

5. Apply potential solutions and share findings: As part of the spirit of inquiry and action research process, the group applies the new solutions or outcomes in their classes and the school workplace and shares their findings and results with group members.

Study groups reflected on the results and effectiveness of the strategies they used, decided whether to continue working as a group on the same learning need during the second semester or switch to another need, and updated their action plan with the actual results.

6. Assess findings and generate new solutions: The group assesses the findings and results from Step 5, evaluates their progress and effectiveness toward the desired outcomes, and creates new potential solutions.

Groups regularly readministered the baseline assessment task to students and examined samples of student work to understand how the changes they were making in their classes were affecting student thinking and understanding. Later in the semester, representatives from all of the study groups met for a third Instructional Council meeting to share interventions and what they were learning about improving student learning.

7. Iterate to desired outcomes: The team considers intermediate findings, results, and solutions, and modifies them accordingly by repeating Steps 3–6, as often as necessary, until the team is satisfied with the final outcomes.

During the 2005–2006 school year, a study group at Bunn Elementary assessed the results of their work with students at the end of the fall semester and then decided whether to continue working on the same need or to shift their focus to a new need.

Recheck Phase

8. Recheck group synergy and comentoring: The team must also periodically recheck its levels of synergy (using the Synergy Checklist) and comentoring, and make appropriate adjustments to continue to satisfy the criteria of Steps 1 and 2.

For a midyear Instructional Council meeting, the principal asked each study group to complete the Checklist for WFSG Process Guidelines in Resource D and to share their findings with other groups.

LEARNING COMMUNITIES

The ability to collaborate—on both a large and small scale—is one of the core prerequisites of modern society . . . without collaborative skills and relationships, it is not possible to learn and continue to learn as much as you need in order to be an agent for social improvement.

Michael Fullan (1993, pp. 17–18)

Definition of a Learning Community

As Fullan highlighted, the collaborative, learning, and improving relationships in a community is the essential nature of a learning community.

A *professional learning community* or *learning community* is a community, large or small, which can effectively collaborate, experience, and learn and then collectively share learning across the entire community and apply the new learning to improve the community and its members.

DuFour and Eaker (1998) tell us in their book, *Professional Learning at Work*, that in professional learning communities "educators create an environment that fosters mutual cooperation, emotional support, and personal growth as they work together to achieve what they cannot accomplish alone" (p. xii). Here is their outline of the key characteristics of professional learning communities (pp. 25–29):

- Shared vision, mission, and values
- Collective inquiry
- Collaborative teams
- Action orientation and experimentation

- Continuous improvement
- Results orientation

What follows are thoughts from DuFour and Eaker (1998), as related to learning communities:

"The school that operates as a professional learning community recognizes that its members must engage in the ongoing study and constant practice that characterize an organization committed to continuous improvement" (p. xii).

"The most promising strategy for sustained, substantive school improvement is developing the ability of school personnel to function as professional learning communities" (p. xi).

"The most critical question educators must confront as they consider an initiative to create a professional learning community is this one: Do we believe in our collective capacity to create a better future for our school?" (p. 286).

Learning teams are themselves small professional learning communities, and they are also the building blocks for larger learning communities. They are the subgroups in the community that separately collaborate, experience, and learn and then collectively share and apply their knowledge and know-how meaningfully across the entire community to importantly improve the community and its members.

We have learned only too well from our many experiences that most communities involved in learning are *not* learning communities. The fact is that genuine learning communities are difficult to develop. The fundamental "lesson learned" here is this: To create an effective learning community, you must first develop strong learning teams across your community!

Whole-Faculty Study Group Schools as Professional Learning Communities

Learning teams are critical building blocks for creating learning communities. So, if groups in a school are functioning effectively as learning teams, how do you move them to the next plateau to turn your school into a learning community? The best process we have seen for doing this is the approach utilized in the WFSG System.

WFSG Goal and Process

The goal of the WFSG System is to focus the entire school administration and faculty on creating, implementing, and integrating effective teaching and learning practices into school programs that will result in an increase in student learning and school improvement.

The WFSG System, as described in Chapters 1 and 2 and in Murphy and Lick (2005), is a job-embedded, self-directed, study group–driven approach to professional development and action research designed to build communities of learners in which professionals continuously strive to increase student learning and improve schools.

Table 3.1 highlights key principles of professional learning communities, as articulated by DuFour and Eaker (1998), and compares them with key principles of the WFSG approach (Murphy & Lick, 2005).

Table 3.1 Comparing DuFour and Eaker's (1998) Elements of Professional Learning Communities With the WFSG Approach

Professional Learning Communities	Whole-Faculty Study Groups
Theoretical framework with guiding principles, tools, and examples	Practical, structured, job-embedded, self-directed, student-driven system to create professional learning communities that increase student learning
Shared mission, vision, and values	WFSG guiding principles: • Students are first. • Everyone participates. • Leadership is shared. • Responsibility is equal. • The work is public.
The focus is on instruction, curriculum, assessment practices, and strategies for improving the effectiveness of schools	WFSG study groups address "how and what" staff teach (instruction, curriculum, and assessment practices).
The question that drives change must be enhanced student achievement	WFSG Guiding Question: "What are students learning and achieving as a result of what teachers are learning and doing in study groups?
Collective inquiry	All study groups engage in cycles of action research to improve student performance.
Collaborative teams	In WFSG schools, all certificated staff organize themselves into study groups of 3–5 members.
Time for collaboration built into the school day and year	Within the school day, WFSG study groups meet weekly for 45–60 minutes or biweekly for 90–120 minutes.
Highly structured meetings	Study groups plan meetings in advance, rotate leadership, prepare and post meeting logs, and use protocols for examining student work.
High levels of trust	Group norms, size limits, and shared leadership help each study group develop trust.
Action orientation and experimentation	Study groups experiment with new teaching strategies and content, act in their classrooms on their plans, and reflect on the impact.
Continuous improvement	Continuous improvement occurs for study groups, schools, and the WFSG National Center.
Results orientation	Every study group improves student learning in their classrooms each year.
Role of the principal	The principal is the primary sponsor within a school, providing support, encouragement, and pressure, and modeling WFSG principles and best practices.
Role of teachers as professionals	The WFSG System embodies the National Staff Development Council standard for teacher involvement in learning communities.

The driving force in the WFSG process is its self-directed study groups as they function *as learning teams* and do action research. Such learning teams do the following:

- Produce learning communities and set common goals, support member interdependence, empower participants, and foster active participation
- Plan and learn together, construct subject-matter knowledge, and engage broad principles of education that modify perspectives, policies, and practices
- Immerse everyone in sustained work with ideas, materials, and colleagues
- Cultivate action researchers, producing, evaluating, and applying relevant research
- Struggle with fundamental questions of what teachers and students must learn, know, and apply (Murphy & Lick, 2005, pp. 177–178)

Among the key "collective sharing and applying" elements in the WFSG approach toward creating a schoolwide learning community are the following:

- At the onset, administrators and faculty members, as a collective group, commit themselves to the WFSG System and a shared vision, mission, and general plan, requiring everyone's best efforts for improving the school and increasing student learning in the school.
- Once the aforementioned commitments are made, the collective group analyzes relevant student and school data to identify the priority student needs that study groups will address.
- After priority needs have been established, each faculty member decides which priority-need study group he or she will join, and then each group becomes a self-directed team and develops an action plan for what the members will do when the group meets to address their specific student need.
- Study groups employ the "practical learning–team design process" to become a synergistic-comentoring team and engage in effective collaborative action research, including the plan-act-reflect cycles.
- As study groups meet and address their action plan, they post logs of their efforts publicly for everyone in the school to see, and the principal or a designee reads and responds to all logs, providing such things as general responses, advice, assessment, encouragement, and offers of support
- Monthly, a different representative of each study group meets together with the principal and the other members of the Instructional Council, the schoolwide coordinating body, to collectively share their efforts and findings, new knowledge and know-how, problems and successes, needs and wishes, and future actions
- Extensive communication mechanisms are provided among study groups and with other groups and offices, including showcase times, bulletin boards, newsletters and brochures—printed and electronic, videos, exhibits and seminars, and special involvements for students, parents, and the PTA, district, superintendent, and board officers and staff, and the general public
- Midyear and end-of-the-school-year celebrations and show-and-tell programs are held to show appreciation and recognition for the work study groups are doing, and for groups to have fun and do creative things to inspire others and raise the status of learning at the school.

DuFour and Eaker's (1998) six "key characteristics of professional learning communities," (i.e., shared vision, mission, and values; collective inquiry; collaborative teams; action orientation and experimentation; continuous improvement; and results orientation), are illustrated in the elements of the WFSG approach described earlier.

The WFSG System has been implemented in hundreds of schools and several thousand study groups in those schools. Where properly implemented, the system has been successful in facilitating schoolwide action research, schoolwide change, and the enhancement of student learning (e.g., see Joyce et al., 1989; Murphy, 1991, 1992, 1995; Murphy & Lick, 2005).

In his recent doctoral dissertation research, Koenigs (2004, p. 60) stated the following:

> Professional learning community models, such as the Whole-Faculty Study Groups System, show great promise to positively affect teachers' instructional practices and school culture if thought and care are taken during the implementation process.

The following example involves the Springfield Public Schools, where almost all of the 51 schools are implementing the WFSG System. It illustrates how the schools in that district, using the WFSG System, created professional learning communities in their schools and shared and applied their knowledge and know-how effectively to turn their schools and school system into successful learning communities with exceptional results.

A School District Example of WFSG Learning Communities

Learning Community Results in Springfield

School year 2000–2001 found, on the Annual Performance Rating of the Missouri accreditation process, that the Springfield (Missouri) Public Schools were only one point above the cutoff for "provisional accreditation." Subsequently, it implemented a major improvement process in approximately 90 percent of its schools with the WFSG System being a central feature (Lick, 2006, p. 95).

On their last three annual accreditation reports, the district scored 100 out of 100 points on their Annual Performance Rating and earned the state's coveted "Distinction in Performance" award (Lick, 2006, p. 95; Lick & Murphy, 2007, p. 275).

The Missouri Commissioner of Education, D. Kent King, said the following:

This award is unique and demanding, because it requires districts to demonstrate growth and progress across the board. Districts must show improvement or high performance at every level—elementary, middle, and high school. (Lick, 2006, p. 95)

In March 2007, the Springfield Public School District was one of five in the state to receive the 2007 Missouri Staff Development Council (MSDC) Commissioner's Award of Excellence for Professional Development. The award honors Missouri school districts with quality professional development that is data-driven, job-embedded, and results-based. Springfield Public Schools demonstrated how professional learning positively impacts students and teachers and how practices are aligned with national standards for professional learning. (http://springfieldpublicschoolsmo.org/ Administration/PIO/archive/06_07/march/AwardExcellence3–7-07.htm)

The WFSG System is a key component of the district's professional development program.

As the third-largest school district in Missouri, the 51 campuses of the Springfield Public School District demonstrated wide variances in performance and were seeing little districtwide improvement. To fulfill their vision of academic excellence for all students, they had to face the reality of their data and implement a change process that began with a focus on student learning, moved to process alignment at all levels, and continued with district-level support for introducing study groups and an uncompromising expectation for results. In their successful approach, they found seven key lessons learned:

1. A clear and uncompromising focus on student performance is required.

2. Accountability created a sense of urgency.

3. Systematic and well-aligned planning models caused meaningful reflection and resulted in action appropriate for the stated goals.

4. The WFSG System was a systematic and well-aligned implementation model for school improvement plans.

5. A sense of urgency was harnessed to facilitate change.

6. District leaders had to provide organizational changes and support required for effective implementation.

7. Schools improved and student performance increased when effective, well-aligned models were combined with dedicated professional teachers, focused district leaders, and supportive board members.

CONCLUSIONS

In this chapter we introduced the concept of learning teams and discussed and illustrated the process for study groups becoming learning teams. We described the fundamentals and key characteristics of professional learning communities, showed how learning teams are critical building blocks for learning communities, and explored how, using a major change process, such as the WFSG System, schools could be turned into professional learning communities with the potential to increase student performance and improve schools.

At the beginning of the chapter we framed two guiding questions. The first, "Do schools implementing schoolwide action research function as professional learning communities and do their study groups function as learning teams?" was followed by our answer, "It depends."

- *Schools implementing schoolwide action research function as professional learning communities when they*
  o *enable study groups to share and learn from each other*
  o *embed the work of study groups in the school's improvement plan so that study groups take direction from the improvement plan*
  o *like experimental laboratories, generate content, materials, and instructional practices that improve student learning and that other faculty adopt and use.*

If schools implement schoolwide action research without providing opportunities for sharing and learning among study groups and do not connect study group work to their improvement plan, they will not become learning communities.

Our second guiding question has two parts: "How do study groups become actual learning teams to improve teacher practice and enhance student learning?" and "How do schools become professional learning communities to improve teacher practice and enhance student learning?"

The answers to both questions are a function of "how they operate" and "what they do."

- *Study groups become learning teams by how they operate.*

    Study groups that embrace the synergy norms in how they work together will become learning teams. Study groups improve teacher practice and enhance student learning by

    o following the action research process described in Chapter 4 ("how they operate")

    o working with content and instructional practices that are directly related to the learning needs of their current students ("what they do")

- *Schools become professional learning communities when their study groups become learning teams and when study groups are sharing and learning from each other.*

    Schools become professional learning communities that improve teacher practice and enhance student learning when

    o the student learning needs that study groups address are driven by the school improvement plan and data

    o each study group is improving teacher practice and student learning for the students its members serve

    o faculty are adopting and using content and best practices proven successful in other study groups

    o the work of study groups is an integral part of the school improvement plan

In Chapter 4 we build on the material from this chapter and earlier chapters to discuss and illustrate the steps in the schoolwide action research process and what study groups do at each step.

4

Conducting Schoolwide Action Research

Guiding Questions

- **What are the steps in the schoolwide action research process, and what do study groups do at each step?**

- **Does the schoolwide action research process change depending on whether a school is an elementary, middle, or high school?**

In the Whole-Faculty Study Groups (WFSG) approach to schoolwide action research, the guiding question for the entire faculty is this: "What are students learning and achieving as a result of what teachers are learning and doing in study groups?" (Murphy & Lick, 2005). Collaborative action research is what teachers are learning and doing in study groups. What teachers do in their study group work is Step 6 in the WFSG Decision-Making Cycle (DMC): Implement the Study Group Action Plan. The WFSG DMC is described in Chapter 2. Figure 2.1 in Chapter 2 shows the DMC and Figures 2.2 and 2.3 provide the template for the study group action plan.

Each study group engages in action research around each student need it addresses. The steps in the action research cycle include the following: (a) Assess needs and establish baseline and target performance, (b) research content and best practices and develop expertise, (c) plan interventions, (d) implement interventions and monitor, and (e) look at student work and data and assess changes. Then study groups evaluate student performance to decide whether to start a second collaborative action research cycle around the same student need or to start a new cycle focused on a different student learning need.

In this chapter, we explain why each step is important, describe what study groups need to do to implement the steps successfully and to document and share their work, and suggest options study groups might consider in tailoring the steps to their specific context. For each step, we provide examples from study groups to demonstrate how the same process can be implemented in elementary, middle, and high schools. We conclude the chapter with lessons learned from WFSG schools about implementing schoolwide action research to improve teacher practice and student learning.

SCHOOLWIDE ACTION RESEARCH STEPS

In schoolwide action research, each individual study group follows the same collaborative action research process with the following steps:

- Assess needs and establish baseline and target performance
- Research content and best practices and develop expertise
- Plan interventions
- Implement interventions and monitor
- Look at student work and data, assess changes, and decide the next step

Figure 4.1 illustrates the action research process or cycle that each WFSG study group follows. The process begins in the lower left portion of the figure with "Students are assessed." This assessment, which might be through school, district, or state assessments, observations, or surveys, occurs prior to Step 1in the WFSG DMC. In Step 2 of the DMC, the faculty collectively create a master list of student learning needs. In Step 4, the faculty form study groups around categories of student needs. In Step 5, each individual study group selects the specific student learning needs its members want to address for their students. Each study group's cycle of action research begins with "assess needs" and continues through "decide next steps—to start a new cycle but continue working with the same need or to start a new cycle working on a new need."

The circular arrows on the right side of the figure illustrate the iterative nature of teachers working to use new practices and content in their classrooms.

In this chapter, we describe the steps in the action research cycle that each study group follows and answer the following questions for each step:

- Why is this step important?
- What are some examples of the work that study groups do in this step?
- What needs to happen to make this step a success?
- How might this step be tailored to your specific context (options)?
- How might study groups document and share their work on this step?
- How much time should study groups spend on this step?

The next two chapters in this book closely relate to this chapter and elaborate on the collaborative action research steps described here. Chapter 5, "Putting Action Into Action Research: Improving Teacher Practice," goes into greater detail on how

Figure 4.1   The Action Research Process for WFSG Study Groups

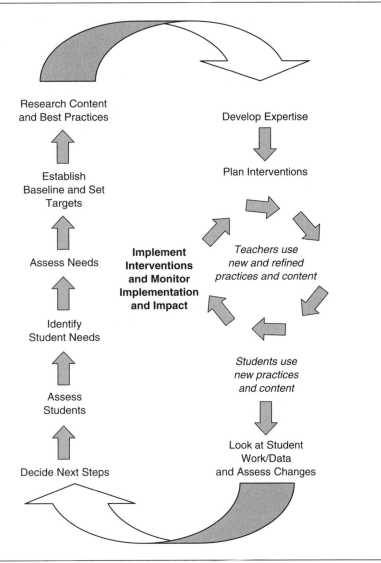

study groups change teacher practice and design classroom interventions that connect three domains of understanding—about students, the content, and teaching. Chapter 6, "Putting Action Into Collaborative Action Research: Improving Student Learning" describes how study groups know whether the changes they make in what they teach and how they teach impact student learning and whether the impact of study group work on student learning can be seen in student performance results on schoolwide, district, and state assessments.

Examples in this chapter come from the action plans and logs from study groups in different WFSG schools in the United States and Canada. The schools are Bunn Elementary School, Bunn, NC; Clarke Middle School, Athens, GA; Crooked River Elementary School, St. Mary's, GA; Hawthorn Middle School North, Vernon Hills, IL; Hubbard Primary School, Forsyth, GA; Northside High School, Warner Robins,

GA; Paul Robeson High School, Brooklyn, NY; Qualicum Beach Middle School, Qualicum Beach, BC; and Village Oaks Elementary School, Stockton, CA. Some of the study group materials can be found in Murphy and Lick (2005). Other materials come from the authors' collections of study group artifacts.

Step 1—Assess Needs and Establish Baseline and Target

There are three components to this step—assess needs, determine baseline student performance, and establish targets for improvements in student performance. These are important first steps in collaborative action research because these steps help teachers define exactly what they should focus on as they research and design classroom interventions to improve student performance. Schmuck (2006) refers to action research that begins with data as *responsive action research*, responding to the needs identified in the data.

Assess Needs

Once a study group has decided which of its student learning needs to address first, the group's next task is to analyze the student need to determine the skills, knowledge, and attitudes students must have to demonstrate proficiency with regard to the need.

Following are some questions to consider:

- What are the content skills and knowledge required to demonstrate proficiency for the need?
- What should students be able to "do" with the skills and knowledge, and what are the performance tasks that demonstrate understanding?
- What is the level of quality that students should reach to demonstrate proficiency, and how do we assess student work for each performance task?

At Clarke Middle School, one study group chose higher-order thinking skills as its category and "demonstrate problem-solving skills" as the student need. As group members started working on their action plan, they realized they needed to be more specifics about problem-solving skills and identified a set of subskills: Compare/Contrast, Synthesizing, Applying Knowledge to New Situations, Listening for Details, Hypothesizing, and Using Vocabulary Prompts. With feedback from the principal about not trying to do too much, the group decided to narrow the focus to the first three subskills.

Determine Baseline Student Performance

The next study group task is to determine for their students where they currently are with regard to the skills, knowledge, and attitudes they must have to demonstrate proficiency. Setting realistic targets and measuring actual changes in student performance relative to specific student learning needs depends on knowing where students are now on each of these needs. This is establishing a *baseline*.

Usually, schools identify student learning needs based on district or state assessment results for all of the students in the school. These data might be disaggregated, though, for groups of students identified by grade level, gender, income, ethnicity, English language proficiency, or special needs. However, these data are usually not organized by specific class or specific learning need, so teachers who have formed a study group around a set of student learning needs identified with schoolwide data often don't have detailed information about how students in their classes this year perform relative to the student needs they have chosen to address. Another reason for taking time to collect data on student performance relative to the chosen student needs is that teachers may not have samples of student work directly related to the need.

Collecting baseline data on student performance involves developing or identifying an assessment task, creating a scoring checklist or rubric, deciding which students to assess, administering the task to students, evaluating student responses for levels of proficiency and areas of strength and weakness, and summarizing results.

Study groups create two products when they conduct the baseline assessment. The first product is the *quantitative data on levels of student proficiency.* Groups use these data to set improvement targets to achieve by the end of the grading period, semester, or year. The second product is the *qualitative data on areas of strength and areas of weakness* with regard to students' skills, knowledge, attitudes, and behaviors related to the learning need. Groups use these data in Step 2, Research Content and Best Practices and Develop Expertise, to decide what to change in content and pedagogy to improve student performance.

Following are some questions to consider:

- What are the characteristics of our students' performance in the area of need we have identified?
- Which skills and concepts do they understand and how well?
- Which skills and concepts do they not understand and why?
- Are there different levels of understanding for different groups of children, and if so, why?
- Based on the analysis we have done, how would we describe the performance of our students relative to this need right now?

At Hawthorn Middle School North, a math problem-solving study group was working on students' ability to answer appropriately the extended response math word problems on the Illinois Standards Achievement Test (ISAT). They decided to use as an assessment task of one math word problem taken from a recent ISAT test and the ISAT rubric to score student work samples. They modified the instructions to first ask students to restate the problem in their own words before solving the problem because they wanted to find out if students understood what the word problem asked them to do before they tried to solve it. The group focused its data collection on just their sixth-grade students.

At Hubbard Primary School, the phonics study group collected baseline data on students' ability to recognize letters and sounds of the alphabet. After deciding how many letters and sounds a student had to recognize correctly for mastery, the group found that 12% of their kindergarten students could recognize alphabet letters in September, but that only 2% recognized sounds.

At Northside High School, a study group focusing on sequencing events in reading, writing, and mathematical processes in complete sentences asked students to write a paragraph that they would evaluate with a scoring rubric. They found that 71% of students were at the need improvement level on writing skills, 29% were at adequate or approaching proficiency level, and 0% were at the exemplary level.

Establish Targets for Improvements in Student Performance

After collecting and analyzing baseline data, the next study group task is to establish a target date and performance targets for expected improvements in student skills, knowledge, and attitudes relative to the student learning need. This is an important task for study groups, because establishing targets for students in their classes gives study groups a clear goal for their work together and it connects study group goals for improving student performance to schoolwide and district performance goals.

Study groups often pick target dates that coincide with the end of grading periods, allowing sufficient time between the time they collect baseline data and the target date for trying out interventions in classes and assessing their effectiveness. Study group targets are SMART learning goals—Specific, Measurable, Attainable but challenging, Relevant, and Time-Bound (Conzemius & O'Neil, 2002).

Following are some questions to consider:

- As a result of our study group work, what improvements in student performance do we want to see by the end of the year?
- How are we going to monitor changes in student performance on this need throughout the year?
- For which students are we going to monitor changes in student performance?
- How often are we going to check for changes in student performance?
- How can we display and chart our students' performance throughout the year?

The math problem-solving study group at Hawthorn Middle School North decided that the percentage of their sixth-grade students scoring above a Level 2 (completely correct response) should increase from an average score of 41% to 50% between December and March.

At Hubbard Primary School, the phonics study group realized in September from its baseline data that learning sounds was harder than recognizing letters, so the group set different performance targets for each skill for January—90% letter recognition and 60% sound recognition.

Between mid-January and the end of March, the Northside High School study group decided it wanted to improve student performance on learning to increase the percentage of students at the exemplary level from 0% to 10%, reduce the percentage of students at the needs improvement level from 71% to 30%, and have 60% at the adequate level instead of 29%.

Make This Step a Success

We find that study groups are the most successful with this step in the action research process, Assess Needs and Establish Baseline Data and Targets, when they do the following:

- Work on one student need at a time. Often study groups have identified several student learning needs as a focus for the group's work. We strongly recommend that study groups start with one specific learning need and go through each step in the action research cycle with that need before turning to a second need. Working on one need makes it much easier to stay focused and enables the group to see success within a reasonable amount of time.

- Clearly define a student learning need to specify the skills, knowledge, and attitudes students must be able to apply to demonstrate proficiency in the need.
  This may require a study group to identify external resources that define the skills and knowledge embedded within a need.
- Find or create a classroom assessment task and scoring rubric everyone in the group can use, even if teachers teach different content or grade levels.
- Design the assessment task, instructions, and scoring guide so that they can distinguish different levels of performance, such as proficient, almost proficient, and struggling, and can elicit what students were thinking and understanding as they completed the task.
- Use the same assessment tasks during the year to assess student progress. The power of study groups comes from the collaborative work. The best assessment tasks have a limited number of questions or prompts and require students to demonstrate their thinking and understanding. Since calculating class averages on an assessment task reveals little about differences in levels of student performance within a class, we recommend that study groups identify students by level of proficiency and by subgroup in schools with achievement gaps between student subgroups. From examining the resultant student work, study group members can both determine each student's level of proficiency and gain insights into why students are having problems with the need. Once a group creates an assessment task, the task can be used periodically, during the period the group is working on the need, to assess the effectives of interventions the group tries and, at the end, to determine whether students achieved their performance targets.
- Set targets for improved student performance for students at each level of proficiency. Performance targets should be in the same format as the baseline data. If the study group specifies levels of proficiency in the baseline data, then the group should set targets for students at each level. Create charts showing baseline student performance by proficiency level and relevant student subgroups for each teacher's class, then create a composite chart for the study group and transfer information to the study group's action plan.
- Keep for future reference all of the work students produce for the baseline assessment. New questions often surface as a study group starts working on the need about what students understand, and the group may wish to reexamine the work samples.

Tailor This Step to Your Specific Context

1. Choose a Specific Need: Sometimes study groups are not sure which specific need is the most appropriate starting point for their students. In this situation study groups can design a baseline assessment to collect data on several related needs and use the results to help them decide where to focus.

   For example, a study group has decided to focus on improving reading comprehension, but is not sure with which aspect of reading comprehension students are having greater difficulty: identifying the meaning of unfamiliar words, or drawing inferences, or whether both are problems, but for different groups of students. The group could design a baseline assessment task that provides a reading passage with questions to answer. Some questions would relate to identifying the meaning of unfamiliar words and others would address drawing inferences. For each student, the group would have two scores, an unfamiliar word score and an inference score. The group analyzes the scores for each teacher's class(es) and decides which specific need to address first and which students to target. The data from the assessment becomes their baseline data.

2. Choose a Sample of Students: One way this step is tailored to fit a study group's specific context is by teachers choosing to assess a sample of students instead of all students for baseline data and student work examples. Ideally, study group members might want to assess all of their students to collect baseline data and work examples relative to a specific student learning need. However, collecting and analyzing data for 20–30 students in a class is time consuming and middle and high school teachers often have four to six classes. Some groups choose to focus instead on a representative sample of students in their classes and follow the progress of these students throughout the year. Other groups choose to focus their study group work on a particular group of students, such as low achieving students or special needs students. This makes regular data collection and analysis and looking at student work examples more manageable.

3. Choose an Assessment Task: Another strategy for tailoring the work in this step to a group's context is to model assessment tasks after state or district assessments, as the math problem-solving group did. Many study groups create or use assessment tools and tasks modeled after the district or state assessments so that students are introduced to tools and tasks they will encounter on these assessments.

    However, many state and district assessments rely on multiple-choice questions, which are useful to determine levels of proficiency, the percentage of correct answers, but provide no information on what students were thinking about or understanding as they chose answers. We encourage study groups to supplement multiple-choice questions with other questions that ask students to explain orally or in writing why they chose one response over others. The math problem-solving group modified the instructions they gave students to ask them to explain the word problem before solving the problem to check on reading comprehension.

4. Use the Internet and District Resources to Look for Assessment Tools, Tasks, and Rubrics: Don't reinvent the wheel! There are lots of Web sites available on the Internet that offer assessment tools, tasks, and rubrics. Check the materials in instructional programs used in your school or district in each content area for performance tasks and assessment rubrics. Tap into knowledgeable people in your study group, school, or district. Invite them to come to a study group meeting to share their expertise and resources. Many districts have content-area specialists who have resource materials that teachers can use to adapt or locate assessment tasks and rubrics.

Document and Share Work

Study groups document and share their work in this step in a variety of ways. They update their action plan to add their assessment tasks and summarize baseline data and targets. They attach copies of assessment tasks, scoring rubrics, and data analyses to the study group log for the meeting in which they were discussed and keep copies in their study group binder. They keep samples of student work from the baseline assessment for comparison with student work as the group monitors progress. Study groups share their work on assessing needs and establishing baselines and targets in Instructional Council meetings and in faculty meetings, and data from the baseline assessment and targets can be posted in teachers' classrooms.

Time Spent on This Step

Typical amounts of time to spend on elements in this step are as follows:

Step	*Time Required*
Analyze the student need for underlying skills, knowledge, and attitudes.	Part of one study group meeting (before the meeting, the group may need to identify resources that define the skills and knowledge embedded in the need).
Decide on an assessment task, scoring rubric, and data collection procedures.	Part of one study group meeting (if members search for tasks and rubrics between meetings).
Analyze baseline data from initial assessment and set performance targets.	One study group meeting (if data are organized before the meeting).

Step 2—Research Content and Best Practices and Develop Expertise

The purpose of this step in the action research process is to identify the content skills, knowledge, and instructional practices teachers should have to design classroom interventions to address the specific problems their students are having relative to the identified student learning need. This step is focused on building teacher expertise in the identified student need—it is targeted at professional development. The goal of study group work is to improve teacher practice to improve student learning. The WFSG System is built around the assumption that student learning will not improve significantly if teachers keep doing what they regularly do in classrooms. Teachers in study groups focus on improving what they teach and how they teach. The question isn't "Did I cover X?" but "Can my students demonstrate understanding of X through how they use and apply it?"

This step has three components: develop an action hypothesis, research content and best practices to use, and develop expertise.

Develop an Action Hypothesis

To start this step, each study group should first develop one or more action hypotheses about what they believe they need to change in class content and pedagogy to improve student performance. The action hypothesis provides a focus for researching content and best practices and developing expertise. The action hypothesis is what Sagor (2005) and Robinson and Lai (2006) call a "theory of action" about the causal relationships that drive performance. Schoolwide action research is a process for testing these study group action hypotheses.

An action hypothesis is an "If, then" statement—If I change X in my teaching, then students will improve their performance in Y. For example, a study group has determined that their students are weak in identifying the meaning of unfamiliar words in a reading passage. In examining samples of student work, they realize that students are not recognizing prefixes and suffixes or compound words and are not using context clues to determine meaning. The group's action hypothesis might be, "IF we teach and help students to recognize prefixes, suffixes, and compound words and to use context clues, THEN they will improve their ability to find the meaning of unfamiliar words."

The question to consider is this: What do we need to change or strengthen about what we teach (the content) and how we teach (instruction and assessment strategies) to improve student performance relative to the specific student need we have identified?

A reading study group at the Bunn Elementary School developed an action hypothesis around recognizing the main idea in any given passage. They reasoned that if they used graphic organizers to help students identify the main idea in reading passages, students would improve their ability in their writing to state a main idea and develop it.

Research Content and Best Practices

The beginning point for research lies in digging deeper into the action hypothesis. Is students' lack of skill or knowledge due to students not being taught or students not remembering or not mastering the skill or knowledge?

In the reading example shown earlier, the group might first ask their students whether their lack of ability in identifying the meaning of unfamiliar words was because they and former teachers hadn't taught the students to recognize prefixes and suffixes or compound words and use context clues, or because the students had been taught and either did not remember or could not apply what they had learned. The responses the group receives from students will help them to decide whether they need to teach new content or teach previously taught content in new ways for student mastery. They may even decide they need new ways to teach new content.

Study groups naturally share their own content knowledge, instructional practices, and experiences with students, but this is not the end to researching content and best practices. WFSG expects every study group to increase its collective expertise regarding its student need by seeking outside resources.

In the reading example, the group would seek resources to answer these questions: What do reading specialists say are the different skills and knowledge that proficient readers use to find the meaning of unfamiliar words? What instructional practices have proved effective in helping students similar to our students become proficient with these skills?

There are many different kinds of resources teachers can use to build expertise. Resources can be the teachers' guides for instructional programs the school is implementing, or for materials connected with school and district initiatives, such as a writing initiative and ongoing professional development on differentiated instruction or quality teaching and learning. Resources can be found at state departments of education, professional associations, and on the Internet.

And resources are people, other staff in the school and district, or in other districts. Many districts have content and instructional specialists who can help study groups quickly identify content and effective practices. Groups can invite "expert voices" to a study group meeting to share their knowledge and skills. With each resource, the guiding question is this: How can this resource help us better teach our students in the areas where they need to improve?

Following are some other questions to consider:

- What are our strengths in addressing this need? What do we know we do that works?
- What are others already doing or what resources already exist to address these needs?

The phonics study group at Hubbard Primary decided after reviewing baseline data that they needed input from a speech teacher on teaching consonant and vowel sounds. The speech teacher met with the group and shared information on which sounds are easy or hard for kindergarteners to learn and strategies and resource books for teaching sound recognition.

After assessing their students' comfort and fluency with writing, a cross-discipline writing study group at the Paul Robeson High School decided to get copies of Learning to Write, Writing to Learn (Indrisano & Paratore, 2005) and use this book as a resource for developing strategies group members could try out with their students.

Many schools and districts have multiyear initiatives to strengthen faculty knowledge of pedagogy and content related to student learning needs. Study groups can select specific student learning needs for which they can apply the strategies and knowledge they are already learning. For example, the Laurel Mill Elementary School in Franklin County, North Carolina, is part of the district's Reading First initiative. The K–3 teachers receiving training through the Reading First initiative decided to form study groups that focused on their students' reading needs that they could address by applying what they had and were learning in their Reading First training.

Similarly, in the Hawthorn School District in Vernon Hills, Illinois, the district has invested heavily in building teacher expertise in "6 + 1 Trait Writing" and the Writer's Workshop. In the two middle schools, teachers formed several study groups to address student writing needs and apply what they had been learning in their professional development.

These are examples of linking ongoing professional development and whole-faculty study groups with improving student achievement, just as Joyce and Showers recommended in their 2002 book, *Student Achievement Through Staff Development.*

The point to keep in mind is that time set aside for ongoing professional development can be used to support the need of study groups to develop expertise without having to add more time for study group meetings.

Develop Expertise

Proactive study groups plan for their own professional development and get help as needed. One strategy study groups use to develop their expertise is to see instructional practices in action, rather than just reading about them. The group arranges to observe another teacher who is successfully implementing the practice. Another is to model practices in study group meetings by teaching the practice to colleagues before deciding whether to try the practice out on students.

Following are some questions to consider:

- In which areas do we need to develop our expertise?
- What do we need to do to develop our expertise?
- What resources or support do we need to help us develop our expertise?

The math investigators study group at Bunn Elementary School decided to visit each other's classrooms to observe how math centers, with investigative math activities, were being used by students at different grade levels.

Make This Step a Success

We find that study groups are the most successful with this step in the action research process, Research Content and Best Practices and Develop Expertise, when they do the following:

- Have a clearly articulated action hypothesis that focuses research for content and best practices.
- Seek "expert voices" outside of their study group to increase their expertise in the identified student learning need.
- Identify instructional strategies that can be used with students across content areas and grade levels.

Successful study groups resist the urge to spend the year researching and developing expertise and begin using new learning in classrooms so that students benefit. Rather than trying to learn everything they can about a need, they limit the scope of research and learning and plan to learn more in the next action research cycle. For example, a reading study group might limit its focus to just teaching decoding in its first action research cycle.

Tailor This Step to Your Specific Context

1. Recognize Different Levels of Expertise: Many study groups have members who teach different grades and subjects and have different levels of expertise about the content and best practices related to the need the group is addressing. Different members of the group may need different levels or types of professional development to develop their expertise around the group's need. Some members may need additional support or need to watch another member teach the strategy before they feel comfortable enough to try the strategy in their classroom. The school's instructional specialist can be a helpful resource.

2. Use Protocols: When members bring articles or other written resources into study group meetings to share, members can use protocols to structure the discussion, such as the Jigsaw protocol developed by Aronson and Patnoe (1997) or the Final Word protocol, developed by Averette and Baron (n.d.).

Document and Share Work

Study groups document and share their work in this step in a variety of ways. They let their principal and other study groups know that they are looking for resources. They list sources for content and instructional best practices in the resource section of the action plan and keep copies of materials found in study group binders with logs of the meetings in which the materials were shared and discussed. They share copies of research and best practices with study groups working on similar needs and at faculty meetings or Instructional Council meetings, put copies in the school's resource center in the faculty room or library, and post copies and Web links to the school's study group Web site or electronic portfolio.

Time Spent on This Step

Typical amounts of time to spend on elements in this step are as follows:

Step	*Time Required*
Clarify the group's action hypothesis, decide what content and practices members need to build their expertise and plan how to acquire it.	One study group meeting
Share resources and discuss implications for students.	One to two study group meetings, depending on the scope of research
Develop expertise in content and promising practices.	One to two study group meetings plus visits with teachers using the practice

Step 3—Plan Interventions

The heart of collaborative action research is the intervention—what teachers try out in their classrooms to help improve student understanding and learning. Steps 3, 4, and 5 are the central action research steps of Plan-Act-Reflect.

An intervention could be introducing new content knowledge and skills or an instructional strategy, such as mnemonics or graphic organizers, to help students learn important concepts. An intervention could extend for part of a class period to a week or more. In study group meetings, members help each other think through and plan classroom interventions.

Planning an intervention for action research builds on lesson and unit planning. As in planning lessons or units, a study group planning an intervention has to think about and articulate what they expect students to think and do during the intervention, and as a result of the intervention, what they will do before, during, and after the intervention, what resources they will need, and how they will assess changes in student learning as a result of the intervention.

Assessing changes in student learning means comparing student performance before and after an intervention—a pretest and a posttest. For example, to assess how well students can compare and contrast before and after introducing Venn diagrams, a study group would ask students to complete a compare-and-contrast task before the intervention and after, making sure that the content and vocabulary in both tasks were of similar levels of difficulty. If the group has just collected baseline data on student performance, the baseline data might be used as the pretest data.

As action researchers, study groups are also concerned about assessing the effectiveness of the interventions they try with students: Is this an effective intervention for improving student performance in X? This extra dimension means that groups first need to pay attention to how the intervention is actually implemented and how students actually respond during the intervention. Then, the group compares what actually happened with what they planned to determine what changed and how these changes may have affected results with students.

How an intervention is implemented really means how proficient the study group members are in teaching the content or strategy the study group has selected to use. In the Concerns Based Adoption Model (CBAM), there are levels of use of an innovation, with teachers progressing from mechanical use to routine use to integrated and renewing use with practice, feedback, and coaching (Hall, Loucks, Rutherford, & Newlove, 1975). If study group members are using a new strategy with students, they need to develop their proficiency with the strategy to expect to see gains in student learning.

At the Daniel Hale Williams Preparatory School of Medicine in Chicago, the Problem-Solving study group faced this challenge in their work during the 2005–2006 school year. The group decided to use a strategy called "Quiet Conversations" to help improve students' problem-solving ability. The strategy has students working in groups of three. One member of the group solves the problem. A second member of the group critiques the solution by the first student, identifying strengths and weaknesses. The third member then critiques the second member's critique. Then the three students change roles and solve another problem.

The group found when they first tried using this strategy in classes that the first students were not clear on what constituted a "good" problem solution and the second and third members weren't clear on what a "good" first and second level critique looked like. They spent several months observing each other's classes, debriefing what happened with students, examining student work, and refining their teaching of the strategy. By the end of the semester they were seeing clear improvements in students' ability to solve problems and critique each other's work.

A second component to assessing the effectiveness of an intervention focuses on students' learning, interest, and engagement. In teaching students to use a new strategy, like a graphic organizer, teachers want students not only to develop proficiency in using the strategy but also improve their performance on the need, such as writing, by doing so. Improved learning encompasses both of these elements. The effects an intervention has on student interest and engagement can only be observed while the intervention is taking place.

Following are some questions to consider:

- What will we do in our classrooms to improve students' performance?
- If we are adapting or using a strategy that others have used, how do we modify it to reflect the characteristics or needs of our students?
- What do we expect students to think and do during this intervention?

- What changes do we expect to see in samples of student work?
- How will we monitor what happens during the intervention—what we do and what students do?
- How will we assess the effectiveness of the intervention—on student understanding and on student interest and engagement?

At Qualicum Beach Middle School, a literacy study group wanted to improve their students' ability to take notes and use notes effectively. The group's members decided to introduce to their students the "Power Notes" strategy of note taking that requires students to create hierarchical notes with the most important ideas identified and subpoints clustered under each main idea. In a study group meeting, teachers planned how they would introduce the strategy and tasks they wanted students to do—use power notes to write a speech and then use power notes to deconstruct another student's speech. For assessment, they decided they would (a) evaluate the quality of each students' notes using a rubric before and after teaching "Power Notes," (b) compare the student's speech with the notes to see if the hierarchy of ideas in the power notes are reflected in the writing, and (c) compare one student's power notes of another student's speech with the other student's original power notes.

Make This Step a Success

We find that study groups are the most successful with this step in the action research process, Plan Interventions, when they do the following:

- Keep it manageable.
    Start with a simple intervention to keep the work reasonable and build confidence in the action research process.
- Use backward planning.
    First, define what you want students to think and do to demonstrate their improvement with regard to the learning need after you have tried the new intervention; then, build the intervention activities to accomplish this.
- Create the assessment tasks, tools, and scoring rubrics—and try them out on each other—before starting the intervention.
- Select assessment tasks for the intervention that are similar to the assessments used to collect baseline data.
    This will help you determine whether students have improved since the baseline assessment.
- Plan to teach the intervention more than once to see if students respond differently the second or third time.
- Let students know that you are engaged in action research to help them, and involve them as coresearchers by developing strategies to capture their reactions and thinking as they participate in the intervention.
- Plan to use other study group members or a video camera to observe the intervention with students.

It is hard to watch students carefully when one is trying out a new intervention and remember all the midcourse corrections one makes in teaching in new ways. Study group members help each other by observing students during an intervention. Teachers also set up a video recorder to tape student activity during the intervention and review the tape later, either individually or in the next study group meeting.

Tailor This Step to Your Specific Context

Some study groups that want to go more deeply into refining classroom instruction explore Japanese lesson study. Catherine Lewis (2004) describes lesson study as a process that small groups of Japanese teachers engage in to systematically examine their practice, with the goal of becoming more effective. This examination centers on teachers working collaboratively on a small number of "study lessons." Working on these study lessons involves cycles of planning, teaching, observing, and revising the lessons.

Document and Share Work

Study groups document and share their work in this step in a variety of ways. They attach copies of the lesson plans, assessment tasks, scoring rubrics, and observation tools they create for the intervention to the logs of the meetings in which these items were developed or discussed and save copies of these documents in their study group binders. They share these materials with colleagues at Instructional Council meetings, grade-level or content-area meetings, and faculty meetings. They also place copies in the school's resource center or post them on the school's Web site.

Time Spent on This Step

Typical amounts of time to spend on elements in this step are as follows:

Step	Time Required
Plan the intervention.	One to two study group meetings, including modeling the practice
Plan assessment and observation.	One study group meeting

Step 4—Implement Interventions and Monitor

Trying out interventions in the classroom is the action in action research. This step takes place in classrooms, not in study group meetings.

Like any good field researcher, study groups involved in action research document what really happens in the classroom, both by the teacher and the students, when trying out an intervention. Teachers keep track of what they do and the adjustments they make during the intervention, either through a journal or by watching a lesson that has been videotaped. They collect student work samples and monitor students' interest and engagement in activities.

Following are some questions to consider:

- How well are we implementing this intervention and what can we do to improve our proficiency with this intervention?
- What adjustments did we make in the intervention as we implemented it and why did we make these adjustments?
- What effects are the interventions having on student interest and engagement?
- How might we improve this intervention when we use it again?

At the Crooked River Elementary School, the Math Facts study group tried a number of different interactive strategies to help students learn addition, subtraction, multiplication, and division. In a study group meeting to review the results of several interventions, teachers said they really noticed the importance of using multiple sources for teaching and learning concepts and that they have to seamlessly integrate the materials so that students don't feel a lack of coherence as they move from one learning approach to another.

Make This Step a Success

We find that study groups are the most successful with this step in the action research process, Implement Interventions and Monitor, when they do the following:

- Assess student learning and understanding before and after the intervention.
- Document the adjustments each teacher makes to the intervention as they implement it.
- Teach the intervention more than once to see if students respond differently the second or third time.
- Observe each other teaching the intervention and debrief and refine the intervention.
- Monitor student interest and engagement as well as their work, using colleagues or a video camera to help capture and observe student reactions.

Tailor This Step to Your Specific Context

1. Involve Students in Learning Experiments: Involving students as participant-observers as teachers try out interventions in classes encourages them to be more conscious of, and reflective about, their own learning and provides the study group with more information about how interventions are affecting students.

2. Keep a Journal or Field Notes: Like any good researcher, teachers need to document what really happens in classrooms, both by the teacher and students, when trying out an intervention. Some teachers use two-column notes with the left-hand column for notes taken during or immediately after the intervention and the right-hand column for reflections, analyses, and connections.

Document and Share Work

Study groups document their implementation of interventions for two purposes—to bring information back to their study group meetings to help the group assess the effectiveness of the intervention and, if the intervention is effective, to be able to share detailed information and teaching tips with other teachers. Teachers keep their observations and notes in a journal or in field notes in their study group binder.

In addition to their own observations, teachers collect student work samples and record students' performances on the assessment tasks. Teachers will want to bring back to their study groups both data about student performance and samples of student work for the next step in the action research cycle, looking at student work and data.

Time Spent on This Step

Implementing and monitoring interventions takes place in classrooms with students, not in study group meetings. Therefore, interventions occur between study group meetings.

However, study group members may want to schedule a special meeting to revise the intervention, based on the reactions to students while members are involved and results from looking at student work and performance data, and assessing changes (i.e., the next step in the action research cycle for study groups).

Step 5—Look at Student Work and Data and Assess Changes

This step has three components: looking at student work, looking at student-performance data obtained from assessment tasks, and assessing what changed and why and planning next steps.

Study groups look at student work samples and performance data because this is the evidence of the effectiveness of the interventions the group has tried. Looking at data and work samples helps the study group identify in which areas students are improving and where students are still struggling. The advantage of collectively looking at student work and student performance data is that each study group member brings different perspectives to the data and work samples. Assessing changes answers the "so what" question: What have we learned and what further improvements do we need to make?

Looking at Student Work

Looking at samples of student work together as a group is a basic strategy that all study groups should use:

> Whole-Faculty Study Groups look at student work as part of a data collection process that documents the current conditions related to a study group's essential question. Student work indicates to what degree a student is or is not meeting one or more standards or identified student needs that a group is addressing. Student work that is examined by a WFSG is aligned with the essential question and the specific student needs that are stated on a group's Study Group Action Plan. (Murphy & Lick, 2005, p. 144)

One of the key features of this approach to looking at student work is that less is more. In a 45- to 60-minute study group meeting, the group might examine only a small number of samples of student work, such as all members examining one student's work or each member examining work from a different student on the same assignment. The work samples have no names and no grades or teacher marks on them to influence the group's conversation about the work. Teachers look at student work for evidence of critical thinking, knowing skills, facts and concepts and being able to apply them, and misconceptions and patterns in errors. They also look for evidence that the student understood the assignment task and instructions.

A second key feature is the use of protocols to guide the examination of student work and structure the group's conversation:

A protocol consists of agreed-upon guidelines for a conversation and it is this structure that permits a certain kind of conversation to occur. . . . A protocol creates a structure that makes it safe to ask challenging questions of each other; it also ensures that there is some equity and parity in terms of consideration of each person's issues. (Murphy & Lick, 2005, p. 145)

There are a number of different protocols for looking at student work (see, for example, McDonald, Mohr, Dichter, & McDonald, 2003). Study groups decide at the preceding meeting what work will be examined, how many samples will be reviewed, which protocol to use, and who will be the presenting teacher, facilitator, recorder, and timekeeper.

One protocol for looking at student work that many WFSG schools use is the "Wows and Wonders" protocol shown in Figure 4.2. This protocol is a variation on the Tuning Protocol (Blythe, Allen, & Powell, 1999) and was first used by ATLAS Learning Communities in its implementation of the WFSG System in ATLAS schools beginning in 1997. The protocol is designed to give the presenting teacher feedback about a sample of student work and has several distinctive features. The presenting teacher poses a focusing question in Step 1 to guide the group's feedback and does not participate in the feedback discussion, Step 4. He or she only listens and takes notes. In Step 4, the facilitator adheres to equal amounts of time that are allocated for "wows" and "wonders" and instructs the group to frame concerns or negative feedback about the work as "wonders" so the presenting teacher doesn't feel angry or threatened by the feedback.

Following are some questions to consider when looking at student work:

- What does this work tell us about what students are thinking, and what questions does it raise?
- What does this work tell us about students' understanding of important skills, concepts, and attitudes, and what questions does it raise?
- What does this work tell us about our teaching or the performance task we asked students to do, and what questions does it raise?
- What does this work tell us about students' interest and engagement in the task, and what questions does it raise?
- What are the implications of what we see, or of the questions we raise, for our next steps?
- Are the interventions we are trying out in our classrooms helping students build and demonstrate understanding?

At the Village Oaks Elementary School, the Fluency Flyers study group used the Wows and Wonders protocol to guide the group's conversation about an audiotape reading by three students of "Jellybean Soup." They found that students' fluency was considerably better than their intonation.

In the writing study group at Paul Robeson High School, one teacher brought in a sample of student work from a writing exercise in environmental science where students had to write two paragraphs about taking a journey from school through the solar system, visiting every planet. The group used the Wows and Wonders protocol to guide their conversation about the student's work. Teachers were impressed by the student's relaxed response, which revealed both factual knowledge and imagination. They wondered whether the wording of the assignment was explicit enough to generate the results the teacher wanted, whether students were familiar with the genre of scientific journal entries while traveling, and whether working with students to create a rubric or set of criteria for a journal of a journey would be helpful.

Figure 4.2   The Wows and Wonders Protocol for Looking at Student Work

Whole-Faculty

Study Groups™

Wows and Wonders
A Protocol for Looking at Student Work in Study Groups

**(Wows and Wonders is a modified version of the
Tuning Protocol and is used by ATLAS Communities)**

Before you begin, select a facilitator and timekeeper to keep the conversation on task and moving. Remember your group norms.

1. **Presentation of student work: 3 minutes**

   Participants listen while the Presenting Teacher presents the work, for example:

   - assignment or prompt that generated the student work
   - student learning goals that inform the work
   - evaluation format (rubric, test, etc.) if appropriate

   Presenting Teacher gives the "focusing question" – what feedback s/he wants

2. **Clarifying Questions: 2 minutes**

   Participants ask the Presenting Teacher clarifying questions, matters of fact (How many students do you have in this class? What kind of prior experience did this student have?).

3. **Examination of work: 3 minutes**

   Participants look at the work (without talking), taking notes on the strengths they see and the questions they have, while keeping in mind the focusing question – what feedback the teacher wants.

4. **Feedback: 20 minutes total time**

   WOWS! 10 minutes: While the Presenting Teacher only listens and takes notes, the participants talk among themselves expressing positive/affirming feedback and expressing the strengths they see in the work, such as:

   I like the way . . .

   It is exciting to see . . .

   The student really seems to . . .

   The obvious strengths are . . .

   WONDERS! 10 minutes: While the Presenting Teacher only listens and takes notes, the participants talk among themselves posing questions to help or to push the thinking of the Presenting Teacher, such as:

   I wonder why . . .

   The gap between what was intended and what is seems to be . . .

   I wonder what would happen if . . .

5. **Reflection: 5 minutes**

   Presenting Teacher talks about what s/he has learned from the feedback. This is not a time to defend oneself, but a time to explore further interesting ideas that come out of the Feedback.

6. **Debrief: 5 minutes**

   Facilitator leads an open discussion about the experience.

Looking at Student Performance Data

In a study group meeting, teachers share the data on student performance that they have from preassessment and postassessment tasks given to students in relation to a specific intervention. They also share copies of the assessment task and the scoring guide or rubric used to evaluate the student products. They format and label data so that they are easy to understand and, wherever possible, disaggregate the data by important or relevant student subgroups and present data by proficiency levels rather than letter grades.

In analyzing the data, the study group first focuses on what they see in the data (e.g., patterns, trends, and outliers) and for similarities within and among groups of students. Then they shift to discussing what might be the causes behind significant patterns, trends, and differences or similarities in the data, in terms of how the intervention was implemented and what students were and were not doing and understanding.

Following are some questions to consider:

- Did the intervention improve student understanding and performance?
- Was the intervention more or less effective in improving student performance than other practices or strategies?
- Are all of our students improving at the same rate?
- Why are some students improving more slowly or more rapidly than others?
- What changes do we need to implement to help students who are still lagging?

The phonics study group at Hubbard Primary found, in analyzing data on letter recognition, that students knew more of the capital than lowercase letters and that scores on letters that looked similar were lower than on letters that looked different. This discovery led them to exploring strategies for teaching the differences among similarly shaped letters. Some of the teachers involved their students in creating classroom data graphs so the children could monitor their progress. By January, the group reported that they had exceeded their target on letter recognition (95% vs. the target of 90%) and just missed their target on sounds (55% vs. 60% mastery).

A math study group at Qualicum Beach Middle School focused their work on determining whether a program of regular practice in math computation skills would improve performance. Using a similar pretest and posttest, teachers assessed changes in student performance in their Grade 6, 7, and 8 classes after three weeks of regular practice. Overall, they found about a 5% increase in performance with variations by grade and gender, with the greatest gains by boys and eighth graders. In analyzing the data, they discussed whether they would have had greater gains had they spread the practice over the entire year and whether they needed to use different teaching strategies for girls and boys.

Assess What Changed and Why and Plan Next Steps

This is a logical extension of the preceding steps, looking at student work and at performance data. It begins with summarizing what happened—whether there were changes in student learning, interest, and engagement as a result of the intervention.

Next the study group uses the information gathered from teacher observations and from looking at student work samples and performance results to develop explanations for why the changes did or did not occur and for why the intervention may have yielded different effects for different students. At this step, the study group is revising or updating its action hypotheses from Step 2 based on the results from the intervention they have implemented.

Finally, the group plans next steps. If the intervention was unsuccessful or partially successful in improving student learning, the group could decide to modify and improve the intervention and try it again with students, perhaps focusing on students who did not improve. They can also decide to keep working on the same need but try a different intervention now that they have a better understanding of their students' needs.

If they decide the intervention was successful and they have met their student performance targets, the group may be ready to set higher targets and continue working on the same need.

The focus of a study group's work in a second cycle of action research around the same student learning need flows directly from the answers to the questions raised in the assessment of the first cycle.

If the group meets its performance targets in one need, it can choose to move on to the next learning need and start a new action research cycle.

Regardless of what the study group decides to do next, the group should plan strategies for helping students maintain and use the proficiencies they have developed.

Following are some questions to consider:

- As a result of this intervention, in what areas have students improved and why?
- In what areas have students not improved and why?
- Which students are improving and in which areas and why?
- Which students are not improving and in which areas and why?
- How have the results from this intervention changed our thinking about our action hypothesis?
- What improvements should we make in this intervention?
- How can we become more proficient in this intervention?
- Is this intervention effective enough to share with other teachers?

Make This Step a Success

We find that study groups are the most successful with this step in the action research process, Look at Student Work and Data and Assess Changes, when they do the following:

- Take time in their discussions of student work and performance data to summarize key findings and implications before ending the meeting.
- Compare the findings from looking at data derived from scoring student work to the findings from looking at student work.
- Plan in advance for a meeting on looking at student work or looking at student data so everyone knows the purpose of the meeting and has the materials they need to be productive.

For the next year, the math study group at Qualicum Beach Middle School wants to expand its repertoire of basic skills teaching strategies, create tools to support students, refine its assessment tools, and experiment with single-gender math classes.

The higher order thinking skills study group at Clarke Middle School wants to continue working on thinking skills with an emphasis on identifying content-specific vocabulary that promotes higher order thinking skills and lesson plans their members and other teachers can use to integrate higher order thinking skills into every lesson.

The literacy study group at Qualicum Beach Middle School wants to collect a series of short texts to use as pretests and posttests for taking power notes and to extend note taking to address how to integrate notes from different sources to construct paragraphs.

Tailor This Step to Your Specific Context

1. Look at Student Work over Time: Instead of trying to look at student work from an entire class of students, monitor student work over time from a representative sample of students, such as a higher performing student, a near proficient student, and a struggling student. Create portfolios for each student being tracked with work samples, data, and reflections from students and the study group about their work

2. Use Charts: Create charts to track students' performance over time on the learning needs being addressed by the study group.

Document and Share Work

Study group members attach data about student performance on assessment tasks and samples of student work to the study group log for the meeting in which the work and data were discussed and place copies in their study group binders. The study group logs provide space for summarizing study group conversations about looking at student data or looking at student work and decisions regarding next steps.

Study groups share the interventions they used and their findings with other study groups at Instructional Council meetings and faculty meetings. Many WFSG schools have processes (see Chapter 6) for sharing among all staff, effective practices identified and tested by individual study groups, and for incorporating these practices into a school's improvement plans.

Time Spent on This Step

Typical amounts of time to spend on elements in this step are as follows:

Step	*Time Required*
Look at student work.	One study group meeting (45–60 minutes) for in-depth conversations about 1–3 samples of student work. In a longer time block, teachers could examine several sets of work samples. Study group members should decide at the preceding meeting who will bring work and whether a protocol will be used.
Look at student data.	One-half to one study group meeting to analyze student performance data from assessment tasks. Study group members should decide at the preceding meeting who will bring the data and whether a protocol will be used.
Assess changes.	This discussion could either be included in a meeting focused on looking at student work samples or data or scheduled at a follow-up meeting.

CONCLUSIONS

This chapter has described and illustrated the following steps study groups take as they implement cycles of action research to address student learning needs:

1. Assess needs and establish baseline student performance and desired targets.

2. Research content and best practices and develop expertise.

3. Plan interventions.

4. Implement interventions and monitor.

5. Look at student work and data and assess changes.

For each of these steps, we explained why each step is important, described what study groups need to do to implement the step successfully and document and share their work, and suggested time allocations and options study groups might consider to tailor the step to their specific context.

There are several key points that study groups should remember as they conduct action research:

- *Focus on one student learning need at a time.*

    Study groups often identify a set of student learning needs that the group's members want to address in their study group meetings and class-rooms. There are several challenges with using the action research cycle simultaneously on several student needs. Limited meeting time is a big challenge. Most study groups meet for 45–60 minutes weekly. It is hard to have thoughtful, substantive conversations on multiple topics in a limited amount of time. A second major challenge is the time study group members spend outside of study group meetings locating assessment tasks, researching and planning interventions, and analyzing data. If the study group is focusing on only one student learning need, it is easier for members to divide up the work so that no one person feels overwhelmed. The higher order thinking skills study group at Clarke Middle School decided to focus on just three of the six problem-solving skills listed in their action plan.

- *Clearly define expectations at the beginning of the action research cycle.*
    - *The underlying skills and concepts to address the student learning need*
    - *The performance task(s) to use to assess student progress*
    - *Baseline student performance*
    - *Desired targets for improved student performance*

    Each of these help study groups clearly define the work they want to accomplish in their study group meetings. "Unpacking" the chosen student learning need by looking at student work samples, analyzing disaggregated student data, and observing and interviewing students helps each study group determine which specific skills and concepts different groups of their students need to improve their performance. The Fluency Flyers study group at Village Oaks Elementary School used student data to pinpoint which alphabet letters and sounds were more difficult for their kindergarten students.

    As action researchers, study group members use their analysis of the skills and concepts students need to develop to decide at the beginning of the action research cycle what performance tasks they will give to students to assess their baseline performance and monitor changes in performance during the school year. By using the same type of performance task at different points during the year, study groups know that they are comparing apples to apples. The math study group at Qualicum Beach Middle School used the same format and types of problems for its pretest and posttest math computations.

Determining where individual students, groups of students, and classes as a whole are now with respect to the student learning need is the baseline performance. Targets are where study group members want their students to be at the end of the action research cycle. Targets should be specific, measurable, and apply to every student. They also should be based on results of performance assessments that teachers or the school give rather than on performance on state or district standardized tests. The reason for this is that it is often months before teachers get the results back from the state and district standardized tests—too late to make data useful for improving instruction with current students.

The phonics study group at Hubbard Primary set measurable targets for learning improvements and then raised its target for alphabet letter recognition and lowered its targets for alphabet sound recognition based on what they learned from their baseline data and student work samples. The math problem-solving group at Hawthorn Middle School North is using word problem tasks that are similar to problems on the state test so they can monitor performance throughout the year, rather than wait months for the state test results.

- *Use "expert voices" to help research and plan interventions.*

  Once study groups have determined precisely in what skills and concepts their students need to improve, they begin to research and plan interventions to try out in their classrooms. Most study groups begin by sharing strategies that they are already using, but this should be only the first step in identifying interventions. Study groups need to reach out to other study groups in their school, teachers in other schools, central office content specialists, and expert voices beyond the district to find strategies that work for the types of students they serve. Through comments on their study group logs, study groups can also ask the principal to help them locate resources. The writing study group at Paul Robeson High School chose a book on writing to guide their study group's learning and classroom interventions. The phonics study group at Hubbard Primary invited a speech teacher to meet with the group to build their understanding of the issues children face in learning sounds and to share different teaching strategies.

- *Try out interventions more than once and monitor implementation.*

  In trying to determine whether a specific intervention really helps students learn, it is good research practice to try the intervention more than once. Teaching an intervention more than once is also essential in developing proficiency with an intervention. Each study group becomes "expert" in the intervention. At the Laurel Mill Elementary School, study groups teach other groups how to use the strategies and interventions they have mastered.

  Many study group members all try the same intervention in each of their classes and compare student reactions and performance. Realizing that classes can have good and bad days, teachers also use the same intervention more than once in their class and look for similarities and differences in students' reactions and work. The literacy study group at Qualicum Beach Middle School tried using the "Power Notes" note-taking strategy in a variety of classroom activities to assess its applicability.

- *Look at student work samples and at data on student performance to assess changes in learning.*

  Looking at student work samples and at data on student performance helps study groups determine whether specific interventions are having the desired impact and whether students are improving performance. More importantly, careful examination of work samples and data often reveals areas of weakness that may require further refinements in the interventions or new interventions. The Math Facts study group at Crooked River Elementary School looked at student work samples and data to determine the effectiveness of its different strategies for learning math facts.

- *Plan ahead to complete at least one action research cycle during the school year.*

  In our description of the tasks involved in each step, we provided estimates of the amount of time study groups might spend on each step. We estimated that study groups need 10 to 15 meetings to complete one action research cycle. If study groups met three to four times per month, this suggests that they could complete one cycle in three or four months and two or three cycles in a school year. We have found that study groups sometimes get bogged down in researching and building expertise in possible interventions—searching for the "perfect" strategy—and run out of time to implement the interventions, monitor student reactions, and carefully examine student work samples and data to assess the impact of the interventions. Our advice is to start small, with manageable interventions that members can master relatively quickly. Don't try to change everything all at once. At Village Oaks Elementary School, where study groups started their work in February, rather than in the fall, each study group chose one specific need to address between February and May.

- *Document and reflect on the study group's work at each step to build expertise and capacity.*

  Another problem with study groups trying to accomplish too much during the school year is that they do not feel they have the time to document the work they are doing and reflect on what they are learning—about their students, about their content knowledge and pedagogy, and about their work together as a study group. Murphy and Lick (2005) describe the four stages that study groups go through—forming, grumbling, willingness, and consequence—and the goal of developing synergistic groups that exhibit common goals, interdependence, empowerment, and participative involvement. Study groups progress through these stages and become more synergistic by taking time to be reflective and purposeful about their work. Just as they use student work samples to assess student understanding and learning, study groups use the documentation of their own work to assess their own learning and improvements.

At the end of each school year, study groups are asked to assess their work by addressing these questions:

- *Did we do what we said we would do in our action plan?*
- *What changes in what and how we teach have our study group members made as a result of our work together as a study group?*

- *Did our study group work result in improved student performance in the learning needs we addressed?*
- *Did our study group follow the WFSG process guidelines and did we work together effectively?*

Without ongoing documentation of their work in the cycles of action research, study groups will not have the data they need to answer these questions. At Clarke Middle School, every study group was asked at the end of the year to identify successful practices for improving student learning and to submit them for whole-faculty consideration for inclusion into the School Improvement Plan for the following year. At Hubbard Primary, Crooked River Elementary, Village Oaks Elementary, Paul Robeson High School, and Qualicum Beach Middle, all the study groups engaged in year-end reflection, sharing, and celebration of their study group work and made plans for continuing the action research cycle the following year.

With these key points in mind, every study group can successfully use the action research cycle to improve practice and increase student learning.

Chapter 5 relates how to move from a discussion of action research to actions that improve teacher practice.

Putting Action Into Action Research

Improving Teacher Practice

Guiding Question

■ How do study groups move from discussion to action that improves teacher practice?

Schools in the first year of implementing the Whole-Faculty Study Group (WFSG) schoolwide action research process often devote considerable energy to creating the time for study group meetings, forming study groups, and establishing mechanisms to support study groups as they meet regularly. But improvements in teacher practice and student learning only occur if study groups go beyond "business as usual." Whether faculty have formed cross-grade or discipline study groups or single grade or discipline study groups, this chapter focuses on moving study groups beyond a superficial application of the action research process and minor tinkering in classrooms to serious discussions of what they teach and how they teach.

Changing Teacher Practice

Changing teacher practice is connected to specific student learning needs. Which practices to change depend on the nature of the specific student learning needs.

Grateful acknowledgment to the School Improvement Network for information on study groups used in this chapter.

Is the learning need about skills or content, about knowledge or understanding, or about application or proficiency?

For example, "improve and enlarge vocabulary" might be one item listed on a high school's master list of student needs. But how teaching practices must change depends on what "improve and enlarge vocabulary" really means. Does it mean to define and identify more words appropriate to the subject? Does it mean using more vocabulary words appropriately in speaking and writing? The teaching practices to change or improve are different for each of these questions. When a study group decides on the student learning need it wants to address, one of its first actions is to discuss what the need encompasses and means in the context of their students, their standards, and their curriculum.

The Hawthorn Middle School North in Vernon Hills, Illinois, developed the following set of student learning needs (see Figure 5.1) as they met as a whole faculty to examine student performance data in math, reading, and writing (Steps 1 and 2 in the WFSG Decision-Making Cycle, or DMC). These are the types of specific student learning needs schools seek to identify for schoolwide action research. The faculty grouped similar needs into categories (Step 3 in the DMC) and formed study groups based on these categories and the specific needs within each category. Student learning needs, such as shown in Figure 5.1, may appear in several categories.

Changing teacher practice relates to changing what is taught and how it is taught. What is taught is content. Besides facts, concepts, principles, and procedures, content includes the enduring understandings (Wiggins & McTighe, 1998) or generative topics (Blythe et al., 1998) that are central to the discipline(s), engaging for students, and providing opportunities for multiple connections.

How content is taught is pedagogy. We ask study groups to use "task analysis" (Kirwan & Ainsworth, 1992) or "backward mapping" (Wiggins & McTighe, 1998). That is, we ask them to first define the performances students should be able to do at the end of a lesson or unit to demonstrate their mastery and understanding, and then, to work backward to plan how they will introduce the lesson or unit and engage students, and how they will structure learning experiences to build the skills and concepts students will need to successfully complete the culminating performances.

In planning learning experiences, we encourage study groups to identify and use instructional strategies that transcend a particular subject or grade level. Mnemonics and summarization are two examples of instructional strategies teachers can use with students to address learning needs in different subjects and grade levels. Mnemonics is a strategy to help students remember information by associating that information with rhymes, acronyms, and acrostics. Marcia Tate (2003) provides examples of mnemonic techniques to use with students at the elementary, middle, and high school levels in a variety of subjects. Rick Wormeli (2005) identifies 50 different summarization techniques that encompass individual or group written, oral, artistic, and kinesthetic activities.

At Qualicum Beach Middle School in Qualicum Beach, British Columbia, one of the math study groups addressed improving students' basic-math computational skills. They realized from their pretest data that many students were not fluent with the basic computational skills that should have been mastered in elementary school and that they needed to teach these skills. They also discovered that it was more effective to spread teaching, review, and practice of basic skills throughout the school year rather than to treat basic skills as a separate unit of instruction.

Figure 5.1   Student Learning Needs, Hawthorn Middle School North, September 2005

Students need to:

1. Retain vocabulary

2. Practice informational comprehension

3. Identify important information when interpreting text through analysis, evaluation, or comparison and contrast

4. Identify important elements of the problem of a text

5. Demonstrate knowledge of math principles and concepts that result in the correct solution of a problem

6. Increase computation skills

7. Identify important elements of a problem

8. Demonstrate use of models, diagrams, symbols, or algorithms to represent and integrate concepts

9. Demonstrate how to explain the solution of problems

10. Improve and enlarge vocabulary

11. Solve word problems

12. Use higher-order thinking skills to solve problems

13. Use conventions appropriately when writing

14. Be aware of audience when completing writing assignments

15. Integrate materials and skills learned in class when writing

16. Demonstrate ability to organize data

17. Demonstrate basic use of measurement

18. Demonstrate the knowledge of geometric concepts

19. Increase knowledge of organization and voice as it pertains to "6 + 1 Trait Writing"

20. Improve sentence fluency

21. Demonstrate knowledge and vocabulary related to math concepts

22. Develop ideas for writing

23. Improve ability to measure in math and apply it to real-life situations

24. Demonstrate word analysis and vocabulary development

25. Demonstrate the ability to comprehend expository passages

26. Demonstrate proficiency in comparative quantitative math

27. Demonstrate understanding of algebra and analytical methods

28. Demonstrate the ability to edit and proofread work

29. Read and follow directions

30. Justify math procedures in written form

Source: Used with permission from Dr. John Ahlemeyer, Hawthorn Middle School North.

During the 2005–2006 school year, the Phonics Study Group at Bunn Elementary School worked on discriminating and identifying rhyming word pairs and the beginning and ending sounds in real words. The group engaged students in a variety of activities to develop discrimination skills. They found that the more often children said and wrote rhyming and word-family words, the higher their degree of accuracy for discriminating and recognizing rhymes. They also found that working explicitly on rhyming words helped students with their third need, discriminating ending sounds of real words. They said identifying ending sounds was the most difficult need for their students to grasp because students were so used to listening for the beginning sounds. They realized the importance of exposing children to the ending sounds at the beginning of the year and practicing these throughout the year instead of waiting to introduce them at the end of the school year.

While the aforementioned examples provide focus on classroom teachers, many study groups include other staff such as teaching assistants, librarians, counselors, and technology specialists, who interact with students on a regular basis, but are not classroom teachers. For these study group members, changing their practice means focusing on what they want students to do or learn as they interact with students and the content, and how they interact with students and the pedagogy to help students do or learn what is expected.

At Qualicum Beach Middle School, the annual school-growth plan has three goals— improving literacy, numeracy, and social responsibility. The educational assistants, counselor, the first-nations support person, the principal, vice principal, and the child and youth care worker chose, for the 2004–2005 school year, to form three study groups focused on needs related to the social responsibility goal. The student needs they chose to address were to develop socially responsible behavior showing tolerance toward others in the school and community, demonstrate appropriate interactions with others, and develop and use leadership skills in the school and community.

The WFSG schoolwide action research process is built on the following, simple, *theory of action:* The work that study groups do together results in changes in what and how members teach. Changes in what and how teachers teach lead to changes in student learning. No changes in teaching practices equals no changes in learning.

There are several caveats to this theory of action:

- Some changes in practice are more effective than others in improving learning and some changes may have little or no impact.
- Most changes in practice take repetition or reinforcement before their impact on learning is seen.
- Some changes are more effective for some students than others.

Therefore, significant improvements in learning will probably require different interventions, repetition and reinforcement, and differentiating instruction.

High-Quality Study Group Work to Improve Teacher Practice

High-quality study group work in improving teacher practice is *focused, rigorous, substantive, and collaborative,* which we discuss in the pages that follow.

Characteristics that describe each of these four areas come from the 15 WFSG guidelines (see Figure 5.2) and from the WFSG rubric (see Resource A; Murphy & Lick, 2005; Murphy, 2007a). The WFSG rubric is an innovation configuration (Hall & Hord, 2001) in that it identifies and describes the different components of an innovation, the

WFSG System. The components of the WFSG System are context, process, and content, the same three components as in the National Staff Development Council's (2001) Standards for Staff Development. Going deeper into each component, the WFSG rubric describes the practices or behaviors within each component at different levels of implementation: not yet, beginning, developing, and advanced.

The WFSG guidelines (Murphy & Lick, 2005, p. 87) describe the key contextual factors and process behaviors that an individual study group addresses and that the schoolwide WFSG System exhibits. These guidelines, shown in Figure 5.2, distinguish WFSG from other collaborative designs and are reflected in the advanced implementation level of the WFSG rubric.

Focused Study Group Work

Study groups that have internalized the question, "What do students we are teaching now need for us to do?" are *focused* on changing their practices during the current school year as they address the learning needs of the students in their classrooms. They are not focused on aligning curriculum or creating grade-level or schoolwide benchmark assessments or developing units to be implemented the following year. Their action plan and logs indicate that they are engaged in cycles of action research in their group. Members establish baseline and targets, identify best

Figure 5.2 WFSG Process Guidelines

1. Determine study group membership by who wants to address a set of data-based student needs identified through a process that involves the whole faculty.

2. Keep the size of the study groups between three and five members.

3. Establish and keep a regular schedule, meeting weekly or every two weeks.

4. Establish group norms and routinely revisit the norms.

5. Establish a pattern of study group leadership, rotating among members.

6. Develop a study group action plan by the end of the second study group meeting.

7. Complete a study group log after each study group meeting.

8. Have a curriculum and instructional focus that requires members to routinely examine student work and observe students in classrooms engaged in instructional tasks that are a result of the study group's work.

9. Use a variety of learning resources, both material and human, that serve as the "expert voice" to the learners.

10. Use multiple professional-development strategies, such as training, to accomplish the study group's intended results.

11. Reflect on the study group's work and the impact of current practice on student performance.

12. Recognize all study group members as equals.

13. Expect transitions or shifts in the work.

14. Assess study group work to determine whether there is evidence that the targeted student needs have been improved.

15. Establish a variety of communication networks and strategies.

practices, develop lessons, use lessons in classrooms, and reflect on results within repeated cycles of inquiry.

Members are confident that the work of the group will impact student learning and they hold themselves accountable for attaining results. The action plan is a living document and kept in front of the group at all times. The group meets weekly for at least an hour or for three or four hours per month to accomplish their goals. Their meeting logs indicate a sense of urgency around identifying and using interventions in their classes that are effective for their students. Every study group meeting is planned in advance so that each member knows its intent and what to bring or prepare. The size of the study group is relatively small, between three and five members, to enable the group to function effectively.

The following vignette describes a study group at the Bunn Elementary School focused on completing one cycle of action research over six meetings in a two-month period. This vignette also includes feedback to the group from the principal, Jewel Eason (Bunn Elementary School, 2006b).

The Radical Readers Study Group Cycle of Action Research

One of the study groups at Bunn Elementary School, during the 2006–2007 school year, was the Radical Readers. The group was composed of five members, one third-grade teacher, two fourth-grade teachers, and two fifth-grade teachers. They chose to work together on student needs related to reading comprehension. Three of the teachers had worked together in a reading study group the previous year. The study group met once a month on the district's earl- release day and at other times during the month at mutually convenient times.

The first student need they addressed was the ability to read and comprehend cause and effect within any given passage. Their study group completed one cycle of action research on this need between September 11 and November 15.

Collect Baseline Data: *In their log for the September 11 meeting, the group reported as follows: "Each member of the group will give their students a pretest on Cause and Effect. We will use the STARS (Strategies To Achieve Reading Success) series book (appropriate to the grade level) to assess each student's current level of knowledge. This will be our baseline percentage to begin our individualized teaching strategies. Each member will grade their pretests and provide a class average to present at our next meeting. Also, during the week, each teacher will gather materials and/or strategies relative to cause and effect and bring this to the next meeting along with their pretests."*

At the next meeting on September 20, the group shared their baseline data with class averages ranging from 47% to 78%. They set a target date for mid-October and each teacher set a target for improvement in the class average on cause and effect.

Identify Content and Best Practices and Plan Interventions: *In their log, they noted the following: "We had a lengthy discussion on the strategies we will be using in our class. We all agreed that we needed to provide the definition for cause and effect first. Everyday examples should also be provided." The group also shared with each other materials from two Web sites, one with primary, intermediate, and upper level activities related to cause and effect, and another with forms and guides, with strategies and graphic organizers attached. They planned to share at their October 2 meeting the materials and strategies they used with their students and their comments and results from using these strategies.*

Debrief Implementation Refine Interventions: *During their October 2 meeting, teachers discussed strategies used within individual classrooms. They found that using everyday examples tend to work better to explain cause and effect than using a textbook to teach. One member brought in a list of books to accompany lessons using cause and effect. They wrote the following in their log: "We examined the Laura Numeroff series and found many examples within those texts. This list has books we personally own or could easily get from our BES library. Awesome Web site that has about 35 graphic organizers (cause and effect included). . . . We do not feel our students are prepared for a posttest. Therefore, we will continue to teach cause and effect using various sources and graphic organizers. Posttest results will now be November 6th."*

At their October 11 meeting, the group prepared for the Instructional Council meeting, where one of their members would represent the group to share what they were doing and learning, and to learn from other groups. They also noted in their log that they were using graphic organizers and questioning techniques in their classes to improve students' understanding of cause and effect. They reported that they were seeing "more organization and detailed thinking" and that the strategies helped "students understand consequences and relate cause and effect to real life situations." The principal, in her feedback to the group, asked whether the group was seeing improvements on a daily basis.

When the group met next on November 6, they responded in their log to the principal's question: "We feel we are seeing a daily improvement in the understanding of cause and effect. However, it's a consensus that it seems easier for the students to understand cause and effect when it relates to real life than when they have to pull it from a passage."

Look at Student Work and Data: *At the meeting, the group reviewed information from the Instructional Council meeting. One member, whose class had the lowest average on the pretest, brought in his test results. They reported the following in the log: "His class has shown a vast improvement in test scores. He incorporated test-taking strategies along with the cause and effect strategies we have been discussing amongst our group. One particular strategy used among all of us is to [have students] read the questions before they read the passage. We shared student work and will have our posttest results next Wednesday. One member is absent today but left Web sites for the group to explore. Due to the time, we did not review these sites together. However, we will review these individually and discuss them at our next WFSG meeting."*

Here is the principal's feedback on the log: "Your group is doing a wonderful job. Thank you for the thorough answer to my question. It is interesting the way Randy's kids are really showing improvement. What test-taking strategy did he use—was it the one listed of reading the questions first? Sounds like we need to share that information with the rest of the faculty so they can hopefully boost their results also!! Thank you for the work outside of the group. I look forward to hearing about what you found."

At the next meeting on November 15, the group shared their posttest results and updated their action plan with these results. Their updated action plan is shown in Figure 5.3.

Assess Changes and Plan Next Steps: *All five teachers reported increases in their class averages from their students' posttests. The averages ranged from 70% to 87% and the increases from the pretest ranged from 5% to 40%, with an average increase of 14%. They also responded to the principal's question: "Within his classroom, _____ did stress reading the question first. That proved to be a very effective strategy. The group used [his] strategy within their individual classrooms and continued to incorporate the charts and various graphic organizers."*

The group noted in the log that they were ready to share with the whole faculty the graphic organizers and questioning strategies they were using. They said they would continue to review and teach cause and effect within their classrooms until they choose another reading skill at their December 4 meeting.

Here is the principal's feedback on their November 15 log: "I reviewed your Action Plan results. Everyone made great gains. You did a good job of projecting results with your targets. I think you could call this a success!! For reading strategies, we learned of another place to receive materials that will be helpful. When we met with the Reading Plus people on the 17th we found that new elements to the program have to do with printable materials to boost these skills. See Jackie and Eddie about help with specific reading skills.

(Continued)

(Continued)

> *I believe you will be thrilled to see what diagnostic information you will be able to get from the Reading Plus program on the students that you are sending to this program. Great job and thank you for answering my question."*
>
> **Provide Year-End Reflections:** *At the end of the 2006–2007 school year, the study group reflected on its work with cause and effect: "This skill was easier to teach among the two needs we focused on this year. There were more charts, graphs, diagrams, etc. we could use to teach this strategy through whole group and small group instruction. Our results concluded that the use of organization and detailed thinking strategies helped students relate cause and effect to real life situations. Our data from our Action Plan shows a significant growth in Cause and Effect among each teacher's class. In only a few months time, there was more than a 10% increase in Cause and Effect scores within the majority of each classroom!"*
>
> Source: Used with permission from Jewel Eason, Bunn Elementary School.

Figure 5.3 presents the action plan for the Radical Readers study group whose work during the fall semester 2006 is described in the vignette. This action plan is the third update of the group's action plan. The first version had some of the activities checked, and some resources listed on the first page. On the second page, the group listed their need and the data source, but no data. The second version was updated with the baseline data and targets, and the group had projected completion by October 11. In the third update on November 15, the group added in the additional resources they had found and inserted their actual results.

Rigorous Study Group Work

Study groups engaged in *rigorous work* to improve their teaching practices demonstrate in their action plan and logs that they are following the WFSG guidelines and the action research steps. In study group meetings and other settings, group members believe in collaboratively using qualitative and quantitative data from several sources for diagnosing their students' instructional needs, setting improvement targets, evaluating effectiveness of instructional strategies, and monitoring progress toward targets. The study group uses a common classroom assessment to collect baseline data, monitor student progress every 6–12 weeks, and assess results at the end of the marking period, semester, or year on the study group's chosen student learning needs.

Their logs tell a rich story of dialogue and action around student learning and indicate that they examined key issues deeply and challenged each other's assumptions, evaluating all input for its value and usability. Looking at student work together using protocols is the heart of the work. This approach is used routinely on varying levels and content, and leads to further changes in teachers' practice. Study groups regularly reflect on the their work and the impact of current practices on student performance.

During the 2005–2006 school year, the second student need that study group No. 4 at the Laurel Mill Elementary School worked on was improving students' ability to compare and contrast ideas in the passages students were reading. In the spring, the group introduced Venn diagrams as a visual strategy for comparing and contrasting with kindergarten and first-grade students completing class diagrams and older students completing individual diagrams. While classroom assessments showed that 90% of their students became proficient with using Venn diagrams, the group reported in their May 3 log that their third- and fourth-grade students had trouble answering written compare-and-contrast questions about reading passages when they had not first completed a Venn diagram.

Figure 5.3   The Radical Readers Action Plan on Cause and Effect

Whole-Faculty

WFSGs

Study Groups™

WFSG Action Plan for Group # 5 – Radical Readers

School BES   Date: 11-15-06

Group Members: C. Beddingfield, Grade 4; A. Joyner, Grade 3; R. Kagarise, Grade 5; A. Murray, Grade 5; M. Watts, Grade 4

What is the general category of student needs the group will address? READING

State the <u>specific skill</u> within the general category the group will target.		Check and list the specific actions the group will take when the study group meets.
Students need to: Demonstrate the ability to read and comprehend cause and effect within any given passage.	***Standard(s):*** Gr. 3: 2.04 Gr. 4: 2.05 Gr. 5: 2.05	***We will:*** ☒ **D**iagnose students' current levels of performance (relative to need) ☒ **D**evelop assessment tools ☒ **I**dentify strategies/materials to address need ☐ **P**lan lessons for how each member will use the strategy/material ☐ **D**evelop/design materials to address need ☒ **D**emonstrate/practice strategies members have used or will use ☒ **A**rticulate strategies we use ☒ **E**xamine samples of student work for evidence of student understanding ☒ **A**ssess results of using strategies in our classrooms ☒ **Other:** Plan and implement a lesson, using various resources within our individual classrooms and bring in student work and replan based on results
Beside each student need, indicate the STATE STANDARD(s) that will be addressed when members target the need. Only give the code or number of the Standard.		

ESSENTIAL QUESTION that will guide the group's work:

How can we use Guided Reading to improve each student's reading skills and/or abilities?

Our resources are:	Our norms are:
At least one of the following resources will be used <u>during</u> study group meetings. CARS I, STARS, CARS II, Study Island, AR Extensions in Reading, Be a Better Reader, Guided Reading observations, Web sites, Curriculum Resource Teacher from BES & other schools, Book Room, Leveled Books - Web sites for cause and effect: www.longman.com/ae/marketing/sfesl/tests/grade4 and www.hartcourtschool.com/activity/trophies/rsr/build/RR_e_5_28.htm and www.quia.com (go to cause and effect)	1. Arrive/end on time 2. Listen and respect others' opinions 3. Stay on topic 4. Give constructive advice 5. Share work load

(Continued)

Figure 5.3 (Continued)

State <u>specific</u> student need that is being targeted – *Students need to:*	Data Sources: What type of pre/post assessments will members give to document current performance level?	Baseline: What percentage of students meet performance standards **when work begins**? **9-20** (DATE)	Target: What do members **predict** will be the percentage after interventions **10-11** (DATE)	Actual: What percentage of students meet performance standards after interventions? **11-15** (DATE)
Increase ability to recognize cause and effect within a given passage.	Using STARS (Strategies to Achieve Reading Success), we will have data to represent each student's basic understanding of cause and effect.	Beddingfield: 68% Joyner: 78% Kagarise: 47% Murray: 68% Watts: 63%	Beddingfield: 75% Joyner: 83% Kagarise: 70% Murray: 80% Watts: 75%	Beddingfield: 73% Joyner: 86% Kagarise: Murray: 79% Watts: 70%

Source: Used with permission from Jewel Eason, Bunn Elementary School.

This example illustrates one of the challenges that study groups face, ensuring that students can transfer learning from one context, "compare and contrast" with Venn diagrams, to another, responding to compare-and-contrast questions.

At Bunn High School, the Golden Girls study group, composed of teachers in math, social studies, career and technical education, and special education, also addressed comparing and contrasting ideas using Venn diagrams. They had different students in the fall and spring semesters. They regularly brought samples of student work to their study group meetings and used the "Wows and Wonders" protocol to examine the work samples together and offer suggestions for improving the work.

The fifth-grade study group at Royal Elementary School worked, during the 2005–2006 school year, on making inferences in the first semester and using context clues in the second semester. While student performance on making inferences improved from 55% proficient in September to 73% proficient in January, the group did not reach their target of 80% proficient. In reflecting on why they did not reach their target, they decided that they might have had better results at the end of the semester if they had reviewed making inferences each week and continued to give students reading passages and questions dealing with inferences.

When the group switched to working on context clues, they discovered that they did not allow enough time for all of their students to answer all of the questions on the pretest. They also realized from looking at student work samples that using context clues was difficult for students to master because of the different types of context clues and because some students were trying to answer questions without reading the passage carefully. As a result, they decided to create a series of minilessons to scaffold and simplify the process for students. In May, the group gave students a posttest using context clues and found that performance improved from 42% proficient in February to 70% proficient in May.

The third-grade study group at Royal Elementary School worked on sequencing events and identifying the main idea during the 2005–2006 school year. They regularly examined student work and included summaries of these discussions with their meeting logs. In reviewing student work on sequencing events, they found that students did better with concrete activities, such as putting events written on note cards in a proper sequence, than sequencing events written on a sheet of paper. They found that students responded better to verbal instructions than written instructions and that they had an easier time identifying key order words when the order words were at the beginning of a sentence. After practicing identifying order words, they were surprised to discover that students then expected all sentences to have order words and had difficulty bridging one step to the next without order words included in the sentence. They also discovered that the length of the posttest affected results. When they gave students fewer questions on the posttest, they found that student results improved (79% proficient vs. 47%) and were more consistent with the work students had been doing in the activities.

Substantive Study Group Work

Study groups engaged in *substantive work* actively seek multiple sources to push themselves to higher levels of understanding of academic content and effective pedagogy. They incorporate materials and strategies from school and district initiatives and existing programs into the group's work. They identify and use instructional strategies that are effective across grades and content areas. As a result of their work together, members incorporate new content and strategies into their repertoire for continued use and revise curriculum units accordingly. Study groups share with others their results from using new strategies and materials in classrooms.

The Radical Readers study group at Bunn Elementary expanded their knowledge about teaching cause and effect by searching for Web sites on the Internet. Study Group No. 4 at Laurel Mill Elementary School shared the methods and materials each member was already using to teach vocabulary and together examined materials from the Voyager K–3 literacy system that the school had adopted. Their principal and the district's director for elementary education also suggested resources to the group. The fourth-grade study group at Royal Elementary School used a study group meeting to examine their Science Research Associates Reading kits to determine how to use the materials to help students learn how to make inferences and draw conclusions.

When the fifth-grade study group at Royal Elementary School reflected in May 2006 on which strategies were effective in improving students' ability to use context clues, they reported that the strategy they found most helpful was asking students to choose a set number of words in the reading passage and write them in a graphic organizer. Students were then asked to write down the meaning of the words as they came to them and record clues that helped them to decide on the meaning. Students would then look up the meaning of the words in the dictionary, write the definition on their graphic organizer, and compare the two meanings. If they were different, the students would go back to the text to try to find clues that supported the correct meaning.

At the end of the 2005–2006 school year, the principal at Bunn Elementary School, Jewel Eason, asked each study group to reflect on the work they had done that year and describe what they knew at the end of the year that they did not know before. The Radical Readers group, composed of third- and fourth-grade teachers, wrote the following:

Working in a group that includes consecutive grade levels has been extremely beneficial in that we can compare skills, objectives, lessons, etc. It has been an enlightening experience because of the similarities among group members and among our students.

Focusing on one skill at a time has been most successful. It has taught us, as teachers, how important it is to be organized and consistent in teaching all skills throughout the curriculum. Our group has found it is necessary to have a multitude of resources and information on any given skill. We value the opinions and resources others have given us and have used them to meet the different learning modalities within our classrooms.

By assessing our students we have been able to compile all information and choose what topics need to be focused on within our classes and grades. This forced us to take a more thorough and subjective look at all of our materials we currently have available and found certain materials are more beneficial with one skill while others may be more sufficient for a different skill. We have become more aware of how important all of our resources are and how we must teach outside of the text. The need to pull from other resources, including methods and ideas from other countywide schools, has been vital to the success of our WFSG (Bunn Elementary School, 2006a, p. 12).

At Western Harnett High School, the Great Minds study group illustrates, in the vignette that follows, how a study group experiments with a number of different strategies to improve student performance.

Changing Teacher Practices at Western Harnett High School

Western Harnett High School, located near Lillington, North Carolina, in rural Harnett County, started implementing WFSG in January 2006. One of the study groups formed during the 2006–2007 school year was "Great Minds," composed of a geometry teacher, a physical science teacher, a health and physical education teacher, and a special education teacher. In the spring semester, they decided to work on students' test-taking skills and their essential question was this: "What strategies can we use to improve the test-taking skills of our students?"

Before collecting baseline data on their students' test-taking skills, the group decided that students first needed to see improving test-taking skills as a strategy to help them achieve their short-term and long-term goals. They designed a goal-setting exercise where students were to set three long-term and three short-term goals and then share their goals in a small group with other students. The group reported in its meeting log that the results were positive for the students and that many of them opened up about their dreams and some of the obstacles they faced. In follow-up to the goal setting exercise, teachers focused students on the accomplishment of their short-term goals, emphasizing academic success and test-taking skills.

They decided to use as their baseline assessment tool the regular end-of-unit tests in the subjects taught by each teacher in the study group. These tests consisted of 20–25 multiple-choice and short-answer questions. They set three performance bands for each test based on the number of questions answered correctly—not yet (below proficient), Level 3 (proficient), and Level 4 (advanced). They found that 54% of their students were below proficient, 36% were proficient, and 10% were advanced. The goal at the end of the semester was to improve student performance, with a target set of 46% to 70% of the students scoring proficient or above on end-of-unit tests.

The group found that students were making careless mistakes on simple questions they knew how to answer. They watched students taking tests and observed that students were not using any active reading strategies, such as underlining or highlighting, to understand reading passages or the questions. They also found that students would not even try to answer harder, more complicated questions.

To find out more about how students saw themselves, they gave students a set of 10 statements describing student behaviors and asked them to rate themselves according to those behaviors. The group also asked students who were not performing well on tests to reflect on reasons for that.

From the student self-reflections, the group realized that they had been undermining students' ability to prepare for tests by handing out teacher-prepared notes on units or by writing notes on the whiteboard for students to copy. From this realization, the group decided to teach students how to take their own notes. They taught the Cornell note-taking process and made taking notes a mandatory part of preparing for the end-of-unit tests until students became comfortable with the process. And, they shared examples of good notes from fellow students.

In addition to working on note taking, the group also taught students three different strategies for attacking test items:

- *Answer every easy question first and then go back and do the harder ones.*
- *Start at the first question and keep going question by question until you reach the end, never leaving a question until you have answered it fully or made an educated guess.*
- *Answer the hardest questions first, then go back and do the easy ones.*

They also taught students "general rules of engagement" for test taking, such as answering every question, using underlining or highlighting to identify key information and instructions, and eliminating obviously incorrect answers. They created a one-page handout midsemester that summarized these strategies and guidelines and gave it to students to refer to when they took an end-of-the-unit test. After every in-class test, they gave students a second handout that asked them to reflect on whether they thought they were successful on the test and to describe what they would to differently to improve their grades on the next test. The self-assessment was particularly useful in getting the students to take responsibility for their performance on tests, and for the ones that needed more or a different kind of instruction, the form provided an opportunity for them to say that.

The teachers taught students to analyze the tests. Students identified which questions were the hardest to answer, analyzed the questions to determine why the questions were hard to answer, and proposed strategies for dealing with similar questions in future tests.

The group also realized that some of its students needed more support than others to improve their test-taking skills. They created cooperative groups to prepare for tests and invited the school's peer tutors to work one-on-one in class and after school with students needing additional support.

They were successful in meeting their targets for improved performance on end-of-unit tests, and the geometry and physical science teachers observed that most of the students were using the test-taking skills they had learned on the state "End of Course" tests.

Several students made dramatic improvements in their academic performance during the semester. One student went from being a shy "C-" student to a confident "A" student. Another student moved from failing to passing. Group members felt that these successes were due to students' impression that their teachers really cared about their success, realizing through the goal-setting and self-reflection activities that they needed to take personal responsibility for improving their own performance and experiencing success from using the test-taking strategies.

Source: Denise King, Western Harnett High School.

Collaborative Study Group Work

Study groups engaged in *collaborative work* ensure that all members are active in planning, teaching each other, and examining student results from all the members' classes. Each member willingly takes his or her turn leading the group. All members do what they agree to do. All feel responsible for the success of the group and hold each accountable to the group's norms. Members respect and appreciate differences, empathize with each other, and consider all input. They are genuinely open with one another about their strengths and weaknesses and willing to give to each other whatever support is needed.

Members rotate in attending the Instructional Council (IC) meetings, discuss and use information from the IC meetings, and tie what the study group is doing to what other groups are doing. Members routinely observe in each other's classrooms and pre-conferences and postconferences within the group. They routinely do joint work, meaning that the group works as one in the development of lesson components and uses each other's results in modifying the work. They value their work and indicate that study group work is meaningful and saves them individual preparation time. Members engage in a rich dialogue with those giving it feedback, evaluating all input for its value and usability. They anticipate transitions or shifts in the work and plan accordingly.

Study group members frequently seek out and use work from other study groups at the school. They continually refer to the school improvement plan and their role in meeting schoolwide goals. In addition to posting materials and sharing at IC meetings, groups make presentations, place items in the school newsletter, and hold celebrations.

This description of collaborative study group work is a depiction of synergistic learning teams presented in Chapter 3.

David Wilm's dissertation (2006) focused on teachers' perceptions in a Midwestern school district of the value of the WFSG professional development model and how it is incorporated into their daily work. He found that most teachers understood the purpose and mission of WFSG and felt that the system as implemented in the district provided opportunities for them to explore new instructional approaches or helped build new skills to identify strategies to better meet the needs of their students. Seventy percent of the respondents indicated that they would recommend this model of professional development. The findings suggest that some teachers have implemented different instructional strategies, curricular ideas, and assessment practices after participating in WFSG and that WFSG allowed teachers to meet, collaborate, and share in a collegial manner. Similar to Koenigs' research reported in Chapter 3, respondents found WFSG to be supportive and collaborative when time was well used and focused.

During the 2005–2006 school year, study group No. 4 at the Laurel Mill Elementary School worked on improving students' reading skills. The cross-grade group, with teachers from kindergarten, first grade, third grade, fourth grade, and music class, spent most of the school year focused on improving students' vocabulary and their use of it in writing. Their study group logs illustrate several forms of collaboration.

At their December 12 meeting, they decided to visit each other's classrooms to observe how vocabulary was being taught by each member. They also reported in the same log that at the recent IC meeting, they learned what other study groups were doing to collect data about student learning and decided that they needed to reevaluate how they were collecting data. This led to discussions in subsequent meetings about how each grade level chooses vocabulary words, decides how many words are appropriate, and decides how and how frequently to assess vocabulary mastery. The feedback on the log from the principal, Ms. Ferrell, pushed their thinking as a group: "What about not focusing on how many words but asking the students how a new word relates to words they already know. Help them understand how new words fit into their previous knowledge and give them ideas of how to use the new words." (Feedback on the 2/13/06 log)

At Laurel Mill Elementary School, several structures support collaboration within and among study groups. First, the four IC meetings, scheduled for October, January, April, and June, are collaboration opportunities for each group to share strategies that are being used with students and the impact of these strategies, as well as the challenges the group is facing.

Second, one-hour Staff Connections meetings, which are scheduled in October, November, January, February, and March, are collaboration opportunities to showcase the work of specific study groups for the whole faculty. At the October Staff Connections meeting, the Reading First study group, K–3 teachers, who are working on phonics and decoding skills, shared a list of informative and interactive phonics and reading Web sites and shared an initial sound activity to stress beginning sounds of words. Each table had to choose a digraph or blend card (ph, tr, ch, etc.) from a bag. On the card also was a word beginning with that sound. Each table's task was to come up with a sentence using their word and containing as many other words that contained their sound, and then share their sentence with the other tables.

At the November Staff Connections meeting, Reading Team 1 shared a strategy for practicing comprehension of vocabulary words related to their need, identifying and describing author's purpose. They used the "cinquain" poem format. They modeled how to write a cinquain, with Line 1, one word, Line 2, two adjectives to describe the word in Line 1, Line 3, three action verbs that relate to Line 1, Line 4, a four-word sentence about Line 1, and Line 5, one synonym to Line 1. Staff, along with students, then wrote their own cinquains, covered Line 1, read them to a partner, and asked the partner to guess the word on Line 1.

Third, all of the study groups were engaged in classroom walk-throughs, visiting each other's classrooms and telling students about the purpose of the walk-throughs.

Helping Study Groups Improve Teacher Practice

Establish and Maintain Focus

Principals and district leaders can help study groups keep their work focused on changing current practice and improving student learning when they do the following:

- Follow the WFSG DMC
- Provide other structures for other student and teacher needs
- Find and protect time for study group meetings
- Articulate expectations and ensure accountability
- Encourage study groups to set short-term targets for improving student learning

Follow the WFSG DMC

In the WFSG DMC (Murphy & Lick, 2005), Steps 1 through 4 are explicitly designed to ensure that study groups are organized around specific student learning needs. The whole faculty, working together, analyzes data on student learning, develops a master list of specific, data-based student learning needs, creates categories for grouping needs, makes choices about the needs to address during the current school year, and forms study groups. The student learning needs are those that are evident in the work that students produce, can be addressed through how and what teachers teach, and enable academic success (Murphy & Lick, 2005, p. 115). This focus excludes such teacher needs as organizing their classrooms into learning centers or aligning the taught curriculum with state content standards, and perennial student needs such as attending school regularly or being respectful.

Steps 5 and 6 focus the work that study groups do. In Step 5, study groups develop action plans within the first three study group meetings. The action plan (see Figure 1.2) guides and focuses the group's work. It specifies the group's essential question, the student needs the group will address, the actions it will take, the resources it will use, the norms it will follow, the data sources the group will use to assess changes in student learning during the school year, baseline data, performance targets, and actual results. Each study group revises and updates its action plan as it implements cycles of action research in Step 6 (see Chapter 4).

Step 7 focuses the year-end assessment of the WFSG schoolwide action research process on the accomplishments of each individual study group. When study groups are launched, faculty are reminded that at the end of the school year, the work of each study group will be assessed by asking the following questions:

- Did we do what we said we would do in our action plan?
- What changes in what we teach and how we teach has each of our study group members made as a result of our work together in our study group?
- Did our study group work result in improved student performance in the learning needs we addressed?
- Did our study group follow the WFSG process guidelines and did we work together effectively (Clauset, Parker, & Whitney, 2007, p. 131)?

Provide Other Structures for Student and Teacher Needs

While school staff are accustomed to working together in grade-level or content-area groups, they are not necessarily accustomed to study group work. Usually, the focus of the work in grade-level or content-area group meetings is on issues such as aligning curriculum and instruction, identifying and selecting instructional materials, analyzing district and state test data, placing students, addressing discipline issues, and conferencing about students. To keep study group work focused on improving student learning, schools need other structures to provide for other school and teacher needs.

At Elbert County High School, teachers for the 2005–2006 school year formed cross-grade and cross-discipline study groups focused on specific student learning needs. But they also kept their department meetings so they could work on aligning course content to the Georgia Performance Standards.

At Bunn Elementary School, study groups are also organized cross-grade by student need. But grade-level teams meet two times per week to analyze their grade-level effectiveness and organize plans for the coming week. The school's curriculum resource teacher meets with each grade level during their curriculum planning meeting. Grade chairmen then meet once a month to evaluate and plan for the total school program as members of the School Improvement Team. (Bunn Elementary School, 2005, p. 11)

Find and Protect Time for Study Group Meetings

Study groups need to meet frequently and regularly—weekly or biweekly—to change practice and improve student learning. Finding time for study groups to meet is the first task administrators should address in planning for schoolwide action research. Study group meetings should be part of the staff's professional responsibilities and time should be provided within contractual time schedules. In Chapter 7, we describe some of the different strategies schools have used to find time. Murphy and Lick (2005, pp. 56–59) offer 22 different strategies schools have used to find time for study group meetings.

Once study groups are formed and start meeting, the next priority is protecting study group meeting time. This is a key responsibility for school and district administrators. This means developing a calendar for the year that specifies study group meetings, IC meetings, and the end-of-year celebration and sharing meeting. It also means administrators do not schedule meetings or class coverage that would pull members away from their study group meetings. If study groups regularly meet on early-release days, then administrators do not cancel study group meetings for other types of meetings.

In Franklin County Schools, time on the districtwide, monthly, early-release days is set aside for study group meetings with the expectation that all study groups meet between these early-release days. Each school is also expected to schedule regular IC meetings and include these meetings in its own calendar. At Laurel Mill Elementary School, one of the norms for the IC meetings is that no meeting will be canceled.

Articulate Expectations and Ensure Accountability

School administrators can articulate expectations and ensure accountability for focused study group work by following the WFSG DMC, giving study groups timely feedback on action plans and logs, and through IC meetings.

Clarifying WFSG Expectations

At the Daniel Hale Williams Preparatory School of Medicine in Chicago, the principal, Delores Bedar, sent out a memo to staff after they formed study groups clarifying the expectations for study group work and sharing among study groups. Parts of the memo follow:

Whole-Faculty Study Groups focus on improving student learning in the curriculum goals and objectives relative to the Illinois Learning Standards. Whole-Faculty Study Groups are self-governing groups of professionals. They organize and lead their own meetings, establish their own norms, choose what needs to be addressed, develop an action plan to guide their work, and implement cycles of action research aimed at improving student learning by changing what and how they teach and assessing the effectiveness of each new strategy they try.

Each study group must meet for a minimum of 1 hour each week.

Study groups implement cycles of action research to improve student learning in the needs they are addressing. The action research steps are:

1. *Analyze student needs to decide what to focus on, establish baseline performance, and set targets.*

2. *Identify and select best practices.*

3. *Plan interventions.*

4. *Discuss actions taken in classrooms and to what degree interventions worked.*

5. *Look at student work, assess changes and decide what the next steps are.*

6. *Monitor student progress and determine corrective action.*

7. *Assess end-of-the-year results and plan for next year.*

(Continued)

(Continued)

We recommend that you align your work by marking period. Collect baseline data and set targets at the beginning of each marking period and collect actual results at the end of each marking period to compare against your targets.

Whole-Faculty Study Groups are a place to connect our professional development to our teaching.

Each study group is expected to incorporate concepts and strategies from professional development in Differentiated Instruction (DI) and Assessment into the assessment tools and classroom interventions members use in their classroom. Each study group member decides which classes or groups within classes to target for improvement.

Sharing the work—*Whole-Faculty Study Groups are expected to share their work with other groups, give constructive feedback to other groups, and receive and consider feedback on their own work. Time will be set aside at monthly after-school AVID meetings for study group sharing.*

In late May/early June, each study group will collect final data on student learning in the student needs the group addressed, update their action plans so they reflect the work they actually accomplished and their final results, engage in a self-assessment of their work reflecting on the WFSG process guidelines, the activities they did in their meetings, and the impact of their work on their teaching practices and student learning, and prepare for an end-of-the-year Accountability Dialogue Session (June 2007).

The data from each study groups' self-assessment will be compiled, analyzed, shared and used to plan for the next cycle of Whole-Faculty Study Groups starting in September 2007.

Reporting Guidelines

1. *Study groups create and update their action plan to guide their work and reflect their results. Study groups create logs for each meeting that document for themselves and others what happened and plans for the next meeting.*

2. *24-hour rule. Study group meeting logs should be submitted within 24 hours of the meeting. We recommend completing the log during the meeting and that responsibility for writing the log is rotated weekly.*

3. *Electronic Action Plans and Logs. All study groups are expected to use the MS Word templates to prepare electronic action plans and logs.*

4. *Study group members should keep copies of their study group action plan, logs, and study group artifacts in their Whole-Faculty Study Group binders.*

5. *Copies of study group action plans and logs will be posted on the bulletin board in the Teachers Workroom (Rm 106).*

Source: Used with permission from Delores Bedar, Daniel Hale Williams Preparatory School.

In Franklin County, principals, such as Kim Ferrell and Jewel Eason, monitor study group action plans and logs and let study groups know if they see problems with attendance, regular meetings, or evidence that groups are not using their time productively. They also use weekly bulletins to staff to reinforce expectations and remind staff of upcoming meetings.

Encourage Short-Term Targets for Improving Student Learning

We have found in the 13 years of national implementation of WFSG schoolwide action research that study groups are more successful in changing practice when they set short-term targets for improving student learning rather than end-of-year targets. Teachers are usually focused on assessing student performance by grading period or semester. Setting short-term targets enables teachers to better align their study group work with the units already planned for the grading period or semester.

In Franklin County, study groups in all 14 schools during the 2005–2006 school year set targets by semester—September to January and January to May. In January, study groups chose to continue with the same need or switched to a different need. In 2006 and 2007, many study groups kept the same semester targets, but other groups set new midsemester targets.

Enable Rigorous Work

Schools and districts can help ensure that study groups engage in rigorous work to change current practices and improve student learning when they do the following:

- Provide timely, constructive feedback on logs and action plans.
- Facilitate visits by members to each other's classroom.

Provide Timely, Constructive Feedback on Logs and Action Plans

One primary responsibility of the principal, and in many schools the assistant principal, is to give regular, timely feedback to study groups on their action plans and logs (Murphy & Lick, 2005, pp. 186–188). Regularly reading action plans and logs and giving frequent feedback to study groups is the way principals can monitor what study groups are doing and provide positive support and constructive pressure for study groups to improve. This is a concrete, purposeful strategy for instructional leadership, enabling more rigorous study group work.

The study group action plan is the single most important document that study groups produce. Action plans identify the student needs a group targets and indicate what targets the group means to meet. If the plan is off target, the group will be off target. Study groups need to know immediately if there are questions or concerns about their action plans.

Study group logs tell the principal, study group members, and other study groups what the group is doing in its study group meetings and how the work connects to the steps in the action research cycle, what strategies group members are using in their classrooms to improve student learning, which resources they are using, what they are planning to do at their next meeting, and what questions or concerns have arisen. Principals use study group logs to give support, guidance, encouragement, and suggestions, and communicate expectations to study groups.

There should be clear written procedures for submitting the study group action plan and logs to the principal, which are distributed to all staff.

In Chapter 7, on the principal's role in supporting schoolwide action research, we return to the task of giving feedback to study groups.

Facilitate Visits to Each Member's Classroom

There are several reasons why it is advantageous for study group members to visit each other's classroom. When study groups are collecting baseline data, members might want to help each other observe students for evidence of interest and engagement in the assessment task. When study groups are trying to identify instructional strategies to use to address their student needs, members of the group, or other faculty in the school, may already be using a strategy that the other members might use. Seeing a strategy in use is more powerful than reading about it. When study group members are experimenting with specific interventions, they might invite other group members to observe their students as they engage in the activities and work associated with the task to collect data on student interest and how students engage in the work.

At Qualicum Beach Middle School, the principal and vice principal had a standing policy for covering classes for teachers so that one teacher can visit another's classroom. All they required is advance notice. They enjoyed the opportunity to interact with students in a different role and found that covering classes kept them connected to the curriculum.

As noted earlier, Laurel Mill Elementary School actively promoted walk-throughs and visits to each other's classroom to observe students engaged in study group work and to see how other members taught strategies.

Promote Substantive Work

Schools and districts can help study groups engage in substantive work to change current practices and improve student learning when they help expand the study group knowledge base and build expertise in content and pedagogy. They enable study groups to improve their practice by assisting them develop a deeper understanding of their students, the content they teach, and effective instructional strategies through professional development that includes observation, modeling, and guided practice. They also aid study groups in locating the people and material resources in the school, the district, and outside organizations that study groups can use at each step of the action research process.

Continuous Quality Improvement in Springfield

The Springfield Public Schools launched, during the 2006–2007 school year, a Continuous Quality Improvement (CQI) process that will be phased in to involve all teachers in all schools. One of the first pilot schools for the CQI process is the K–4 McBride Elementary School. The CQI pilot had two goals: increasing student engagement and improving student achievement. After receiving initial training, the faculty decided to focus their CQI work in mathematics because of their efforts in study groups over the past several years on student learning needs in math and their recent adoption of the Everyday Mathematics program.

The CQI process involved a weekly Plan-Do-Study-Act (PDSA) cycle that mirrored the WFSG action research cycle. Teachers and students set weekly learning goals and teachers guided students through learning activities and diagnostic assessments Monday through Thursday after preassessing their levels of proficiency and understanding. On Fridays, students completed postassessments, discussed with the teacher what worked during the week and what didn't, and set goals for the coming week. Each grade level had their own essential questions posted outside their rooms, along with charts showing students' progress. Students took greater responsibility for their own learning and wanted their graph to be better than other classes.

Teachers in the study groups focused on student engagement and the CQI process, working together to improve their use of the PDSA cycle and strengthen their use of cooperative learning strategies for student engagement, another district initiative. Mr. Range, the principal, saw CQI as a way to reinvigorate the study group process through giving all teachers a common framework for thinking about teaching and learning.

Source: Used with permission from Bret Range, McBride Elementary School.

WFSG schools have often used an instructional or content specialist, working collaboratively with the principal, to support study groups.

In Franklin County, each school has a curriculum resource teacher who works with individual teachers, study groups, grade-level teams, and content-area teams to assist faculty with various areas of professional development, including instructional strategies, classroom management skills, and specific content information. They analyze school data on student learning and share data with faculty, identify and share materials and resources to support instruction, model best practices, teach demonstration classes, monitor instruction, and informally observe teachers and offer constructive feedback. Using the North Carolina Standard Course of Study and Pacing Guides, the elementary and middle school curriculum resource teachers also create the district benchmark assessments that teachers use to diagnose student learning.

The district has formed curriculum study groups that meet monthly and are composed of curriculum resource teachers and teacher volunteers from different schools. At the elementary level, the writing group is using data from last year's writing assessments to identify areas to address in writer's workshops in each school and identify strategies to model for teachers. The reading group is working on lesson plans for leveled books (guided reading) and matching the leveled books to other content areas. The math group is using data from last year's state tests and district benchmarks to identify key concepts to address this year and is developing investigative math lessons for all teachers to use.

The K–8 Hawthorn District 73 provides each school with the services of teaching and learning coaches (TLCs). These coaches analyze student data and help teachers plan interventions for specific students, share and model best practices, team teach, help teachers and study groups plan units, and provide support for districtwide initiatives, such as writing across the curriculum. The district helps each school implement flexible block schedules to provide time within the day for the TLCs to work with teachers and for teachers to work in study groups.

Outside organizations help districts and schools improve teacher and study group expertise. In Louisiana, the state Department of Education has created the Learning-Intensive Networking Communities for Success (LINCS) program to improve student achievement in low performing schools through developing teacher expertise and supporting WFSG. Three national organizations, The Centers for Quality Teaching and Learning, ATLAS Learning Communities, and Learning-Focused Solutions, are working with schools that use WFSG to improve teacher practice. The School Improvement Network's PD 360 program provides study guides and an online and on-demand professional development video that study groups can use to develop their expertise. We describe the work of each of these organizations in the discussions that follow.

Centers for Quality Teaching and Learning

A number of WFSG schools in North Carolina, Virginia, and Georgia use Quality Teaching and Learning (QTL) to provide all of the teachers in a school with a repertoire of research-based instructional strategies that they can use to address specific student needs. QTL is a model-teaching program, focused on research-based instructional strategies and the appropriate use of technology as a tool. QTL emphasizes active engagement of students and professional collaboration to achieve school improvement goals.

Teachers learn and use research-based strategies and technology tools in five days of professional development in a QTL model classroom. The QTL curriculum addresses instructional organizers such as learning styles, brain-based learning, and multiple-intelligences instructional strategies, such as direct instruction, cooperative learning, and inquiry or problem-based learning, and instructional tactics and skills that support a constructivist approach to instruction. It also includes a field study and culminating group presentations. Each strategy, tactic, and skill is presented, modeled, and practiced. Teachers learn practical applications and are able to apply them immediately to their own classroom instruction.

During the 2006–2007 school year, Franklin County began to train teams from all 14 of its schools in QTL strategies and plans to provide training for all staff so that they can use the QTL strategies in their study group work.

Follow-up evaluations by the Centers for Quality Teaching and Learning (2005) show that QTL professional development enhances teachers' use of instructional strategies, particularly with constructivism and brain-based learning strategies, and their willingness to collaborate with other teachers in improving instruction. They also found that teachers reported improvements in student attitude to learning, classroom behavior, and academic performance.

In the 2005–2006 school year, the Centers began to assist schools that had received training in QTL to launch WFSG as a vehicle for deepening the use of QTL strategies and enhancing the impact on teacher practice and student learning. QTL consultants attended WFSG training institutes and partnered with consultants from the WFSG National Center to launch WFSG in QTL schools. During the 2005–2006 school year, QTL consultants worked with two middle schools and one high school in North Carolina and Georgia to strengthen QTL practices through their work in WFSG. In 2006 and 2007, QTL consultants expanded their work to include additional WFSG schools in North Carolina and Virginia (five elementary, seven middle, and one high school).

Centers' staff found, from the two years of work to transition school staff from QTL to WFSG with QTL, that staff in some schools have had little or no experience in working together collaboratively and using action research to improve teaching and learning and that some principals and assistant principals were unprepared for giving feedback and support to study groups.

To address the first concern, the Centers' staff developed a process to build collaboration and action research skills over several semesters for school staffs that need intensive support. After receiving QTL training in the summer, school staff members work collaboratively in small groups on student-centered projects that are aligned with the school's improvement plan and use QTL strategies. Then, in the spring semester, school staff members begin a Focused Collaboration Cycle (FCC) that introduces school staff members to study group work and action research. The following year, staff can either learn new strategies in the fall and engage in another FCC in the spring or move directly into full implementation of the WFSG System. The Centers' staff will pilot the FCC during the 2007–2008 school year.

To address the second concern about the capacity of principals and assistant principals to support student-centered, collaborative schoolwide action research with QTL and WFSG, the Centers expect school leaders to attend staff training in QTL and WFSG and participate in leadership training over a three-year period. This training enables school principals to develop a deeper understanding of the essential elements of successful instruction and increases their capacities as instructional leaders. QTL consultants provide one-on-one, on-site coaching for principals and leaders, and in year two or three, an Instructional Practices Assessment, where every teacher is observed by QTL consultants to present a holistic picture of the actual versus perceived instructional practices prevalent in the school.

The Centers also partner with the WFSG National Center and the Rutherford Learning Group to offer schools a comprehensive school-reform program, Capacity First, which emphasizes QTL and Learning Centered Schools strategies implemented through WFSG.

For more information about QTL, see the Centers' Web site: http://www.qtl centers.org/.

Learning-Focused® Schools

Many WFSG schools in Georgia use instructional strategies and the lesson- and unit-planning model from Learning-Focused Schools to provide a framework for the work of individual study groups in changing teacher practice. Developed by Dr. Max Thompson, the Learning-Focused Schools Model guides teachers in designing learning units that preview the unit with a student learning map and key vocabulary, and offers concept and skill acquisition lessons with essential questions, activities to motivate and activate prior knowledge, specific teaching strategies such as collaborative pairs, mnemonics and graphic organizers, and summarization, extending and refining lessons with minilessons and tasks that emphasize critical thinking skills activities, and a culminating project or product.

The model provides templates for creating units and acquisition lessons, and extending lessons, and offers more than 30 different graphic organizers for teachers to use. It has also developed guides for prioritizing and mapping the curriculum and applying learning-focused strategies to teaching reading, writing, and mathematics. Schools that adopt Learning-Focused Schools as their primary school improvement model receive professional development for staff and leaders, administrative support, and access to the model's toolbox Web site with tools for building lessons and units and links to units and curriculum maps from other schools. The Toolbox Web site contains a sample unit on reading comprehension for middle school students that addresses the types of student learning needs that study groups address, for example, improving skills in summarizing and making inferences, using figurative language, and understanding literary elements.

The model developers report positive gains in student achievement for schools using the program. Data from 391 Title I schools in Georgia implementing Learning-Focused Schools during the 2002–2003 school year show that 80% to 100% of the schools met their annual student-subgroup targets on the Georgia State **Criterion-Referenced Competency Tests** (Learning-Focused School Improvement Model Planning an Implementation Guide, n.d.).

For more information about Learning-Focused® Schools, see the Web site: http://www.learningfocused.com.

Louisiana Department of Education Learning-Intensive Networking Communities for Success (LINCS)

Since its inception during the 2000–2001 school year, LINCS' staff members have worked with 272 low performing schools across the state to provide a framework within which school staff can develop the knowledge and skills they need to present deep content in mathematics, science, and English language arts, infuse teaching with technology, develop standards-based lessons, and authentic assessments. Implementing the WFSG System is the cornerstone of the LINCS infrastructure. All teachers in a LINCS school participate in WFSG.

The LINCS Professional Development Process is designed to assist schools in their efforts to provide the necessary framework for improving student achievement. Field-based LINCS regional coordinators work directly with school and district staff, modeling lessons, observing and coaching classroom teachers, facilitating study groups, and otherwise providing individualized support to schools.

Each school has a LINCS coach who works alongside classroom teachers, modeling lessons, coaching, and providing other feedback as required to support the implementation of standards-based teaching and learning strategies.

University professional development is provided to LINCS schools in their content focus area. Schools send a team of three participants (LINCS Content Leaders or teachers) to the university program for three consecutive summers. Some schools send the same team for three summers but most send different teams each summer. During the following school year, the teachers who attend the university project bring back content and pedagogy to the other teachers by sharing in study group meetings, IC meetings, grade-level and content-area meetings, and school-wide professional development.

Schools are in LINCS for five years. In Year 1, schools get the WFSG process going, have a LINCS coach at least one day each week to assist with study groups and coach teachers in their classrooms, and have a LINCS regional coordinator (RC) assigned to the school to be sure that all requirements are met, conduct monthly professional development for LINCS coaches, and assist study groups and coach teachers in their classrooms.

In Years 2–4, LINCS schools continue study groups, support from coaches and the RC, and add participation in the summer university professional-development project. In Year 5, LINCS schools are expected to be functioning well and planning how the professional learning community will live on without LINCS guidance, assistance, and funding.

In a 2005 longitudinal study, Gansle and Noell (2005, pp. 7–8) assessed the LINCS program's impact on teachers. About 90% of the more than 300 teachers involved in the study took summer courses in mathematics. They found statistically significant improvements in teacher scores on the mathematics content test both immediately after the summer training and during the winter follow-up. These gains indicate that the summer programs were effective in improving teacher content knowledge.

In examining the data from fall and spring observations of random sample groups of teachers (some, but not all, attended the summer university programs) in a random sample of LINCS schools in the second, third, and fourth years of implementation, Gansle and Noell (2005, p. 22) found a high level of cognitive demand, student engagement, and instructionally sound practices in observed lessons in LINCS schools, with improvements observed from fall to spring observations. They also found that teachers in third- and fourth-year LINCS schools outperformed teachers in second-year schools in elements of instruction, the clarity and quality of objectives, the factual accuracy of the lesson, and the developmental appropriateness of the lesson, in both mathematics and English language arts.

For more information about LINCS, see its Web site, http://www.doe.state.la .us/lde/pd/842.html, and several chapters in *The WFSG Fieldbook* (Lick & Murphy, 2007), including "Going Statewide With Whole-Faculty Study Groups in Louisiana," "Enhancing Performance in the English Language Arts," "Implementing Reading and Mathematics Programs," and "Using Data to Improve Student Achievement in Mathematics."

ATLAS Learning Communities

ATLAS Learning Communities, one of the original New American Schools designs and now a national Comprehensive School Reform design, incorporated the WFSG System as its central professional development component between 1997 and 2006. The five major components of the design are teaching and learning, assessment, professional development, family and community involvement, and management and decision making.

Since 1997, the design has been implemented in over 100 elementary, middle, and high schools, large and small, across the United States. Every ATLAS school is assigned an ATLAS site developer who provides ongoing support to teachers, administrators, and staff. Site developers visit schools on the average of one day a week, building improvement capacity by providing assistance in facilitating study group and leadership-team building work, helping to organize professional development activities for the school and district, and ensuring that the ATLAS design is in full operation.

In ATLAS schools, students master skills and content by using what they learn to complete meaningful individual and team projects. Curriculum is designed to help students develop deep understanding of essential concepts, habits, and skills needed for productive work and informed citizenry, and to apply what they have learned in real-world situations.

To help teachers build expertise in using techniques, methods, and strategies that develop deep understanding and incorporate authentic assessment, ATLAS offers, in collaboration with Harvard Project Zero, one of its founding partners, an annual summer institute, Pathways for Understanding, with follow-up support from the site developers and ATLAS teaching and learning specialists. The institute builds on the work of Howard Gardner, David Perkins, and others at Harvard Project Zero on teaching for understanding (Blythe, 1998) and thinking dispositions (Ritchhart, 2002) and focuses on helping teachers and administrators identify the dimensions of understanding and visible-thinking routines, and applying them to designing curriculum, instruction, and assessment for understanding.

Beginning with the 2006–2007 school year, ATLAS has modified the study group design and procedures to put a greater emphasis on developing students' thinking and understanding. Even with the shift, ATLAS still expects study groups to develop a plan to improve student thinking and understanding; engage in inquiry cycles; look at student work using protocols; collect data about student learning; rotate responsibilities for leader, recorder, and presenter of student work; keep a journal and portfolio of their meetings; and share their work publicly.

For more information about ATLAS Learning Communities, see the Web site: http://www.atlascommunities.org/.

The School Improvement Network

Teachers often want to see best practices in action, not just read about them. In 2006, the School Improvement Network, which has produced professional development videos since 1991 as *The Video Journal of Education,* launched PD 360, an on-demand resource that allows study groups to instantly access full video programs and specific segments within programs that relate to the student learning needs that groups are addressing. Study groups can search the PD 360 on-demand database for video segments that contain content or instructional strategies that group members can use in their classrooms.

In addition to providing best practice examples of strategies being demonstrated in classrooms, PD 360 also provides study groups with follow-up tools to help teachers understand how to implement improved practices. Reflection questions assist teachers as they think about how to apply their learning and digitized guidebooks, which are full of discussion questions and group activities and support facilitators in preparing 30–45 training session around each segment. Schools can create their own customized library of video segments and align the video segments to state, district, and school standards.

For example, a high school study group addressing a student need to improve reading comprehension in different content areas could access one or both of the following programs to help the group decide which strategy or strategies to use in their classes. They could then develop a deeper understanding of how to use the strategy by watching the video segments together and using the activity and discussion suggestions in the guidebook for each program. PD 360 allows study group members to focus specifically on the segments of a video program that meets their needs:

- *Reading in the Content Areas—Secondary* has segments on power thinking and power notes, selective underlining, identifying the author's craft, creating active student conversation strategies such as think-pair-share, using active strategies for learning such as concept maps, using formal and informal writing activities, and doing classroom walk-throughs to look for evidence of students using the strategies.
- *Thinking Maps to Graphic Organizers—Secondary* has segments on how to construct and use eight different thinking maps for defining in context, describing attributes, comparing and contrasting, inductive and deductive classification, identifying parts of a whole, sequencing, identifying cause and effect, and seeing analogies.

For more information about PD 360 see the School Improvement Network's Web site: http://www.schoolimprovement.com/info/pd360.cfm.

Foster Collaborative Work

Schools and districts can help study groups engage in collaborative work to change current practices and improve student learning when they do the following:

- Facilitate collaboration within and across study groups.
- Connect study group work to school improvement plans.

Facilitate Collaboration Within Study Groups

Choosing to be in a study group based on a desire to work on the same student needs does not automatically ensure that members of a group work together collaboratively or that the group becomes an effective team.

The WFSG System fosters collaboration by encouraging and expecting it. When a school's faculty accepts the WFSG System for their school, they understand that study groups are self-governing groups of professionals who are to work together collaboratively for the entire year. The roles, structure, and guidelines for study groups are specifically designed to demonstrate that study groups are not traditional committees and that study group meetings function differently from grade-level, content-area, or department meetings. After study groups are formed, all study groups follow a checklist for the first three meetings that puts structures in place to foster collaboration. Study groups develop and write down their norms, potentially including the synergy norms for genuine teams discussed in Chapter 3. They also develop a schedule for rotating the roles of leader, recorder, and IC representative.

Principals, assistant principals, and WFSG consultants monitor the initial study group logs and action plan for evidence that groups are following the checklist and incorporate reminders into their feedback.

Self-reflection is another way to foster collaboration within study groups. The Synergy Checklist given in Chapter 3, as one approach to self-reflection, is a way to determine if the group's collaboration is synergistic and the group is functioning as a genuine team. Often at the second or third IC meeting, when study groups have had about 10 meetings, principals will ask group members to reflect on how they are doing in terms of process and content. Resource A in Murphy and Lick (2005) offers several status checks that study groups can use for self-reflection.

Using protocols in study group meetings is a third way to foster collaboration. Protocols are scripts for structured group conversations that promote focus, equal participation, and active listening—all qualities of good collaboration (cf. McDonald, Mohr, Dichter, & McDonald, 2003). The "Wows and Wonders" protocol, an example of a protocol for looking at student work, is shown in Chapter 4, Figure 4.2. The WFSG National Center includes training in using protocols for text-based conversations and looking at student work in training for schools implementing the WFSG System.

Ideally, study groups, as members work together, become more like genuine teams and learning teams as discussed in Chapter 3, and, as a result, more productive and effective over the course of the school year.

Research on team development, as Murphy and Lick describe, suggests that teams go through developmental stages of forming, grumbling, willingness, and consequence (2005, p. 101). Unfortunately, some groups get stuck, often at the forming or grumbling stages. Like getting a car out of sand, the longer a group is stuck, the harder it is to help members get unstuck. Generally, groups get stuck because of context, process, or content issues. Murphy and Lick (pp. 191–198) describe an eight-step technical assistance process that principals, an instructional specialist, a district staff person, or a WFSG consultant can use to determine the symptoms, diagnose the causes, and help the group improve. For those rare individuals who refuse to collaborate, they can be invited to form a study group of one with the same responsibilities and expectations as a group of five.

The three-year QTL process with the Focused Collaboration Cycles, described earlier in this chapter and developed by the Centers for Quality Teaching and

Learning, is a strategy for building staff collaboration skills while also building teacher skills in creating student-centered learning and action research.

Facilitate Collaboration Across Study Groups

The WFSG System is designed to foster collaboration across study groups. (See the WFSG Goals and Process section of Chapter 3 for a brief summary of collaboration across study groups.)

Making the Work Public

One of the guiding principles of the WFSG System is that the work is public. WFSG schools publicly display hard copies of study group action plans and logs for teachers, students, and parents to see and use electronic networks and Web sites to gather and display study group work.

In the Hawthorn School District, for instance, all study groups post their logs and action plans to a district Web site that any teacher and any study group can access. The Web site is supported by Rubicon International, which also offers the Atlas Curriculum Mapping software. The Web site provides templates for study group action plans and logs, and has the capability of linking study group work to specific state content and performance standards and the ability to attach assessment tasks, rubrics, samples of student work, and web links to action plan and logs.

For more information about Atlas Curriculum Mapping software and the WFSG add-ons, go to the Rubicon Web site at http://www.rubicon.com/AtlasCurriculum Mapping.

In Franklin County, schools are using the districtwide Moodle course management software to foster sharing among study groups. Each school has folders for each of their study groups with action plans and logs and the countywide-administrator study groups also have folders. All of the posted work is public and open to all district staff.

Some WFSG schools set up areas in their professional development libraries for study group reference materials and study group products. Many schools use newsletters for staff and parents to share the work of study groups. At Bunn Elementary School, the principal shares work from study groups in her weekly newsletter to staff. Other schools, such as the Arbor Hill Elementary School, have a WFSG bulletin board at the entrance to the school where study groups take turns displaying their work.

Instructional Council Meetings

WFSG schools use IC meetings as a key vehicle for both sharing work among study groups and improving the quality of work. The IC (Murphy & Lick, 2005) generally consists of representatives from each study group, the principal, and perhaps representatives from the Focus Team that helped launch WFSG in the school. Study groups rotate their representative to the IC meetings, reinforcing the WFSG principle of shared leadership. Most schools provide a focus for each IC meeting, which are held every four to six weeks. The first IC meeting, usually held after the third study group meeting, focuses on sharing study group action plans and giving constructive feedback to each group. The second IC meeting often focuses on baseline assessment tools and strategies and findings from the data. Subsequent IC meetings address the changes in teaching practices that groups are experimenting with in their classrooms and groups' assessment of the effectiveness of these practices on student learning. Midyear IC meetings may focus on midyear results and a status check on how groups are doing in following the WFSG guidelines. End-of-the-year IC meetings often include reflecting on study group accomplishments and the status of study groups relative to the indicators in the WFSG rubric. The most effective IC meetings are those which require study group representatives to prepare in advance and bring materials and artifacts to the meeting and use protocols to structure the meeting, ensuring participation by all and constructive feedback to every group.

IC meetings are also used for professional-development workshops, where professional development is provided for the IC representatives, who then share their learning with their study groups at their next meeting. WFSG consultants, in follow-up visits to schools, use IC meetings for professional development in action research skills, using protocols for looking at student work and understanding how to use common instructional strategies in cross-grade and cross-discipline study groups. Schools use IC meetings for workshops on school or district initiatives such as differentiating instruction and writing across the curriculum.

Small schools with few study groups often choose to turn staff meetings into IC meetings with all study group members present rather than just one representative per study group.

Resource F in Murphy and Lick (2005) contains illustrative agendas, preparatory materials, and examples of IC meeting minutes.

Year-End Reflection, Sharing, and Celebration

All WFSG schools are expected to end each school year with Step 7 in the DMC and a year-end celebration and sharing meeting.

Step 7 is the evaluation step, an opportunity for individual study groups to reflect on their work and for the school as a whole to assess the year's implementation of the WFSG System. The evaluation process begins with each study group reflecting on its impact on student learning, changes in members' teaching practices, both content and strategies, the extent to which their action plan accurately reflects the group's work, and the degree to which the group followed the WFSG guidelines. Schoolwide evaluation includes sharing the results from individual study group assessments, using the WFSG rubric to determine how much progress the school and its study groups have made toward advanced implementation and the areas they need to improve the following year, assessing the impact of decisions made about time for study group meetings and the process for forming groups, the quality of the data used to determine student learning needs, the quality and timeliness of principal feedback to study groups, and the quality, timeliness, and appropriateness of resource and professional-development support for individual study groups.

The year-end celebration and sharing meeting is a special opportunity to recognize the time and effort that staff have invested in study groups over the school year, celebrate the accomplishments, and share the work produced. Many WFSG schools schedule the celebration and sharing time for a half-day early-release day or professional day near the end of school. They plan the program and the sharing, arrange food and music, decorate the meeting space, and invite central office staff and school board members—all to signify that WFSG work is not "business as usual."

Connect Study Group Work to School Improvement Plan

Study group work connects to school improvement plans in several ways. First, the data-derived goals in the school improvement plan for improving student learning informs the selection of data used by the whole faculty in Step 1 of the DMC. These goals may also inform the decision about whether all study groups should address one category of student needs, such as writing, or whether groups can address any of the categories of student needs created for the master list of student needs identified in Step 2 of the DMC.

A second way the school improvement plan influences study group work is through schoolwide curricular or instructional initiatives embedded in the plan. At the Daniel Hale Williams Preparatory School for Medicine, the entire faculty is involved in a yearlong professional-development program around differentiating instruction. They have decided that all of their study groups will apply the strategies they are learning about differentiating instruction to each study group's work on specific student learning needs.

Third, study groups are written into the school improvement plan as a primary vehicle for achieving the plan's goals for improving student learning—rather than asking teachers to work in study groups and to work in other groups on the same goals. At Bunn Elementary School (2005), the 2005–2008 School Improvement Plan states that the study groups are the vehicle for getting much of the work done and that teachers will work to improve student performance in reading, writing, and mathematics through their work in WFSG.

Fourth, study group work in one year shapes the school improvement plan for the following year. The work that study groups do on specific student learning needs creates a rich collection of classroom-assessment data that the school can use to supplement state and district data about student learning. These study group data can be used in Step 1, Data Analysis, when study groups are relaunched during the next year.

Since each study group operates as an experimental laboratory for identifying instructional practices that are effective for the school's students, those effective practices that individual study groups have tested can be incorporated into next year's school improvement plan for wider use by other staff.

Clarke Middle School developed a formal system for incorporating study group best practices into the school improvement plan (Murphy & Lick, 2005, pp. 291–295). In April, a school leadership team asked each study group for recommendations for best practices that the group felt would be beneficial for other teachers and students. They were asked to describe the practice and provide evidence of its effectiveness. All of the recommendations were collected and shared with the entire faculty. On a professional day, staff worked in groups and together to review the recommendations and develop a prioritized list of practices to be incorporated into the plan and implemented more widely the following year.

Connect Study Group Work to Teacher Improvement Plans

In many states, teacher recertification is linked to continued professional development (PD). Teachers must develop a personal PD plan and accumulate credits for recertification, based on hours devoted to PD related to their PD goals. Since the expectation for every study group is that study group members will improve their knowledge and practice relative to specific student learning needs over the course of the school year, their study group action plan can serve as the member's personal PD plan. There is no need for a separate plan. Similarly, in states that allow it, time spent in study group meetings can count toward the hours required for recertification credits. Defining study group work as PD work helps teachers see that study groups are not something extra, they are the work.

In Massachusetts, teachers must renew their teaching certificates every five years by demonstrating that they have engaged in PD related to the content and pedagogy of the area of their certificate (see www.doe.mass.edu/recert/2000guidelines/appa.html). Each teacher is responsible for designing an Individual Professional Development Plan, with personal PD goals aligned with school and district improvement goals. Teachers must earn 150 Professional Development Points (equivalent to 150 clock hours) for recertification. WFSG schools in Massachusetts allow teachers to incorporate their study group work into their individual PD plans and to earn PD points for their study group meetings.

In Springfield, Missouri, the district requires teachers to have 12 hours of on-site professional development each year. Teachers may fulfill this requirement with their WFSG study group work.

CONCLUSIONS

This chapter has focused on one of the two central goals of schoolwide action research, improving teacher practice. In schoolwide action research, this relates to the steps in the action research process in which study groups research and identify interventions that change what and how they teach for specific student learning needs, build expertise in the content and strategies, plan and implement interventions in their classrooms, and assess the effectiveness of these interventions through looking at student work and assessing changes in performance.

We have found that study groups improve teacher practice when their work is focused, rigorous, substantive, and collaborative. Drawing on the WFSG rubric with its delineation of the characteristics of advanced implementation of the WFSG System and schoolwide action research and examples from study groups in the United States and Canada, we have defined what each of these four areas mean in terms of how study group members work together and what they do.

For each of these four areas, focus, rigor, substance, and collaboration, we have then described what school leaders, district staff, and outside organizations are doing to help study groups engage in high quality work that improves knowledge and practice.

There are several key points to remember about strengthening study group work for improving teacher practice:

- *Professional development becomes "data- and demand-driven."*

   If the guiding question for study groups is, "What do our students need for us to be learning and doing in study groups?" then the guiding question for a school's PD program is, "What do our study groups need to help them more effectively address our students' learning needs?" It is data-driven because the student learning needs are derived from student learning data and the study group learning needs are based on data from study groups— their action plans and logs.

   It is demand-driven because what PD to offer and when to offer it depends on the specific needs and timing for individual study groups. Within three or four weeks of forming study groups in the fall, a principal knows from the action plans and logs the needs each of the school's study groups are addressing, the resources that they have identified, and their thinking about appropriate assessment tasks. This is sufficient information to identify immediate needs as well as anticipate resource and PD needs when the group analyzes its baseline data and begins to identify content and instructional strategies.

Many WFSG principals set aside funds for resource materials and outside professional development that study groups can access. Purchasing a set of three to five copies of a resource book for a study group to use provides the school with a resource other groups can also use. Other schools set up resource bins for each study group so that staff can share resources and materials.

- *Each study group and each study group member has different needs and different areas of expertise.*

    Educators often talk about the need to differentiate instruction for students to recognize multiple intelligences and different learning styles, interests and levels of prior knowledge and skills, but fail to apply the same principles to designing PD opportunities or help study groups and their members improve practice. Every study group and every member has areas of strength and areas to improve. Just as with students, the challenge within and across study groups is to recognize and utilize strengths and build capacity in areas to improve. Study groups can always get better.

- *Both pressure and support are important.*

    The mantra WFSG consultants use with principals in WFSG schools is the importance of continual pressure and support. Research on team effectiveness and productivity (Hackman, 2002) has shown that teams are most effective when they are engaged in meaningful and challenging work with clear outcomes and have the autonomy and organizational supports to enable them to plan and execute the work.

    In the WFSG System, the focus on changing practice and student learning within the current grading period or semester provides a sense of urgency to study group work. The action plan template makes these goals explicit, as do the regular IC meetings. Pressure comes from the calendar, reminders from the principal and peers. But too much pressure can lead to fear and paralysis. It is the Goldilocks problem—not too much and not too little.

    As we have noted earlier in this chapter, there are a variety of ways to support study groups, with feedback from the readers and the IC meetings being the primary vehicles. Too much support leads to the classic systems problem, shifting the burden for change from the study group to the support person. Too little support and the group gets frustrated, confused, and angry.

- *This work is about changing the school culture.*

    Fundamentally, the WFSG approach to schoolwide action research is about changing the culture of the school. It embodies distributive leadership (Spillane, 2006) with study groups operating as self-governing groups of professionals sharing ownership and leadership for their group. It fosters a culture of collaboration within and across study groups, shared responsibility for the success of all students, experimentation and risk taking (it is OK to try out interventions, and fail and learn from failures), and continuous improvement focused on improving each adult's knowledge and expertise and addressing specific student needs and improving student performance.

Chapter 6 focuses on the second main goal of study group work—using action research to improve student learning.

6

Putting Action Into Action Research

Improving Student Learning

Guiding Question

- Does schoolwide action research lead to improvements in student learning as measured by classroom, school, district, and state assessments?

The "bottom line" for schoolwide action research is improving student performance each year, every year, in the specific student learning needs the school's faculty has chosen to address in their study groups. This chapter focuses on how study groups know whether the changes they make in what they teach and how they teach impact student learning. Using concrete examples from study groups in elementary, middle, and high schools, we show how study groups determine current levels of student proficiency for specific learning needs, assess the effectiveness of teaching interventions, and measure changes in student learning over time.

While every study group is expected to use classroom assessments as their primary vehicle to monitor changes in student learning, it is important to ask whether the impact of study group work on student learning can be seen in student performance results on schoolwide, district and state assessments. This chapter explores these connections through examples from Whole-Faculty Study Group (WFSG) schools and districts and highlights the challenges in ascribing changes in student performance to schoolwide action research.

UNDERSTANDING AND ASSESSING STUDENT LEARNING NEEDS

Study group work to improve student performance for specific learning needs mirrors how medical specialists help patients improve their health.

When a patient visits a medical specialist about a specific health problem, the specialist has already developed an understanding of the symptoms, causes, and treatments for that particular problem. During the visit, the specialist collects information from the patient, first by listening to the patient's description and then by conducting an initial examination. Often, the specialist recommends follow-up diagnostic tests. Using the examination and test information, the specialist frames a diagnosis about the nature of the problem and its probable causes, identifies appropriate treatments, and develops a treatment plan with anticipated outcomes. Treatment might be multifaceted with medication, changes in diet or lifestyle, and therapy. The specialist then confers with the patient about the treatment plan and its implementation. While the treatment plan is implemented, the specialist monitors the patient's progress with follow-up visits and tests and makes adjustments in the treatment plan when there are unanticipated side effects or less than expected results.

Study groups diagnose and solve student learning problems. Step 1 in the schoolwide action research process, assess needs and establish baseline and target performance, is analogous to the medical specialist's initial patient examination and diagnostic testing. The purpose of the study group's discussion about the need and initial baseline data collection is to be able to pinpoint students' learning problems with the need and identify probable causes that can be addressed through the treatment plan, the study group's classroom interventions. In Chapter 4, we referred to this as the study group's action hypothesis.

Understand the Need

Study groups ask and answer the following question: What are the facts, skills, concepts, and attitudes students need to have to be proficient in this need?

Since individual study group members may have different levels of expertise about the student learning need they intend to address, one of the group's first steps should be to share what they already know about the need and then check the literature to see what researchers and other practitioners have written about it.

For example, a middle school study group may have selected "improve reading comprehension" as a student need to address. They then review articles on the components of reading comprehension, share their knowledge, and decide that there are four components to reading comprehension that are relevant to their students: find the meaning of unfamiliar words, read for factual meaning, predict outcomes, and make inferences. These are more specific learning needs than "reading comprehension." We encourage study groups to always focus their work around specific learning needs because it is easier to see results with specific needs.

Collect and Analyze Baseline Data and Establish Improvement Targets

Study group members choose which students to work with to collect baseline data for their study group work, based on what students need and what is manageable.

The group decides whether all members should use the same student sample or whether individual members can have different samples.

Choose a Student Sample

A teacher in a self-contained classroom may decide to collect data from all students or may decide to focus on a particular group of students, such as students who were low performers on last year's state reading test.

If a teacher chooses to collect data from an entire class, a corollary decision is whether to assess the performance of different subgroups within the class, such as by gender, first language, disability, socioeconomic status, or prior performance. This decision might be influenced by school priorities, such as closing achievement gaps among specific subgroups, or by the teacher's own knowledge of students.

A teacher with multiple classes may decide to collect baseline data from all classes or from one or two classes. The teacher could also choose to focus on a particular group of students in one class or the same group of students across all five classes.

Nonteaching study group members, such as librarians, media and technology specialists and counselors, also decide on appropriate student samples.

At Qualicum Beach Middle School, the counselor, child- and youth-care worker, and first-nations support person were working in a study group to improve students' socially responsible behavior in the school. They decided as an intervention to pilot the impact of a video and discussion on tolerance with two eighth-grade classes.

Decide Which Facts, Skills, Concepts, and Attitudes to Assess

Using the reading comprehension example, if teachers in the study group already have some information about their students' performance for each of the four specific reading comprehension needs mentioned earlier, they may decide to start with one need, such as finding the meaning of unfamiliar words, and focus their baseline assessment on that need. If they do not have information about student performance for the specific needs, then the group may choose to assess baseline performance in all four specific needs and then decide which need to address first.

At Northside High School, the Success study group chose four student needs to address: develop study skills, improve organizational skills, develop basic note-taking skills, and demonstrate time management. They decided to give their students a survey to determine which need students perceived as the greatest need. Based on the survey, they decided to start with note taking.

The Reading Rainbow study group at Northside also had four student needs: improve and enlarge vocabulary in all curricular areas, demonstrate the ability to gather and synthesize information, apply content knowledge, and interpret standardized questions. Based on prior experiences with their students, the group began with vocabulary needs.

Choose or Design an Assessment Task

To collect baseline data on students' level of proficiency with the need, areas of strength and weakness, and their thinking processes, the study group needs to give students a task to perform that requires students to use the facts, skills, and concepts required by the need. The group might decide to use an assessment task from a textbook or other resource or design an assessment task.

At each step in designing the task, a study group makes choices that affect the nature and quality of the data collected. Choices include the reading level and content of the prompt, the types of questions asked, and the work that students do.

If the study group has decided to collect data on students' ability to read for factual meaning, then group members might decide that their assessment task will be to have students read a passage and answer factual questions about the passage.

There are two parts to this assessment: the reading passage and the questions. In choosing a reading passage, the group might discuss whether the reading passage should just contain text or also graphs and charts and the appropriate reading level for the passage. Students who can find factual meaning in text passages may or may not be able to find factual meaning in charts, graphs, and tables. If the group decides both skills are important to assess, members might have a reading passage with text and a chart, frame questions for each, and score the answers to the two groups of questions separately.

If a reading passage contains many unfamiliar words for students, they will probably not be able to answer questions about factual meaning if they do not have good skills for finding the meaning of unfamiliar words. The study group will need to think about how to find out whether poor vocabulary or poor word identification skills are affecting students' ability to read for factual meaning.

Another choice is whether all students should read the same passage or whether the content of the passage should be based on the subjects and grade levels each member teaches.

The second part of developing this reading-for-factual-meaning assessment task is creating the questions or tasks that will be given to the students.

In our reading-for-factual-meaning example, one approach that mirrors state and district tests is to ask students a series of factual questions about the passage they just read. Study group members might choose to ask students to respond to short-answer, extended response, or multiple-choice types of questions. They might decide to use the types of questions students typically encounter on state and district tests to give students practice with the types of questions they will encounter on these tests.

Study group members can review student answers to the questions to determine the number of correct responses and which questions were easier or harder for different groups of students. But student answers to these questions do not tell the study group why students gave correct or incorrect answers and what they were thinking or understanding as they answered each question.

Since the study group is concerned about improving reading comprehension, members will want to know how students use the reading passage to locate answers for questions. Which words, phrases, or sentences did students think contained the information they needed to answer each question? Are wrong answers due to not locating the appropriate sections in the passage or not processing the information correctly after locating the information?

Some strategies for discovering more about students' thinking might include asking students to do the following:

- Circle or annotate the parts of the passage they used to answer the question
- Circle or underline any words in the passage they didn't know and guessed the meaning of or skipped, with different notations for guessed and skipped
- Explain, for at least one multiple-choice question, why they rejected the other choices and chose their response

- Cite, quote, or paraphrase specific information from the passage in response to a short-answer question

Study groups do not have to create totally new assessment tasks. They can copy and modify passages and questions from textbooks, supplementary materials, Internet resources, or state and district tests.

Plan Details for Administering the Assessment Task

Once the study group has chosen or developed its assessment task, the group needs to plan the details for giving the task to students. These details include the following:

- What context and instructions to give students
- Whether the task should be a timed task or an untimed task, where students have as much time as they need (and monitor who takes the longest)
- Whether to monitor and observe students' reactions to the task—level of interest, engagement, and off-task behavior while they complete the task
- Whether students should be asked to check their work for accuracy and completeness and, if so, whether they should explain what they did to check or show corrections
- Whether all students provide qualitative information or just a specific group, such as low-achieving students, or a representative sample of students

Compile, Analyze, and Display the Data

As noted in Chapter 4, study groups need to collect two types of data from students about their performance: quantitative data on levels of performance and areas of strength and weakness and qualitative data on evidence of thinking and understanding.

In the reading-for-factual-meaning example, a student's level of proficiency might be based on the number of questions the student answered correctly compared with the standard for proficiency.

Some study groups choose to define performance levels based on those used by their state. In North Carolina, there are four performance levels, with Level 4 being proficient and Level 1 being the lowest. We encourage study groups to use their state-proficiency levels or three performance levels—proficient and above, almost proficient, and struggling or below proficient.

Regardless of how many levels the group decides to use, members need to decide the cut points for each level. In reading for factual meaning, the group might decide to have three levels and define proficient as 8–10 questions correct, almost proficient as 6–7 questions correct, and struggling as 0–5 questions correct.

For study groups to determine proficiency levels for student work samples from the baseline assessment, they develop a scoring rubric or scoring guide for the assessment task. This helps all study group members assess student work similarly.

However, having the same rubric does not guarantee that each study group member will use the scoring rubric the same way and that two members would rate a piece of student work the same. Researchers call this an issue of interrater reliability. Ruth Mitchell (2004) developed a workshop activity that addresses this issue by asking groups to develop a scoring rubric collaboratively, score the same set of work samples individually, compare ratings, and then identify and discuss similarities and differences.

After scoring the student work samples, study group members determine the number and percentage of students at each performance level and can further sort students by relevant subgroups to determine whether there are differences in performance for different subgroups.

In moving from assessment to action, it is important for each study group member to attach student names to the students at each performance level. The following questions might prove helpful in determining this:

- Who are my proficient students and what do I need to do to help them maintain and improve their proficiency?
- Who are my students who are almost proficient and what do I need to do to help them reach proficiency?
- Who are my struggling students and what do I need to do to help them reach proficiency?

Study group members use the scoring rubric to identify areas of strength and weakness by performance level and subgroup. If members mark, on copies of the rubric, each student's rating on each element, they can tally the ratings for each element for students in each performance level and subgroup.

Study groups examine the student work samples collected during the baseline assessment for insights on student thinking and understanding. In the reading-for-factual-meaning example, the study group might select one or several sample student responses from the set of students at each performance level, such as struggling, almost proficient, and proficient, and compare the responses for similarities and differences across the different performance levels. Study group members can also interview selected students about their responses to the assessment tasks.

One issue each study group needs to address as it analyzes its baseline data is whether to present data only for a class as a whole or to disaggregate data for each class by such variables as student ethnic group, gender, first language, special needs, and prior performance. If the school has identified achievement gaps for different student subgroups and is trying to close the gaps, then study groups should also disaggregate their data by the same subgroups, set targets for each subgroup, and track changes in performance over time for each group. Table 6.1 illustrates how a study group member might present quantitative and qualitative student data by proficiency level and socioeconomic status. After each member creates a table with data from his or her class, the study group creates a composite table for all their students in the same format.

After analyzing the data, the study group should create separate tables summarizing the baseline data from each study group member's class and a composite table summarizing baseline data for the entire group. Study groups can use a spreadsheet program to enter data for each class, create a composite table, and create charts of their data.

Establish Improvement Targets

Once the study group establishes performance levels for assessing student proficiency in the chosen need and members have compared performance for different student subgroups, then the group sets improvement targets for each subgroup at each level. Establishing improvement targets requires specifying the time frame and the amount of improvement desired.

Table 6.1   Illustrative Baseline Data Table on Reading for Factual Meaning

	No. Low-Income Students	% of Class	Key Problems	No. Other-Income Students	% of Class	Key Problems	Total No.	Total % of Class
0–59% correct – Below Proficient	10	33%	Finding info and connecting info found to answer choices	3	10%	Finding info and unfamiliar words	13	43%
60–79% correct – Almost Proficient	6	20%	Locating info for questions out of sequence	4	13%	Locating info for questions out of sequence	10	33%
80–100% correct – Proficient	4	13%	Not checking answers	3	10%	Eliminating inappropriate answers	7	23%
Total	20	67%		10	33%		30	100%

We encourage study groups to set time frames and target dates that reflect the amount of time and work members think it will take to improve student performance on the chosen need and align these dates with the end of a unit, a grading period, or semester, when they are already assessing student learning. We have found that an October to May time frame is too long for study groups to maintain focus and provide a sense of urgency, even if members believe they will need to work on the need for the entire school year.

At the end of the time period, every study group has the option to continue to work on the same student need for the next unit, grading period, or semester. In this case, the actual results at the end of the time frame become the baseline data for the next time frame.

Once a group decides on a time frame, members establish the amount of improvement they plan to achieve for students in each performance level and subgroup. Targets should be challenging, but attainable, so that the study group has to change teaching practices to reach the targets. Table 6.2 illustrates how a study group member might set targets for his or her class, with the challenging goals of having the greatest impact on the low socioeconomic status students and ensuring that no students are in the "below proficient" level by November 15. After each member creates a table with baseline data and targets from his or her class, the study group creates a composite table for all students in the same format.

ASSESSING THE EFFECTIVENESS OF STUDY GROUP INTERVENTIONS

The reason study groups begin the action research process with collecting baseline data is to identify the specific skills and concepts students need to master to improve their performance. Then, study groups identify content, strategies, and activities they can use to help students improve their mastery in these skills and concepts. The

Table 6.2 Illustrative Baseline Data and Targets Table on Reading for Factual Meaning

	Baseline Data— Low SES Students— 9/15		Target— Low SES Students— 11/15		Baseline Data— Other SES Students— 9/15		Target— Other SES Students— 11/15		Baseline Data— All Students— 9/15		Target— All Students— 11/15	
	No.	% of Class	No.	% of Class	No.	% of Class	No.	% of Class	No.	% of Class	No.	% of Class
Below Proficient— 0–59% correct	10	33%	0	0%	3	10%	0	0%	13	43%	0	0%
Almost Proficient— 60–79% correct	6	20%	4	13%	4	13%	2	7%	10	33%	6	20%
Proficient— 80–100% correct	4	13%	16	53%	3	10%	8	27%	7	23%	24	80%
Total	20	67%	20	67%	10	33%	10	33%	30	100%	30	100%

Note: SES = socioeconomic status.

content, strategies, and activities the study group identifies are the interventions members will implement to improve student learning.

In essence, each study group identifies two action hypotheses that drive its work on a chosen student learning need. Figure 6.1 illustrates these hypotheses.

Assessing the effectiveness of interventions means that study groups are testing each of their action hypotheses:

- Did changing teaching practices A, B, and C lead to improvements in student mastery of X, Y, and Z?
- Did changes in student mastery of X, Y, and Z lead to improvements in student performance on the chosen need?

Impact of Teacher Interventions

Study group interventions in their classrooms are analogous to a laboratory experiment. In a laboratory experiment, researchers record data about the subjects before treatment begins and carefully document each step of the treatment process and any conditions in the environment that might affect results. After the treatment, researchers collect new data about the subjects to determine the nature and magnitude of any changes. Laboratory researchers repeat the experiment several times to see if they get the similar results each time.

To assess the impact of an intervention, a study group needs to know, for each member and for each class or group, what the classroom environment and the

Figure 6.1   A Study Group's Action Hypotheses

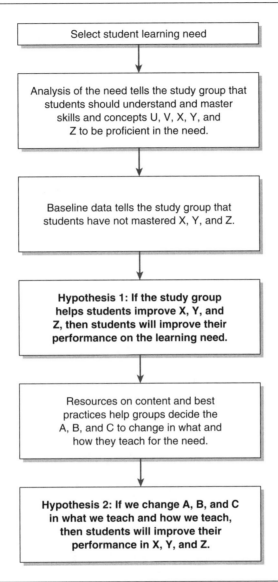

intervention were and how student mastery of specific concepts and skills changed from before to after the intervention. Members also need to try out the intervention more than once with each class or group to determine whether they can get consistent results with the intervention. This is the *heart of the action research process* that study groups follow—planning interventions in their study group meetings, acting on the plans with students in their classrooms, and then reflecting on the results and planning next steps back in their study group meetings. Figure 6.2 illustrates this cycle.

Seeing impact on student learning for an intervention depends on what teachers do and how well they do it. As we indicated in Chapter 4, how well an intervention is implemented depends on how proficient the study group

Figure 6.2   The Whole-Faculty Study Group Action Research Cycle

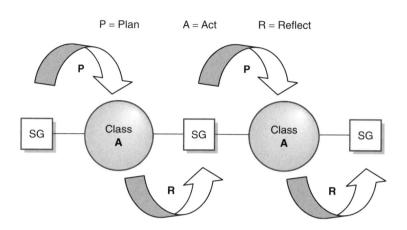

members are in teaching the content or strategy the study group has selected to use. If study group members are using a new strategy with students, they need to develop their proficiency with the strategy to expect to see gains in student learning.

Two techniques that study group members use to document the classroom environment during an intervention and the actual implementation of the intervention are to videotape the intervention or invite another study group member to observe and document.

To assess changes in student mastery of skills and concepts, study group members use pretests and posttests. They also assess the quality of work products produced during the intervention.

Pretests and posttests enable study group members to determine if there are any changes in student mastery after an intervention. Both tests should be similar in design and should assess the specific skill(s) and concept(s) addressed in the intervention. Depending on the skills and concepts addressed, pretests and posttests may be the same as the baseline-assessment task, a part of the task, or an entirely different assessment.

Even if there are changes in learning from the pretest to the posttest, these changes may not be the result of the intervention. To rule out this possibility, study group members assess the quality of the work students do during the intervention. For example, if the intervention involves using a graphic organizer, the teacher reviews students' completed graphic organizers, assesses how well each student mastered the use of the graphic organizer, and compares these results with the changes in the students' learning between the pretests and posttests.

Study group members analyze pretest and posttest results by proficiency level and student subgroup, just as they did with their baseline assessment. In addition, they determine which students improved from pretest to posttest, which ones stayed the same, and which ones, if any, declined.

Since this type of data analysis for an entire class takes time, study group members could select a sample of students, representing different subgroups and proficiency levels, and limit the detailed data analysis to this sample of students.

This process addresses the second action hypothesis: If we change A, B, and C in what we teach and how we teach, then students will improve their performance in X, Y, and Z.

Impact of Student Mastery of Skills and Concepts on Student Performance

As teachers know well, students' mastery of individual skills and concepts in isolation does not necessarily mean that they will be able to use them appropriately together or apply them in new contexts. So the second level to assessing the effectiveness of an intervention is whether students' improved mastery of specific skills and concepts translates into improved performance on the learning need. For example, if an elementary study group has been teaching students to use a graphic organizer to sequence events in a reading passage, can students now sequence events without using the graphic organizer, as on a state test?

One way to assess whether students can make the transfer is to readminister the baseline-assessment task. Study groups should readminister the baseline-assessment task on the target date to assess actual progress. They can also use the same task at regular intervals during work on the learning need to monitor changes in performance.

Another way to assess transfer is to build into the intervention opportunities for use of the skills and concepts in different contexts, such as practicing sequencing events without the graphic organizer.

CONNECTING CHANGES IN CLASSROOM PERFORMANCE TO CHANGES ON ASSESSMENTS

Study groups use classroom assessments as their primary vehicle to monitor changes in student learning. But, it is important to ask whether the impact of study group work on student learning can be seen in student performance results on schoolwide, district, and state assessments. This section provides examples and data from three states: North Carolina, Missouri, and Louisiana.

In identifying data showing the impact of the WFSG System on student achievement, it is important to understand that schools launch the system in a variety of ways with different levels of contact and support from the WFSG National Center. These different launch strategies include the following:

- Launching on their own by (a) reading the WFSG book (Murphy & Lick, 2005) and following the scripts and guidelines in it, (b) viewing the Video Journal of Education's video on study groups and reading the companion book, or (c) attending a WFSG institute or other workshop conducted by Carlene Murphy at state or national conferences
- Launching with direct support from consultants with the WFSG National Center
- Launching with national, state, or district support from people trained by Carlene Murphy

Because of the variety of ways in which schools can implement the WFSG System, it is difficult for the WFSG National Center to know exactly how many schools are currently implementing the system and what results they are achieving. Since its founding in 2002, the WFSG Center has facilitated the networking of WFSG schools that it is aware of through the annual WFSG National Conference and summer institutes for schools which have progressed beyond the initial launch process and want to share and deepen their WFSG work.

There has been no funded, independent, overarching research to date on the impact of the WFSG System on improving teacher practice and student learning. We know of seven dissertations on WFSG by Dwyer (2004), Koenigs (2004), Lasserre-Cortez (2006), Lucas (2000), McLaughlin (1997), Roth (2005), and Wilm (2006). None of these dissertations focused on the impact of the WFSG System on student learning.

However, the Lasserre-Cortez dissertation did include a comparison of school effectiveness scores between schools in the Louisiana Learning-Intensive Networking Communities for Success (LINCS) program with WFSG and non-LINCS schools. We described the Louisiana LINCS program in Chapter 5 and discuss it again later in this chapter. She defined school effectiveness as progress of a school toward achieving accountability goals as measured by Louisiana School Performance Scores, computed each school year from standardized test data and school attendance (Lasserre-Cortez, 2006, p. 15). She found that a sample of 95 LINCS schools had significantly higher growth scores in the 2004–2005 school year than did 70 non-LINCS schools (Lasserre-Cortez, 2006, p. 129).

WFSG Impact on Student Learning in Franklin County Schools

In January 2005, all 14 schools in the Franklin County Public School District, located in central North Carolina north of Raleigh, began implementing the WFSG System to improve student learning. The county is predominately rural and agricultural, but demographics are changing with an increasing Hispanic population and professionals moving north from the Raleigh area in search of cheaper housing. During the period from January to May, each school followed the WFSG Decision-Making Cycle (DMC) to examine data, identify student needs, form study groups, and begin the action research process. The first full year of implementation began in September 2005 and both teachers and administrators felt that during "the second time around," they better understood the WFSG DMC and the schoolwide action research process.

During the 2005–2006 school year, the 115 study groups (32 high school groups in three schools, 26 middle school groups in three schools, and 57 elementary school groups in eight schools) met twice a month from September to May. Most study groups were cross-grade and cross-discipline groups.

Each group was asked to track changes in student learning from September to January and from January to May. Study groups used classroom assessments to collect baseline data and monitor changes in performance. Some groups worked on the same need all year, others selected a different need to address in the second semester. A number of the Franklin County study groups used the Study Island online (http://www.studyisland.com), a North Carolina standards-based learning program to create classroom assessments, monitor student progress, and offer tutorial help for students to supplement classroom instruction.

Performance on District Benchmark Assessments

To help teachers improve student learning, Franklin County began, in the 2005–2006 school year, to administer benchmark assessments for students in Grades 3–12 in subjects assessed by the state. At the elementary level, these benchmark assessments were given in reading and math. Using state and district pacing guides, the school-based Curriculum Resource Teachers met by level with the director of elementary education to decide which concepts were to be assessed in the fall and spring. The types of questions on the benchmark assessments were similar to the questions on the North Carolina End-of-Grade tests. The benchmark assessment was used as a diagnostic tool for individual teachers, not for study groups, and results from the benchmark assessments were returned to individual teachers.

In September 2006, Clauset examined the spring 2006 benchmark data for four elementary schools and one middle school to see if results on the benchmark assessments corroborated the study group's findings from classroom assessments.

Laurel Mill Elementary School

The results from the Laurel Mill Elementary School study groups are similar to the results from other schools in the district. At Laurel Mill, five of the six cross-grade study groups chose to address student learning needs related to reading comprehension and one group focused on student needs in math. Except for Group 2, the other study groups worked on one student need in the fall semester and a second need in the spring semester. Group members created their own classroom assessments to assess baseline student learning and changes at the end of the semester. In most groups, students were given a set of questions to answer. Groups determined the percentage of students able to perform the need by the number of correct responses and the quality of the responses.

For example, in their work during the spring semester on making inferences, Group 1 teachers created the same 10 multiple-choice question assessment for a pretest and posttest. Each question had a short paragraph for students to read. In the pretest, 71% of the students answered 70% of the questions (7 of 10) correctly, with an average score of 70%. In the posttest, the percentage of students answering 70% of the questions correctly increased to 79%, with an average score of 81%.

Table 6.3 shows data for each study group in September and October, the baseline data, and follow-up results in January and May (Murphy, 2006).

As Table 6.3 indicates, all five of the reading study groups found gains in student learning from September to January and January to May. But were there any changes in reading performance in district or state assessments?

For three of the five Laurel Mill reading study groups, Groups 1, 4, and 6, the spring 2006 benchmark assessments for Grades 3, 4, and 5 included concepts the three groups were addressing, as indicated in Table 6.4. Since each of these study groups was a cross-grade group, only one or two classes were assessed on each concept. The composition of each study group is noted in the "Study Group" column. PE means physical education and EC means exceptional children, children with special needs.

To illustrate, Table 6.4 shows that Study Group No. 1 had both of its student needs addressed on the benchmark assessment. "Author's purpose" was the content for two questions on the Grade 5 assessment and "making inferences" was the content for 10 questions on the Grade 4 assessment and three questions on the grade 5

Table 6.3 Changes in Student Learning on Classroom Assessments, Laurel Mill Elementary School Whole-Faculty Study Groups, 2005–2006 School Year

Group No. and Specific Student Needs Listed in Action Plan	Baseline Data % of Students Able to Perform Need September–October 2005	Actual % of Students Able to Perform Need January 2006	Actual % of Students Able to Perform Need May 2006
GROUP 1:			
Author's Purpose	18%	63%	—
Inferences	—	71%	81%
GROUP 2:			
Comprehension	12%	22%	30%
GROUP 3:			
Interpret Illustrations	60%	82%	—
Vocabulary	—	60%	86%
GROUP 4:			
Vocabulary	75%	80%	87%
Compare and Contrast	—	75%	90%
GROUP 5:			
Measurement/Money	67%	82%	—
Estimation	—	40%	46%
GROUP 6:			
Inferences	75%	92%	—
Context Clues	—	70%	90%

Source: Used with permission from Kim Ferrell, Laurel Mill Elementary School.

Table 6.4 Topics Assessed on the District's Spring 2006 Benchmark Assessment, Laurel Mill Elementary School Study Groups

Study Group	Concept on Benchmark	Grade Level/No.Questions/ No. Classes
Group 1 (Grades 2, 4, 5, & PE)	Author's Purpose	Grade 5, 2 questions, 1 class
	Make Inferences	Grade 4, 10 questions, 1 class
		Grade 5, 3 questions, 1 class
Group 4 (K, Grades 1, 3, 4, Music)	Compare and Contrast	Grade 4, 1 question, 1 class
Group 6 (K, Grades 3, 4, EC, Media)	Make Inferences	Grade 3, 9 questions, 1 class
		Grade 4, 10 questions, 1 class

assessment. This means that two of the study group members, the fourth and fifth grade teachers, had benchmark data for their students on needs that the study group was addressing.

Study Group 1 Benchmark Results

Group 1 worked on *author's purpose* during the fall semester. Members reported an increase on classroom assessments from 18% answering 70% of the questions (7 of 10) successfully in the pretest to 63% on the posttest. The spring benchmark assessment had two questions on *author's purpose* for Grade 5 classes. Forty-seven percent of the Grade 5 class for Group 1 answered both questions correctly and 40% answered one of two questions correctly. This benchmark result is roughly comparable to 63% answering 70% of questions correctly on the classroom posttest.

Group 1 worked on *making inferences* during the spring semester. In the pretest, 71% of the students answered 70% of the questions correctly with an average score of 70%. In the posttest, the percentage of students answering 70% of the questions correctly increased to 79% with an average score of 81%. On the spring benchmark assessment, which was administered midsemester, 73% of the Grade 5 students answered 2 or 3 out of 3 questions on *making inferences* correctly and 75% of the Grade 4 students answered 6 or more out of 10 questions correctly. This benchmark result is roughly comparable to 79% answering 70% of the questions correctly on the classroom posttest.

Study Group 6 Benchmark Results

Group 6 worked on *making inferences* in the fall semester and used similar pretests and posttests. From September to January, students increased mastery from 75% to 92%, based on the group's classroom assessments. In the spring benchmark assessment, 86% of the students answered two thirds or more of the questions correctly.

Study Group 4 Benchmark Results

For Group 4, using the benchmark data to compare with student learning on classroom assessments is more complex. There was only one multiple-choice question on *compare and contrast* on the Grade 4 assessment and there were no *compare and contrast* questions on the Grade 3 assessment. So, only one class was assessed on only one question and only 44% of the students answered the question correctly. But from January to May, students increased mastery from 75% to 90%, based on the group's classroom assessments.

In reviewing the study group's logs, it appears that the group did not start working on *compare and contrast* until April, which was about the time the benchmark assessment was given to students. Group members reported that they emphasized the use of visual aids such as Venn diagrams as a vehicle for analyzing a reading passage. In the group's May 3 log, members noted that while their students did well using a Venn diagram, their older students had trouble answering written questions about reading passages when they had not done the diagram. This is exactly what students were asked to do on the benchmark assessment given earlier in the semester. The group concluded that students needed more practice in making the transition from visual aids to mentally processing information.

Royal Elementary School

At Royal Elementary School, study groups were primarily organized by grade level. Seven of the eight groups addressed student needs related to reading. As at Laurel Mill, each study group created its own classroom pretests and posttests.

Table 6.5 shows classroom data for each study group in September and October, the baseline data, and follow-up results in January and May (Murphy, 2006). Group No. 8 is working with students with disabilities. In North Carolina, students with disabilities are referred to as EC students.

As Table 6.5 indicates, all seven of the reading study groups found gains in student learning, using classroom assessments, from September to January and January to May.

The Grades 3, 4, and 5 study groups worked on student needs that were assessed on the spring 2006 benchmark assessments, as indicated in Table 6.6.

Grade 3 Study Group Benchmark Results

The Grade 3 study group reported in the group's action plan an increase in student performance on *main idea*, from 75% to 84% in the spring semester, using classroom assessments. On the benchmark assessment questions for *main idea*, 60% of the students across five classes answered both questions correctly and another 33% answered one out of two questions correctly. Two questions are not enough to distinguish levels of proficiency, but if group members used 70% or 80% correct as their standard for classroom assessments, then the benchmark results from mid-spring are generally consistent.

Grade 4 Study Group Benchmark Results

The Grade 4 study group had three needs addressed by the benchmark assessment. Based on classroom assessments, they reported a combined increase in *drawing conclusions* and *making inferences* during the fall semester from 20% to 80%. The midspring benchmark assessments on *conclusions* and *inferences* showed Grade 4 students performing better on *making inferences* than *drawing conclusions*. Eighty-seven percent of the students correctly answered 6 or more of the 10 *inference* questions and 51% answered 8 of 10 correctly. For the four *conclusion* questions, only 15% answered all four correctly and another 25% answered three of four correctly.

Based on classroom assessments, group members reported an increase in performance on *main idea* in the spring from 70% to 87%. On the benchmark assessment questions for *main idea* in midspring, 44% of the Grade 4 students across five classes answered both questions correctly and another 43% answered one out of two questions correctly. These results are better than the teachers' pretest results and lower than their final results. However, it is difficult to assess levels of proficiency on the benchmark assessment with only two questions.

Grade 5 Study Group Benchmark Results

The Grade 5 study group had one of the group's needs, *using context clues*, addressed on the midspring benchmark assessment. Based on classroom assessments, the group reported an increase in performance from 42% to 70% in the spring semester. On the benchmark assessment, 53% of the students answered all three questions correctly and another 33% answered two of three questions correctly. These results are consistent with the teachers' results.

Table 6.5 Changes in Student Learning on Classroom Assessments, Royal Elementary School Whole-Faculty Study Groups, 2005–2006 School Year

Group No. and Specific Student Needs Listed in Action Plan	Baseline Data % of Students Able to Perform Need September—October 2005	Actual % of Students Able to Perform Need January 2006	Actual % of Students Able to Perform Need May 2006
GROUP 1: Kindergarten			
ABCs	10%	79% (usually 50% by January)	83%
GROUP 2: 1st grade			
Spacing	16%	78%	95%
Complete Sentences			
GROUP 3: 2nd grade			
Sequence Events	60%	82%	—
Match Cause and Effect	—	32%	93%
GROUP 4: 3rd grade			
Sequence Events	65%	79%	—
Main Idea	—	75%	84%
GROUP 5: 4th grade			
Conclusions/ Inferences	20% —	89%	—
Main Idea		70%	87%
GROUP 6: 5th grade	55%		
Inferences	—	70%	—
Context Clues		42%	70%
GROUP 7:	24%		
Vocabulary	—	79%	—
Spell Homophones		74%	76%
GROUP 8: Special Education	17%		
Improve Writing	—	79%	—
Descriptive Words/Phrases		5%	52%

Source: Used with permission from Rob Bendel, Royal Elementary School.

Table 6.6   Topics Assessed on the District's Spring 2006 Benchmark Assessment, Royal Elementary School Study Groups

Study Group	Concept on Benchmark	No. Questions/No. Classes
Grade 3	Main Idea	2 questions, 5 classes
Grade 4	Main Idea	2 questions, 5 classes
	Draw Conclusions	4 questions, 5 classes
	Make Inferences	10 questions, 5 classes
Grade 5	Make Inferences	3 questions, 5 classes

These examples from six study groups illustrate the potential and challenges in using district benchmark assessments to corroborate changes in student learning observed by study groups with classroom assessments. The potential is illustrated by the Grade 4 study group at Royal Elementary for the group's work on *drawing conclusions* and *making inferences*. With 4 to 10 questions for each concept, there are enough questions to distinguish levels of performance among students, and with all five classes taking the same assessment, there is comparative data for each class. The challenges are illustrated by concepts with only one or two questions and, for cross-grade study groups, concepts not assessed for each grade.

Performance on North Carolina End-of-Grade Assessments

North Carolina assesses student performance in Grades 3–8 in reading and math in End-of-Grade (EOG) tests. The state provides data for schools that show the percentage passing (Levels 3 and 4) the EOG tests by grade, the percentage passing by grade and content strand, and the percentage by performance level for all grades tested. The state does not provide, as other states do, release items, item analyses, or performance on specific North Carolina Learning Standards.

Since most study groups at both Laurel Mill Elementary School and Royal Elementary School focused on reading during the 2005–2006 school year, we examined state data on student performance on the EOG tests in the 2004–2005 and 2005–2006 school years. The reading content strands most relevant to the study groups' work are cognition (sequence events, main idea, context clues, author's purpose), interpretation (make inferences, draw conclusions), and critical stance (compare and contrast). Each strand (North Carolina Department of Public Instruction, 2005, p. 6) also provides assessment items that ask students to demonstrate other reading skills. Therefore, student performance on a strand encompasses more than the needs addressed by a study group.

Five of the six study groups had classes with students who took both the 2004–2005 and the 2005–2006 state EOG assessments in reading.

Table 6.7 shows the five study groups, the student needs, the related reading EOG categories, the grades with comparative data, and the findings—whether the 2005–2006 percentage correct was greater than (>), equal to (=), or lower than (<) the 2004–2005 EOG results. The findings shown in Table 6.7 are derived from the data presented in Table 6.8. In the table, "LMES" is Laurel Mill Elementary School and "RES" is Royal Elementary School.

Table 6.7 Connections Between Study Group Needs and Content Categories on the North Carolina End-of-Grade Reading Tests and Changes in Performance From April 2005 to May 2006

Group	Student Need	Reading EOG Category	EOG Results for April 2005 and May 2006	Findings— Weighted Mean % Correct
LMES Group 1	Author's Purpose	Cognition (author's purpose)	Grade 4 (May 2006) vs.	Cognition—4th (May 2006) = 3rd (April 2005)
(Grades 2, 4, 5, PE)	Make Inferences	Interpretation (make inferences)	Grade 3 (April 2005)	Interpretation— 4th (May 2006) > 3rd (April 2005)
			Grade 5 (May 2006) vs.	Cognition—5th (May 2006) > 4th (April 2005)
			Grade 4 (April 2005)	Interpretation— 5th (May 2006) > 4th (April 2005)
LMES Group 4	Compare and Contrast	Critical Stance	Grade 4 (May 2006) vs.	Critical Stance— 4th (May 2006) > 3rd (April 2005)
(K, Grades 1, 3, 4, Music)			Grade 3 (April 2005)	
LMES Group 6	Make Inferences	Interpretation	Grade 4 (May 2006) vs.	Interpretation— 4th (May 2006) > 3rd (April 2005)
(K, Grades 3, 4, EC, Media)			Grade 3 (April 2005)	
RES Grade 4	Main Idea	Cognition (main idea)	Grade 4 (May 2006) vs.	Cognition—4th (May 2006) > 3rd (April 2005)
	Draw Conclusions	Interpretation (draw conclusions, make inferences)	Grade 3 (April 2005)	Interpretation— 4th (May 2006) > 3rd (April 2005)
	Make Inferences			
RES Grade 5	Use Context Clues	Cognition (use context clues)	Grade 5 (May 2006) vs.	Cognition—5th (May 2006) > 4th (April 2005)
	Make Inferences	Interpretation (make inferences)	Grade 4 (April 2005)	Interpretation— 5th (May 2006) > 4th (April 2005)

Table 6.8 (on page 135) displays the data from the Summary Goal Reports for Grades 4 and 5 for the 2004–2005 and 2005–2006 school years for the North Carolina EOG tests in reading for Laurel Mill Elementary School and for Royal Elementary School. The diagonal arrows in the table show the results for the same cohort of students as they move from one grade in April 2005 to the next grade in May 2006.

At Laurel Mill, the three study groups had members who taught fourth-grade students during the 2005–2006 school year. The findings column in Table 6.7 and the data in Table 6.8 show that the Grade 4 students improved their performance in 2005 and 2006 in *interpretation* and *critical stance* compared with their performance the previous year, 2004–2005, as Grade 3 students, on the EOG reading test, but their performance in the *cognition* category remained about the same from Grade 3 to Grade 4.

One group had a fifth-grade teacher. The Grade 5 students had higher performance in both the *cognition* and *interpretation* categories on the May 2006 EOG reading test than they had as Grade 4 students taking the EOG reading test in April 2005.

At Royal Elementary, both the Grade 4 and Grade 5 study groups addressed needs related to *cognition* and *interpretation*. Both cohorts of students improved their performance in May 2006 compared with their performance in April 2005.

Both schools also showed improvements from the 2004–2005 school year to the 2005–2006 school year on the EOG reading test in the percentage of students passing, both for specific grades and for Grades 3–5 combined, and a reduction in the percentage of students below proficiency. Laurel Mill Elementary saw considerable improvement in the percentage passing for the 2004–2005 third- and fourth-grade cohorts as they progressed to Grades 4 and 5 in 2005 and 2006. Royal Elementary saw similar gains in the percentage passing for the 2004–2005 fourth-grade cohort as it progressed to Grade 5 in 2005 and 2006. Table 6.9 (on page 135) shows these data. The diagonal arrows in the table show the results for the same cohort of students as they move from one grade in April 2005 to the next grade in May 2006.

Table 6.8 Performance on North Carolina End-of-Grade Reading Tests by Content Category in 2005 and 2006

Laurel Mill Elementary School			
	Weighed Mean % Correct		
Category 1: Cognition	Grade 3	Grade 4	Grade 5
April 2005	70.1%	61.4%	67.9%
May 2006	37.6%	69.5%	68.8%
	Weighed Mean % Correct		
Category 2: Interpretation	Grade 3	Grade 4	Grade 5
April 2005	62.3%	59.3%	61.5%
May 2006	62.1%	69.4%	64.2%
	Weighed Mean % Correct		
Category 3: Critical Stance	Grade 3	Grade 4	Grade 5
April 2005	56.4%	52.2%	57.7%
May 2006	58.5%	63.0%	52.9%
Royal Elementary School			
	Weighed Mean % Correct		
Category 1: Cognition	Grade 3	Grade 4	Grade 5
April 2005	74.0%	65.9%	72.2%
May 2006	77.1%	75.4%	72.5%
	Weighed Mean % Correct		
Category 2: Interpretation	Grade 3	Grade 4	Grade 5
April 2005	66.1%	61.4%	66.5%
May 2006	74.5%	74.4%	69.5%

Table 6.9 Percentage Passing the North Carolina End-of-Grade Reading Tests in 2005 and 2006

Laurel Mill Elementary School—% Passing End-of-Grade Reading				
Reading	Grade 3	Grade 4	Grade 5	Grades 3–5
April 2005	77%	72%	86%	78%
May 2006	73%	92%	83%	82%
Royal Elementary School—% Passing End-of-Grade Reading				
Reading	Grade 3	Grade 4	Grade 5	Grades 3–5
April 2005	86%	78%	82%	82%
May 2006	95%	90%	90%	91%

WFSG Impact on Student Learning in Springfield Public Schools

Since the fall of 2001, the Springfield Public Schools, the third largest school district in Missouri with 51 schools, has been implementing the WFSG System districtwide as a vehicle to create professional learning communities and improve student learning. By the 2003–2004 school year, 90% of the schools used the WFSG System as the primary vehicle for reaching their academic learning goals in their school improvement plans (Kissinger, 2007).

A 2005 study by Standard & Poor's determined that Springfield Public Schools was among 24 of 366 (6.6%) Missouri school districts in 2002–2003 to outperform demographically similar districts in reading and math proficiency. School districts were identified as "outperforming" under the following criteria:

- They report a higher percentage of students who score at or above state standards on reading and math tests than other school districts that serve similar proportions of economically disadvantaged students.
- They achieve proficiency levels that fall above the threshold for expected performance; simply beating peers is not sufficient.
- They outperform for at least two consecutive years.

Other district initiatives have supported the implementation of the WFSG System in schools and the continued focus on improving student learning. These include introducing a new school improvement planning process that required a data-driven action planning process that solely focused on student performance, "reallocating contract time for professional development from district activities to site activities to provide more time for study groups, allowing their WFSG action plans to be used as the required professional development plan in our teacher evaluation program; and allowing schools to creatively schedule time for study groups to meet during the school day" (Kissinger, 2007, p. 38).

After three full years of implementing the WFSG System, the results from Parkview High School, Cherokee and Pleasant View Middle Schools, and McBride Elementary School are illustrative of the progress Springfield students have made on the Missouri Assessment Program (Springfield Public Schools, 2002, 2005).

While student performance in Springfield continued to improve from school year 2004–2005 to school year 2005–2006, comparisons between 2005 and 2006 results and results from previous years are difficult to make because the state changed from five to four performance levels during the 2005–2006 school year and used different cut scores for the new levels. In the following examples, we present data from 2001 to 2005 separately from the 2006 and 2007 data (Springfield Public Schools, 2006, 2007).

Parkview High School

Parkview High School has 1,516 students, 87 faculty members, and three assistant principals led by a new principal during the 2006–2007 school year. The format for the school's study groups has remained basically the same since the school began implementing the WFSG System in 2002. Expert-voice meetings describing the topics and ways of implementation begin each quarter. Teachers then meet during conference hours once a month in groups of five to eight to discuss implementation and to look at student work. Group composition is cross-departmental. The results of the work are logged on the computer network. All four administrators are responsible for responding to the study group logs.

All assistant principals participate in study groups with assistant principals from each of the other four high schools. The principal is also involved in a high school principals' study group.

The focus during the 2004–2005 and 2005–2006 school years was instructional strategies in Marzano, Pickering, and Pollock (2001), *Classroom Instruction That Works: Research-Based Strategies for Increasing Student Achievement.* Those strategies are aligned with the process skills tested on the state assessment. The focus for the 2006–2007 school year shifted to reading comprehension strategies based on the work of Cris Tovani. Parkview feels that the study group format has played a significant role in growing collaboration and collegiality as well as increasing student achievement.

Before Parkview began study groups, the school was classified as a Needs Improvement School. Since 2001, student performance on the Missouri Assessment (MAP) tests has improved (based on e-mail correspondence with Shela Lovewell, January 22, 2007).

Grade 10 and 11 Results—2001 to 2005

- Communication Arts—Grade 11
  - Levels 4 and 5 (proficient and advanced) increased from 17.0% in 2001 to 26.6% in 2006 (state—22.6% to 22.9%).
  - Levels 1 and 2 decreased from 39.1% in 2001 to 36.4% in 2005 (state—33.8% to 35.3%).
- Mathematics—Grade 10
  - Levels 4 and 5 (proficient and advanced) increased from 8.9% in 2001 to 19.2 % in 2005 (state—12.7% to16.6%).
  - Levels 1 and 2 decreased from 64.7% in 2001 to 52.8% in 2005 (state—56.8% to 53.2%).

Parkview's MAP Results for 2006 and 2007

- Communication Arts—Grade 11—proficient or advanced—state average, 34.7% in 2006, 41.8% in 2007; Parkview, 45.9% in 2006 and 51.2% in 2007.
- Mathematics—Grade 10—proficient or advanced—state average, 26.6% in 2006, 41.0% in 2007; Parkview, 44.6% in 2006 and 43.5% in 2007.

Source: Used with permission from Shela Lovewell.

Cherokee Middle School

The Cherokee Middle School has 900 students and 60 faculty members and has been implementing study groups since 2001. During the 2006–2007 school year, there were 11 study groups. Some groups were organized by grade level, others by content area. Study groups meet weekly or biweekly during the school day.

The student needs that Cherokee study groups addressed were determined each fall by analyzing the previous year's results on the MAP tests in communication arts and mathematics. Using an Item Benchmark Description report, which lists for each test item the type of question, the relevant process standard, the content concept, the item description, the Depth of Knowledge category, the number of points possible, and the average number of points earned, the faculty look for items with high averages to identify areas of strength and items with low averages to identify areas of weakness. For the 2006–2007 school year, groups were working on the following process standards: discover and evaluate patterns and relationships in information, ideas and structures, and reason inductively from a set of specific facts and deductively from general premises.

(Continued)

(Continued)

When they first began using the schoolwide action research process, faculty realized students were having problems answering the constructed-response type questions on the MAP test. Building on the professional development they received for "6 + 1 Trait Writing," a district initiative, study groups focused on improving students' ability to answer this type of question. Teachers explicitly taught students how to answer constructed-response questions and used them more frequently on quizzes and tests.

After seeing improvements on the MAP tests, staff began to shift their focus from the type of question to the content standards addressed in the question and the kind of cognitive processing students were being asked to do. Mr. Apostol, assistant principal at Cherokee during study group implementation, reported the following in an e-mail dated January 10, 2007: "Not only were staff members including constructed-response questions in their assessments, they were also tooling their questions to see if students could demonstrate proficiencies in process standard deficits. That is, teachers tooled some of the questions to determine if they were proficient in 'discovering and evaluating patterns and relationships in information, ideas and structures,'" an area Cherokee needed to improve. Study groups applied the same strategy to content-area deficits in math and communication arts. As a result, the faculty has seen a reduction in the number of content and process deficits from year to year. This is the work behind the school being named one of the most improved schools statewide from 2001 to 2005.

Study group work at Cherokee is supported by the principal, assistant principal, the school's professional development committee, and its district-level instructional support specialist. Together, they help with study group action research cycles, where groups "learn information from an expert voice and create an assessment to improve student performance in areas of deficiencies, and to share with other teachers their experiences. As soon as groups feel that they have established a level of proficiency with their students, they move on to another process standard to improve upon." The principal and assistant principal support study groups by "communicating through logs, finding data for study groups, or sharing success stories at faculty meetings."

Study group work is an integral part of the Cherokee annual improvement plan. The 2006–2007 plan stated the following: "WFSGs and grade-level departments will focus on how to improve student performance on process standards and content area deficits as identified in 'three year trend data.'"

In concluding our e-mail conversation, Mr. Apostol stated the following: "The most important group who benefits from WFSGs is not only our teachers, but our students. By creating time for teachers to meet and involving them in the School Improvement cycle, staff has a vested interest in their study-groups' performance."

Study group work, focused on analysis of the MAP data, has helped improve student performance on the MAP assessments. In March 2006, Cherokee Middle School was named by the Missouri Department of Elementary and Secondary Education one of the top 10 schools in regard to the percentage of students moving into the "proficient" and "advanced" levels, based on the percentage increases from the 2001 administration to the 2005. Cherokee increased its percentage of Grade 7 students achieving the proficient level or advanced in communication arts by 11.6% from 2001 to 2005. By contrast, statewide, the percentage of Grade 7 students moving into the "proficient" and "advanced" levels since 2001 for communication arts decreased by 1.7% (Springfield Public Schools, 2006). Mr. Apostol stated the following in an e-mail dated January 9, 2007: "I believe that our WFSG [approach] has a role in focusing instruction to better enhance student performance."

Grade 7 and 8 Results—2001 to 2005

- Communication Arts—Grade 7
  - Levels 4 and 5 (proficient and advanced) increased from 52.5% in 2001 to 64.1% in 2005 (state—34.2% to 32.5%).
  - Levels 1 and 2 decreased from 16.8% in 2001 to 11.3% in 2005 (state—34.5% to 35.8%).

- Mathematics—Grade 8
  - Levels 4 and 5 (proficient and advanced) increased from 24.5% in 2001 to 28.2 % in 2005 (state—14.7% to 15.5%).
  - Levels 1 and 2 decreased from 32.3% in 2001 to 28.2% in 2005 (state—54.4% to 50.6%).

Cherokee's MAP Results for Grade 7 and 8 Students in 2006 and 2007

- Communication Arts—Grade 7—proficient or advanced—state average, 43.9% in 2006, 45.5% in 2007; Cherokee, 75.1% in 2006 and 74.3% in 2007.
- Communication Arts—Grade 8—proficient or advanced—state average, 42.4% in 2007; Cherokee, 66.7% in 2007 (somewhat lower than the percentage at Grade 7 in 2006).
- Mathematics—Grade 7—proficient or advanced—state average, 45.8% in 2007; Cherokee, 73.1% in 2007.
- Mathematics—Grade 8—proficient or advanced—state average, 40.7% in 2006 and 41.6% in 2007; Cherokee, 73.9% in 2006 and 61.0% in 2007.

Source: Used with permission from Jonathan Apostol.

Pleasant View Middle School

Pleasant View Middle School has 368 middle school students in Grades 6–8. The 2006 to 2007 school year is the sixth year the school has been implementing the WFSG System. Working together in study groups is an accepted part of professional practice at the school. The middle school teachers have some study groups organized by grade-level teams and some by content area. Study groups usually meet twice a month for an hour and complete one or two action research cycles over the school year. Groups choose their meeting times and either meet during the school day or after school. The categories of student needs addressed by the study groups change from year to year, based on data about student learning needs and the goals in the school improvement plan. Study group meetings count toward the district requirement for site-based professional development. Study groups have become a key vehicle for implementing the school's improvement plan.

Dr. Ron Snodgrass, the principal, described the WFSG work at Pleasant View in a January 5, 2007, telephone interview and follow-up e-mails. He said he provides regular feedback to study groups on their logs, offering praise, questions to push the group's thinking, and reminders about the importance of teachers being continual learners on the cutting edge of their profession. One of the district's Instructional Support Specialists also supports study group work at Pleasant View by meeting with study groups and providing resources to support their work.

In the past, the school has had a year-end celebration and sharing of study group work. In 2006, Dr. Snodgrass started monthly afterschool Instructional Council (IC) meetings for sharing among all study groups. He lets study groups know in advance the focus for the meeting and asks groups to bring materials and strategies to share. The representatives attending the IC meetings are expected to share what they learn in their next study group meeting. He also uses his weekly newsletter to staff to share work that study groups are doing.

During the 2006–2007 school year, a number of groups focused on reading comprehension. One middle school study group is focusing on increasing student engagement, a district and school priority. The group is using Kagan's cooperative-learning structures. Groups collect classroom data to monitor changes in student learning as they try out strategies and regularly look at student work using the Wows and Wonders protocol.

(Continued)

(Continued)

For several years, writing has been a major focus for study group work. Based on an analysis of student performance on the state MAP tests, a sixth-grade study group decided for the 2002–2003 school year to focus on improving students' ability to answer questions that required a constructed-response answer. Working in math, science, and social studies, they used rubrics to evaluate student work and help students to restate questions in their own words, used graphic organizers to organize their thinking, wrote explanations in complete sentences, and checked answers against the questions. They shared the concrete strategies they used with other teachers.

During the 2003–2004 school year, the Encore Team study group, composed of music, art, and physical education teachers, focused on incorporating writing into their daily classroom curriculum. Some of the types of writing they experimented with included reports, written descriptions of art work or music, compare and contrast essays, and analyses of physical education assignments. They found that students had a hard time translating thoughts about music, art, and physical education into writing and that frequent practice made this easier for students.

One study group has been working on writing for several years. During the 2004–2005 school year, the group focused on connecting the "6 + 1 Trait Writing" to the minilessons given to students in the Writers Workshop program. Members brought samples of student work to study group meetings to examine it together, against the "6 + 1 Trait Writing" rubric, plan follow-up minilessons to improve specific traits, and identify books with good examples of writing for each trait that they could share with students.

Students' writing performance has improved significantly as a result of study group work. The percentage of Grade 7 students scoring at the proficient or advanced levels on the state communications and arts assessment in the writing content strand increased from 62% in 2001 to 79% in 2005 and 78% in 2006. Grade 6 and 8 students, who took the state assessments in 2006 for the first time, scored 84% and 99% in the proficient and advanced categories. The school has also seen an improvement in students' responses to constructed-response questions.

Grades 7 and 8 Results—2001 to 2005

- Communication Arts—Grade 7
  - Levels 4 and 5 (proficient and advanced) increased from 27.0% in 2001 to 51.2% in 2005 (state—34.2% to 32.5%).
  - Levels 1 and 2 decreased from 37.6% in 2001 to 22.4% in 2005 (state—34.5% to 35.8%).
- Mathematics—Grade 8
  - Levels 4 and 5 (proficient and advanced) increased from 14.7% in 2001 to 21.8 % in 2005 (state—14.7% to 15.5%).
  - Levels 1 and 2 decreased from 52.8% in 2001 to 37.8% in 2005 (state—54.4% to 50.6%).

Pleasant View's MAP Results for Grade 7 and 8 Students in 2006 and 2007

- Communication Arts—Grade 7—proficient or advanced—state average, 43.9% in 2006 and 45.5% in 2007; Pleasant View, 55.2% in 2006 and 59.0% in 2007.
- Communication Arts—Grade 8—proficient or advanced—state average, 42.4% in 2007; Pleasant View, 45.6% in 2007 (still above state average, but 10% lower than the percentage in Grade 7 in 2006).
- Mathematics—Grade 7—proficient or advanced—state average, 45.8% in 2007; Pleasant View, 65.0% in 2007.
- Mathematics—Grade 8—proficient or advanced—state average, 40.7% in 2006 and 46.1% in 2007; Pleasant View, 65.7% in 2006 and 46.4% in 2007.

Source: Used with permission from Ron Snodgrass.

McBride Elementary School

The McBride Elementary School is a K–4 school with 600 students and 30 teachers. The school started implementing the WFSG System during the 2002–2003 school year, and the current principal, Mr. Bret Range, has been at the school since the 2003–2004 school year. Mr. Range described the WFSG work at McBride in a January 28, 2007, telephone interview and follow-up e-mails. During the 2006–2007 school year, the school had eight study groups that were primarily organized by grade-level teams to facilitate meetings during the school day. Specialist teachers joined the grade-level teams. Study groups were expected to meet at least 12 times between September and April to meet district requirements for site-based professional development. Study groups post their action plans and logs in the teachers' lounge and receive regular feedback from the principal. Study groups share their work at monthly faculty meetings and at the biweekly grade-level leaders meetings.

Mr. Range also participates in monthly principal study group meetings. His study group has focused on using classroom walk-throughs to improve instruction. During the 2006–2007 school year, the group used classroom walk-throughs to monitor student engagement and developed an observation checklist to use in walk-throughs. Mr. Range shared his data with his faculty and encouraged study groups to incorporate cooperative learning activities into their teaching.

During the 2006–2007 school year, study groups were working in three main areas of student need: mathematics, reading, and student engagement. Study groups at McBride have been focusing on math for several years in conjunction with the district adoption of Everyday Mathematics. Several study groups shifted their focus to reading to coincide with the district adoption of a new reading program. The other study groups were focusing on student engagement in conjunction with McBride piloting in 2006 and 2007, a new multiyear initiative in continuous quality improvement (CQI) in classrooms. The CQI pilot has two goals: increasing student engagement and improving student achievement. After receiving initial training, the faculty decided to focus their CQI work in mathematics because of their past study group work in mathematics.

The concentrated study group work in mathematics for the last several years has paid off. Teachers were more comfortable using the Everyday Math program and helping students make real-life connections, and they spend more time in class on math. They also learned to use regular biweekly diagnostic assessments to monitor student understanding and progress, a skill they are now applying to their CQI work. The school has seen improvements in student performance on the state MAP assessments in math.

Grades 3 and 4 Results—2003 to 2005

- Communication Arts—Grade 3
  - Levels 4 and 5 (proficient and advanced) increased from 48.3% in 2003 to 50.9% in 2005 (state—34.1% to 35.1%).
  - Levels 1 and 2 decreased from 10.3% in 2003 to 7.0% in 2005 (state—26.4% to 24.3%).
- Math—Grade 4
  - Levels 4 and 5 (proficient and advanced) increased from 54.5% in 2003 to 61.3 % in 2005 (state—37.7% to 43.0%).
  - Levels 1 and 2 changed from 1.1% in 2003 to 7.2% in 2005 (state—20.4% to 16.1%).

(Continued)

(Continued)

McBride's MAP Results for Grade 3 and 4 Students in 2006 and 2007

- Communication Arts—Grade 3—proficient or advanced—state average, 43.3% in 2006 and 43.6% in 2007; McBride, 53.7% in 2006 and 50.4% in 2007.
- Communication Arts—Grade 4—proficient or advanced—state average, 45.9% in 2007; McBride, 50.0% in 2007 (slightly lower than Grade 7 percentage in 2006).
- Mathematics—Grade 3—proficient or advanced—state average, 45.7% in 2007; McBride, 66.9% in 2007.
- Mathematics—Grade 4—proficient or advanced—state average, 44.1% in 2006 and 45.2% in 2007; McBride, 65.8% in 2006 and 64.0% in 2007.

Source: Used with permission from Bret Range.

Williams Elementary School

The Williams Elementary School is a K–5 school with about 300 students and 40 teachers. About 85% of the students are on free or reduced lunch. The school started implementing the WFSG System during the 2002–2003 school year, and the principal, Dr. Lynne Miller, has been at the school since the 1999–2000 school year. Dr. Miller described the school's work with WFSG in a February 15, 2007, telephone interview and follow-up e-mails.

There are eight study groups composed of teachers, aides, and other certificated staff, with six groups organized by grade level that include other staff, a group with special education teachers and aides, and a group with special teachers, such as art, music, and physical education. The groups meet weekly during the school day and submit monthly logs that describe their weekly meetings and lessons they have developed as a group and taught. The format of the logs has changed over time in response to feedback from groups. Action plans and logs are posted on a public display and the principal provides feedback on logs and action plans. She and the school's literacy coach also meet once a month with each study group. Study groups share their work at faculty meetings by presenting minilessons to their colleagues.

The principal and the school's instructional specialist led the faculty through a developmental process for implementing study groups during the first three years that enabled teachers to focus on the content of study group work right from the beginning without getting bogged down in the paperwork. This developmental period is described in more detail in Weiskopf (2007b).

Since the 2002–2003 school year, the school has focused on improving reading and writing. Study groups have been the vehicle each year for connecting the staff development with changing classroom practice. During the 2006–2007 school year, the early elementary groups were working on phonemic awareness and reading skills. The upper elementary groups were working on reading comprehension and writing skills.

The school has also developed expertise in two other district initiatives: peer coaching and classroom walk-throughs. Each year, the school decided to implement these practices differently to keep things interesting. During the 2006–2007 school year, study groups were doing the classroom walk-throughs, along with the principal.

Study groups use a variety of data to guide their work. In addition to the state assessment data, groups use DIBELS, DRA, and SRI diagnostic data, a set of teacher-developed common assessments that students take every six weeks, and mock state tests in math and communication arts. The principal and the literacy coach provide resource options for each study group. Each group selects resources for members to use during the year.

As a result of four years' work with study groups, student performance in communication arts is improving. During the 2005–2006 school year, the school met the state's Annual Yearly Progress targets in both communication arts and math. During the 2005–2006 school year, the state started testing Grades 3 through 5 in both communications arts and mathematics. Grades 4 and 5 had higher percentages in the proficient and advanced levels in communication arts than did Grade 3, and Grade 5 had higher percentages in mathematics for proficient and advanced than did Grade 4.

Grades 3 and 4 Results—2002 to 2005

- Communication Arts—Grade 3
  - Levels 4 and 5 (proficient and advanced) increased from 18.4% in 2002 to 20.8% in 2005 (state—34.1% to 35.1%).
  - Levels 1 and 2 decreased from 59.2% in 2002 to 30.2% in 2005 (state—26.4% to 24.3%).
- Math—Grade 4
  - Levels 4 and 5 (proficient and advanced) increased from 16.3% in 2002 to 28.8 % in 2005 (state—37.7% to 43.0%).
  - Levels 1 and 2 decreased from 32.7% in 2002 to 20.3% in 2005 (state—20.4% to 16.1%).

Williams Elementary's MAP Results for Grade 3 and 4 Students in 2006 and 2007

- Communication Arts—Grade 3—proficient or advanced—state average, 43.3% in 2006 and 43.6% in 2007; Williams, 26.5% in 2006 and 21.7% in 2007.
- Communication Arts—Grade 4—proficient or advanced—state average, 45.9% in 2007; Williams, 29.8% in 2007 (slightly higher than Grade 3 percentage in 2006).
- Mathematics—Grade 3—proficient or advanced—state average, 45.7% in 2007; Williams, 30.4% in 2007.
- Mathematics—Grade 4—proficient or advanced—state average, 44.1% in 2006 and 45.2% in 2007; Williams, 38.5% in 2006 and 48.9% in 2007.

Source: Used with permission from Lynne Miller.

Louisiana Department of Education Learning-Intensive Networking Communities for Success (LINCS)

The State of Louisiana Department of Education began a formal relationship with Carlene Murphy and the WFSG System in 2000. The relationship was established through the Learning-Intensive Networking Communities for Success (LINCS), a statewide initiative to elevate and sustain teacher- and student-content knowledge in low-performing schools throughout the state. As described in Chapter 4, study groups were a key component of the LINCS program, connecting professional development to changes in teacher practice and improvements in student learning.

In a 2005 longitudinal study of changes in student achievement for students in 158 of 170 LINCS schools focusing on mathematics, Gansle and Noell (2005) found that in performance on the Louisiana Educational Assessment Program (LEAP) assessments for Grades 4, 8, and 10, "students enrolled in a LINCS school for one year in 2005 fell further behind state averages by 7.5 points in 2005. Conversely, longer-term participation in LINCS was associated with gains relative to state averages. Those students who were in their second year in LINCS gained 3.75 points over two years, and those in their third year had gained 10.5 points over three years" (p. 36).

In analyzing changes in student performance in the 55 out of 170 LINCS schools that focused on English language arts, Gansle and Noell (2005, p. 46) found that third- and fourth-year LINCS schools exhibited growth on the English Language Arts component of the Iowa Test of Basic Skills in Grades 3, 5, 6, 7, and 9 and surpassed state averages for the first time, while results for first- and second-year schools were mixed. On the LEAP, second- and third-year schools made strong gains in Grade 4 but lost ground in Grade 8. Analyses that tracked individual students indicated that results for students in LINCS schools were generally similar to statewide averages after considering prior achievement and demographic factors.

HOW SCHOOL AND DISTRICT LEADERS HELP STUDY GROUPS IMPROVE STUDENT LEARNING

School and district leaders help study groups improve student learning when they keep the focus of study group work on improving student learning, arranging easy access to student data and providing assistance in using it, offering professional development in action research basics, providing tools to support collecting and analyzing classroom data on student learning, and establishing school and district benchmark assessments.

Focus on Improving Student Learning

In the absence of clear expectations and continual reminders, study group members can lose sight of their primary goal—to improve student learning this year in each of their classes. Without appropriate pressure and support, study group meetings devolve into conversations about curriculum and changes they or others need to make "next year."

The three main strategies principals use to maintain the focus on student learning are as follows: (a) link explicitly and publicly the work of study groups to the academic improvement goals in the school's annual improvement plan, (b) encourage ongoing work on improving learning through feedback on study group action plans and logs, and (c) use IC meetings, faculty meetings, the school Web site, and staff and parent newsletters to share effective best practices and the impact on student learning.

Jewel Eason, the principal of Bunn Elementary School, uses all three strategies to help the Bunn study groups stay focused on student learning. The 2005–2008 Bunn Elementary School Improvement Plan lists the WFSG System as the vehicle for getting much of the work done, and study groups are listed in the action plans as the key groups for implementing specific instructional strategies such as the Four Blocks Literacy Program. After each study group meeting, she provides immediate feedback to each of her nine study groups on their logs and action plans and asks groups to share copies of their assessment tools and results. In her weekly newsletter to staff, she highlights specific practices and accomplishments of study groups and asks them to share, at the regular IC meetings with representatives from each study group, strategies, assessment tools, and results.

Provide Easy Access to Student Data and Help in Using It

State and district data on student learning for the students in their current classes can help study groups determine specific learning needs and important differences in achievement among the different student subgroups when the data is easily accessible. Study groups do not have the time or skill to plow through reams of data to find the relevant data for their students.

In the K–8 Hawthorn School District, the district introduced, during the 2005–2006 school year, new data management software, Just5Clicks, that allows teachers to easily access student data from the Illinois state assessments and the districtwide benchmark assessments in reading, mathematics, and language usage. Just5Clicks can also be used to capture study group data. Building administrators and each school's teaching and learning coach received training in using the software and they, in turn, trained teachers.

Teach Action Research Basics

Engaging in schoolwide action research requires every study group to engage in cycles of action research around the student learning needs the group has chosen to address. As described in Chapter 4, following are the action research steps that each study group follows:

1. Assess needs and establish baseline student performance and desired targets.

2. Research content and best practices and develop expertise.

3. Plan interventions.

4. Implement interventions and monitor.

5. Look at student work and data and assess changes.

Because of their experiences in other types of collaborative work, school staff members tend to be more knowledgeable about some action research steps than others. We have found that most study groups are comfortable sharing teaching practices that they have used and are willing to try them in their own classes. Some groups are also comfortable with expanding their knowledge base by researching content and best practices. Few study groups have had experience in assessing needs, establishing baseline student performance with classroom assessments, setting targets, developing action hypotheses, planning and implementing interventions to enable them to assess the effectiveness of the interventions, and examining student work and performance data together.

During the first year of implementing the WFSG System, we encourage and support schools and districts to provide professional development in action research for study groups as they move through the steps in the action research process. This professional development can occur in faculty meetings and IC meetings, on early release days or professional development days, and during study group meetings.

In September 2005, Carlene Murphy visited all 14 Franklin County schools and met with representatives from each study group for 1.5-hour sessions to provide feedback on the study group action plans and set the stage for beginning the action research process. WFSG Consultant Lynn Bader followed up with a two-day workshop on using protocols for looking at student work to assess student understanding and gauge the effectiveness of instructional strategies. Each school's Curriculum Resource Teacher and two other representatives participated in the workshop and practiced using protocols so that they could share the use of these protocols with their study groups.

In February 2006, WFSG Consultant Karl Clauset visited two WFSG high schools in Georgia and facilitated, during periods within the school day, miniworkshops for study groups at each school on collecting baseline data.

The WFSG consultants also offered workshops on action research skills at the annual WFSG National Conference and at the WFSG Level II Institutes in Augusta, Georgia.

Provide Support for Collecting and Analyzing Data on Student Learning

There are a variety of ways that schools and districts can help study groups identify and use tools to collect and analyze classroom data on student learning. Sometimes study groups need assistance in finding or creating an assessment task for the student learning need they have chosen to address. Study groups may not realize that they can use state test-release items or computer programs such as Study Land, STAR Reading, STAR Math, and PLATO to create diagnostic assessments.

At Northside High School, some study groups created multiple-choice assessments and used the school's OCR scanner and software to read answer sheets and create summary statistics and item analysis information. At Bunn Elementary School, the curriculum resource teacher helped a reading study group locate Web sites that students could use for online tutorials and quizzes as they worked in reading activity centers in each teacher's classroom.

Establish School and District Benchmark Assessments

Study groups as well as individual teachers can use data from school and district benchmark assessments to improve student learning. Many districts are introducing reading, writing, and math benchmark assessments that are aligned with state standards, administered two or three times a year, and return diagnostic data to teachers within weeks instead of months. Study groups can use the benchmark data to compare student performance with the results from their classroom assessments.

The Hawthorn School District gives districtwide benchmark assessments to Grades 2–8 three times a year in reading, math, and language usage using the Northwest Evaluation Association's Measures of Academic Progress. The district also gives fall and spring writing assessments in Grades K–8, which are scored for kindergarten on a six-point scale and for Grades 1–8 on holistic and specific writing traits.

In Franklin County, the district designed and implemented a diagnostic Mock Writing Test that mirrors the North Carolina State Writing Assessment. The elementary writing assessment was given to students every nine weeks. The district also provided a fall and spring benchmark assessment in reading and math in Grades 3–8 and in core subjects at the high school level. The assessments were based on the North Carolina Standard Course of Study and pacing guides and were revised each year.

The Springfield Public Schools have quarterly benchmark assessments in Grades 1–8 in mathematics and communication arts and gave a writing assessment in Grades 6–10 twice a year. High school assessments were part of the semester final exams. Results on the assessments were posted on the district Web site at midyear and the end of the year. Several schools are implementing their own common assessments in other areas and are providing courses on assessment for learning and studying the effectiveness of the classroom instruction.

CONCLUSIONS

This chapter has focused on two steps in the action research cycle that are critical for improving student performance in the learning needs each study group addresses: understanding and assessing student learning needs and assessing the effectiveness of study group interventions. For each of these steps, we have delineated the key factors that study groups need to consider, offered suggestions for how study groups might approach each step, and provided examples from practicing study groups.

We have also addressed a common question about schoolwide action research: Do changes in student learning that study groups see in classroom assessments also lead to changes in district and state assessments? We respond to this question with examples from two districts that are implementing WFSG districtwide: Franklin County Public Schools in North Carolina and Springfield Public Schools in Missouri.

We conclude this chapter with a discussion of the ways in which schools and districts can support study groups in improving student learning.

There are several key points to remember about strengthening study group work in improving student learning:

- *State tests are only one measure of student learning and performance.*

    In the current testing and accountability environment in U.S. states and many provinces in Canada, the paramount measure of successful student learning and performance are the state and provincial annual assessments. Realistically, schools and study groups have to pay attention to improving student performance on these assessments. But educators know that there is more to educating children than state test results. At the Dr. Paul Nettle Middle School in Haverhill, Massachusetts, the school faculty developed a new vision statement in 2006 which included achievement of the following competencies before students enter high school: communicate effectively both verbally and through written expression; demonstrate basic literacy and math skills; work and research independently; demonstrate time management, organizational, and study skills; give independent presentations; think creatively; complete multitask assignments; and develop good citizenship. The characteristics of successful learners in this vision statement are characteristics that can be defined, assessed, and monitored over time. As such, each could become the basis for study group work.

- *Data and documentation are important.*

    Study groups are expected to work with quantitative and qualitative data as they engage in action research on their chosen student learning needs. They use state and district data to identify specific learning problems or groups of students. They use classroom data to establish benchmarks and targets, monitor progress, assess the effectiveness of their interventions, and identify changes in student thinking and understanding. They regularly document the interventions they use with students and work they do in their study group meetings. The documentation study groups provide enables others to build on and use their work and helps study groups remember their work.

- *Study group work is about learning, not just achieving targets.*

    Study groups are expected to set challenging but attainable targets for improving student performance in their chosen student learning needs and to work toward these targets. The underlying assumption is that learning will not improve if study groups do not change what they teach, how they teach, and how they assess, and become proficient in these new ways of teaching, assessing, and using qualitative and quantitative data about students and their learning to improve instruction.

The journey is just as important as reaching the destination. No study group is penalized for not reaching its targets. The important questions are as follows: Why do you think students did not reach the targets? What did you learn in this cycle of action research about designing assessment tasks, planning and implementing interventions, and looking at student work that might help you reach your targets in the next cycle? Study groups can learn as much from not reaching targets as from reaching them.

- *Removing roadblocks.*

  School and district leaders and outside organizations can help study groups be successful in improving student learning by removing roadblocks that make it hard for study groups to do their work. Protecting study group time; simplifying the record keeping and documentation; providing data, assistance, and resources when necessary; teaching action research basics; and connecting study group work to school improvement plans, individual professional development plans, and job requirements all reinforce the message that study group work is *the* work.

- *Communication provides peer support and pressure.*

  When study groups operate in isolation, the burden of providing support and pressure for study groups to improve falls on the principal's shoulders. When study group work is public and there are frequent opportunities for study groups to give each other constructive feedback and share strategies and resources, schools create a shared commitment to continuous improvement.

Chapter 7 shifts the focus from the work of study groups in schoolwide action research to the work of the principal in leading and supporting schoolwide action research.

7

Supporting Schoolwide Action Research

The Principal's Role

Guiding Question

■ **How do principals and other school leaders support schoolwide action research?**

Whole-Faculty Study Groups (WFSG) are professional learning communities at the heart of a job-embedded, self-directed, student-driven, professional development system. Within each school, individual study groups engage in cycles of action research that strive to increase student learning. The principal is a key figure in ensuring the success of schoolwide action research. By "principal" we mean school leaders, which include the principal, assistant principal(s), and instructional or curriculum specialists, who together share responsibility for leading and supporting teaching and learning. In this chapter, we use "principal" as shorthand for school leaders.

The design of the WFSG System mirrors the conceptual framework for the National Staff Development Council's (NSDC, 2001) Standards for Staff Development in Action. Both the WFSG System and the NSDC standards are organized around three domains: context, process, and content. School leaders have a role in all three domains.

149

Within the context domain, the NSDC standard for learning communities is as follows: "Staff development that improves the learning of all students organizes adults into learning communities whose goals are aligned with those of the school and district" (Roy & Hord, 2003, p. 13). The NSDC expectations for teachers (Roy & Hord, 2003, p. 14) are that every teacher "meets regularly with the learning team during scheduled time within the school day to develop lesson plans, examine student work, monitor student progress, assess the effectiveness of instruction, and identify needs for professional learning." This describes what the WFSG System does; it is an approach for creating professional learning communities that target student learning.

Both the NSDC and the WFSG System expect the principal to do the following:

- Create and maintain a learning community that supports teacher and student learning.
- Develop a culture that supports continuous improvement.
- Provide job-embedded professional development to develop teachers' deep understanding and the implementation of research-based classroom practices.

This chapter focuses on how principals and other school leaders accomplish these tasks in leading and supporting schoolwide action research. Its discussion and examples connect with the discussion in Chapter 3 on creating learning teams and learning communities, steps in the action research process described in Chapter 4, and ways in which schools support study groups as they work to change their practice, described in Chapter 5, and improve student learning, described in Chapter 6. The chapter concludes with important lessons learned about the principal's role in supporting schoolwide action research.

John Kotter (1998), in his study of why major initiatives in the private sector usually fail, identified principles for leaders to follow to ensure success in transforming organizations, which is what the WFSG System is all about:

- Establish a sense of urgency.
- Form a powerful guiding coalition.
- Create and communicate a vision.
- Empower others to act on the vision and eliminate obstacles to change.
- Plan for and create short-term wins.
- Consolidate improvements and produce more changes.
- Institutionalize new approaches.

These same principles apply to launching and implementing the WFSG System and any other major schoolwide initiative. The assumption behind these principles is that any major schoolwide initiative, such as WFSG, represents a major shift from "business as usual."

LEADING THE LAUNCH

Establishing a Sense of Urgency

Organizations tend to operate to maintain the status quo and schools are no different. Implementing a new initiative like WFSG is a change to the status quo.

Principals create a sense of urgency for launching study groups based on data about student learning and effective and productive professional learning communities.

Federal and state pressure to ensure that students in every subgroup are proficient in reading and mathematics by 2014 provides every school with ample opportunities for creating a sense of urgency for improving student learning. In addition, most schools have mission and vision statements that define learning more broadly than reaching proficiency on standardized tests, and recognize that they have much still to do to reach these goals. Staff members examining a variety of data together about student learning can create a sense of urgency that supports implementation of a study group initiative as a vehicle for improving student learning. When schools start the WFSG Decision-Making Cycle (DMC), the entire school faculty start with data about student learning.

Another element to creating a sense of urgency is the quality of collaborative work around teaching and learning. While schools have a plethora of committees, teams, and task forces, the fundamental work of creating learning opportunities that challenge and engage students and assess their impact on student learning often takes place in isolation.

But this view of teaching is changing. Roy and Hord (2003) state that every teacher should be part of a learning community: "Staff development that improves the learning of all students organizes adults into learning communities whose goals are aligned with those of the school and district" (p. 13). WFSG is a system for creating professional learning communities that target student learning.

Forming a Powerful Guiding Coalition

Kotter (1998) emphasizes that a smart leader assembles a group of people within the organization, a guiding coalition, to help the leader lead the change effort. He recognizes that the initiative becomes more credible if others beside the titular leader are actively engaged in planning and leading the initiative. In the WFSG System, the Focus Team plays the role of a guiding coalition.

The Focus Team usually comprises the principal and four or five teachers who represent a cross-section of the school faculty. Their primary responsibilities are as follows:

- Attend training to deepen their understanding of the process and to learn how to lead the faculty through the DMC.
- Lead the whole faculty, if one has not already been done, in an orientation to define and explain the system, review the research supporting it, develop understanding of the functions of the system, and present its 15 guidelines.
- Lead the whole faculty through the system's DMC (Steps 1–4) that results in establishing study groups and what they will do.
- Lead the whole faculty through the DMC at the beginning of each school year to establish and confirm the work of study groups.
- Provide continuity on the Instructional Council. (IC; Murphy & Lick, 2005, p. 63)

The Focus Team members are not "experts" in the system. They learn enough about the system up-front to enable them to lead the school faculty through an orientation to the system and the DMC. Teacher members of the Focus Team join teacher study groups and serve as regular, participating members. The principal is often a member of an administrative study group.

Creating and Communicating a Vision

A clear vision answers the question, "Why are we doing this?" The NSDC standards and expectations about learning communities within schools quoted earlier is a vision for transforming schools to benefit both students and staff. Principals can enhance the success of their study groups by creating a vision for the school that incorporates them as a primary strategy for achieving that vision. Kotter (1998) reminds us that it is not enough to create a vision. For the vision to be an effective staff motivator, the guiding coalition needs to communicate the vision repeatedly through every vehicle possible, develop strategies for achieving the vision, and teach new behaviors through the actions of the guiding coalition—"walking the talk." For the principal, walking the talk means protecting study group time, actively and regularly giving feedback and support to study groups, participating in an administrative study group, and being an advocate for study groups to the district and community. For staff members of the Focus Team, walking the talk means being productive members of their own study groups.

Empowering Others to Act and Removing Obstacles to Change

As their staff begins to work in study groups, many principals find that teachers do not believe that they control the work they do in study groups. They keep expecting the principal to tell them what needs to address, or what to put in their action plan, or which strategy to use in their classrooms. This is especially true in schools that have a tradition of "top-down" decision making and leadership. Study groups really do have choices and flexibility to decide what to do. The system also fosters teacher leadership by requiring members to rotate responsibilities for leader, recorder, and representatives to the IC. It breaks from the traditional view that teams and committees have designated leaders; all members share the leadership.

Principals can empower study groups by encouraging and expecting risk taking and nontraditional ideas and strategies in the interventions that study group members try out in their classrooms to improve student learning.

One of the biggest obstacles to the successful implementation of the schoolwide approach to action research is finding time for study groups to meet frequently and regularly and finding time for cross-study group sharing and problem solving.

Find Time

To implement a system, schools need to find time for study groups to meet and for regular IC meetings or other meetings for study group sharing.

Study Group Meetings

One of the first questions school staff have about study groups is about time—how often they will be expected to meet and when they will meet during contract time. Staff members also want to know whether they can form a study group with any other staff members choosing the same category of student need. The principal, focus team, and school leadership team (if applicable) should either decide on a plan to present to staff or decide on options to present to the staff for discussion and reaching a consensus decision.

The WFSG National Center recommends that study groups meet weekly for 45–60 minutes or biweekly for 90–120 minutes within the contract week. Study groups that meet less than biweekly accomplish little because they have no sense of urgency for improving student learning and lose valuable meeting time trying to remember what they were doing at their last meeting. The reason we insist that study groups meet within the contract day or week is that study group work to increase student learning should be a school priority and working in study groups is part of members' professional responsibilities and, as such, should be done "on company time," not on personal time.

The ideal scenario for forming study groups is for staff to form groups around student needs without time constraints. This means all study groups can meet at the same time and day within the contract week, such as on a weekly early release or late-start day.

Some schools have difficulty finding common free time for study groups to meet and choose to form study groups around existing grade-level or content-area teams or with teachers who have the same planning periods.

In forming study groups by grade level or content area, teams that regularly meet together could select one day a week to meet as a study group to develop and implement their study group action plan. The other business that teams have, curriculum articulation, unit planning, identifying resources, and student and parent conferences, can take place on nonstudy group days.

In Step 4 of the DMC, each team member still creates an individual action plan. But, instead of joining a study group with other staff focused on the same category of student needs, the team member reaches consensus with other team members about a set of student learning needs that all members of the team know their students require and can address through the curriculum they teach.

When teachers with the same planning periods form study groups, they also must go through the same consensus process to identify a set of student learning needs that all members of the team can address.

Decisions about when study groups meet and how groups are formed are fixed for the year but can change from year to year. How a school allocates time for study groups in Year 1 is not the way it has to do it in Year 2. For example, a school might have to form study groups in Year 1 around teachers with the same common planning period because it is too late to change the student schedule, but in Year 2, plans can be made ahead to change the student schedule to allow all staff to meet for study groups at the same time.

Murphy and Lick (2005, pp. 56–59) describe 22 different strategies schools have used to find time for study group meetings. Table 7.1 is a condensed version of their list. The important thing to remember is that there are "pots" of time throughout the workday, workweek, month, and year that can be combined and used for study group time: before and after schooltime, afterschool meeting time, and during planning periods and staff development days. As Murphy and Lick (2005, p. 56) said with conviction, "There is time in the school day for teachers to collaborate, if the administration and faculty are willing to change other things!" Figure 7.1 illustrates 18 different ways that schools have used to create time for regular study group meetings within the teacher workday or workweek.

Figure 7.1 Finding Time for WFSG Study Group Meetings

1. Release students early one day a week and add minutes to the other days if necessary.

2. Have a "late start" day once a week when students arrive 30 to 60 minutes later.

3. Have an "early dismissal" day once a week when students leave 30 to 60 minutes earlier.

4. Use teaching assistants to release teachers for study group meetings at different times during the school day.

5. Use teams of parents or business partners to release teachers for the hour their study groups meet.

6. Pair study groups to take each other's classes.

7. Identify a team of five substitutes that spend a day at the school, covering for a different study group each period.

8. Use after-school required meeting time three times per month for study group meetings.

9. Use part or all of a daily team planning period once a week.

10. Permit teachers to earn compensatory time for their after-school study groups.

11. Design an assembly model to give teachers time to collaborate during the school day.

12. Allow teachers to select for themselves when their study group will meet once a week.

13. Redesign a modified day plan that may have been in place prior to the initiation of the study group process.

14. Schedule a weekly common planning period for teachers in the same study group.

15. Enlist college students to spend one day a week at the school.

16. Make allowances for the contract time teachers spend after school in their study groups.

17. Release teachers from their teaching duties for an hour and a half each week with volunteers providing activities for students.

18. Establish a silent reading time for one morning a week with volunteer and aide coverage.

Instructional Council Meetings

The WFSG National Center also recommends convening Instructional Council (IC), IC meetings with the principal and study group representatives after the second study group meetings (when action plans are completed) and after that, every four to six study group meetings. IC meetings typically run for 50–90 minutes and can be scheduled during the school day or before or after classes start. We recommend developing a study group calendar for the year that lists study group meetings, IC meetings, professional development time for study groups, and the year-end celebration and sharing event.

Once study groups are formed and groups begin their cycles of action research, other obstacles may appear that can undermine successful implementation. Principals can eliminate these obstacles to successful implementation when they protect study group time, give frequent feedback and support to groups, help groups locate resources and professional development, incorporate study groups into the school improvement plan, modify school schedules to better accommodate study groups, and include study group work in staff supervision and evaluation. All of these actions signal that study group work is important and valuable work.

Build Consensus

Launching schoolwide action research requires consensus among the staff to embark on the process. Prior experience in working collaboratively also increases the likelihood of a successful launch. How long the consensus-building process takes depends on a number of factors. Contextual conditions determine what is needed.

Many schools can reach consensus quickly. In such schools, the principal or another school leader may simply give a short presentation on schoolwide study groups, followed by the faculty agreeing to such a system. Also, much is currently being written about professional learning communities (PLCs), and speakers invited into districts often speak of the importance of PLCs. Often teachers attending conferences will return with questions about how their schools might initiate a model or design that would provide for more collaboration. When these conditions are present, the need for learning communities and willingness to participate are established. In such schools, identifying the PLC design that fits the school is all that is required to begin a schoolwide study group approach. Consensus can occur in one meeting or as the result of several meetings over a short period of time. If readiness has been established in any number of ways, extending the consensus-building time may dampen the momentum to begin.

One strategy for building consensus is to ask faculty members at orientation activities to share in their reflections, at the end of each session, their questions or concerns about the WFSG System. Then the Focus Team compiles the list of questions and concerns, organizes them into categories, and writes answers to each group of questions and concerns. The questions and answers are distributed to all staff and posted in the faculty room.

Franklin County Schools

In Franklin County, North Carolina, all of the faculties of the district's 14 schools spent the spring of 2004 reading Philip Schlechty's (2002) *Working on the Work*. During the summer of 2004, a member of the Curriculum and Instruction staff attended a WFSG Institute. The representative shared materials with central office colleagues and the resulting decision was that the WFSG System would be the structure through which the faculties would "work on the work" of teaching and learning. The superintendent met with the principals and it was agreed that the WFSG System would be implemented in all the schools beginning in September 2004. By November, the WFSG System had been introduced in all schools and study group meetings began in January 2005. Many of the examples of study group work included in this book are from the Franklin County School District.

Qualicum Beach Middle School

Before launching schoolwide action research at Qualicum Beach Middle School, the principal, Don Boyd, and vice principal, Jessica Antosz, spent two years laying the foundation for collaborative work focused on improving student learning (Antosz, Boyd, & Clauset, 2005).

(Continued)

(Continued)

During the 2001–2002 school year, they introduced grade-level study groups for teachers and provided time during the school day for group meetings, even if it meant covering classes for teachers. These study groups worked on grade-level goals. They altered staff meetings to focus on the sharing of new ideas and materials regarding goal setting and change and supporting the needs of the grade-level study groups.

During the 2002–2003 school year, the principal and vice principal decided to broaden and formalize the work of the grade-level study groups to engage all staff members and to increase the impact of study groups on student learning. They researched various systems for teacher collaboration and attended two training sessions on the WFSG System to learn more. They decided to present the WFSG System to their staff for several reasons: (1) the system could be a vehicle for implementing the annual school growth plan; (2) the structure provided by the system would help staff focus on changing practice and improving student learning; (3) staff members could choose the student needs they wanted to address for their students and could choose to work in cross-grade groups or in grade-level groups; (4) it could involve all staff, not just teachers; and (5) it modeled a collaborative and cooperative school climate, where in study groups, everyone is equal and members share ownership of what they do together.

The principal and vice principal shared WFSG information with their staff and secured support in May 2004 to embark on implementing and establishing the WFSG structure during the 2004–2005 school year. In June, September, and October, staff reviewed results from the Grades 4 and 7 provincial Fundamental Skills Assessments, data from student and parent satisfaction surveys, student grades in classes, student participation and discipline data, and data from gradewide writing samples to identify student learning needs. They organized these needs into three categories—literacy, numeracy, and social responsibility—which became the three goal areas for their annual School Growth Plan.

From a list of 20 specific needs in these three areas, staff (including teachers, assistants, specialists, the vice principal, and principal) chose, in October, the student needs they wanted to work on in study groups. The 40 staff members organized themselves into nine study groups of two to six members with three groups working in each of the three goal areas. In November, study group members worked collaboratively to write an action plan to provide a structure to guide their work for the remainder of the year. The study groups began working on their action plans in December. From December through May, the study groups engaged in cycles of action research on their chosen student needs. During the period from November to May, the principal and vice principal sought regular feedback from staff about issues and concerns that they had about the process and brought in a WFSG consultant to meet with individual study groups. In June, the staff evaluated the impact of study groups on student learning and staff practice and made plans for the following year.

Clarke Middle School

Kenneth Sherman, the principal, and Kim Reynolds-Manglitz, Instructional Lead Teacher (Sherman & Reynolds-Manglitz, 2007), describe a similar process for building commitment and support at Clarke Middle School. Building on several years experience with their "own homegrown, shared decision-making and governance process" (p. 94), the principal and staff spent eight months laying the foundation for WFSG and schoolwide action research. They sent a team to learn more about the WFSG System and receive training in how to launch the system, engaged staff in conversations about the system and responded to questions and concerns, planned how to integrate the system with existing structures and initiatives before launching study groups, and built understanding and support with the superintendent and key district-level staff. Even after the faculty reached consensus to implement the WFSG System, they continued to publicize their work and build broader support. They concluded the following: "We strongly recommend building in enough time on the front end to plan and build commitment, to ensure the WFSG program will take root and succeed" (Sherman & Reynolds-Manglitz, 2007, p. 95).

Regardless of how long faculties take to determine action, what strategies are used in the decision-making process, or how thorough the orientation procedures are, once the WFSG approach or any complex initiative begins, there will still be individuals who will feel some resentment about how decisions were made to begin the initiative. Leaders can expect differences in how individuals respond and the level of consensus among faculty members. Even those individuals who were most willing to begin may become less so when the real work of collaboration begins. We have found the old adage, "It's not real until it's real," to certainly be true. Commitment to the work comes when teachers see the positive impact of study group work on student learning.

AFTER THE LAUNCH, THEN WHAT?

Creating Short-Term Wins

Principals create short-term wins for study groups when they get help to develop their action plans and start the action research cycle within the first three or four meetings and when they see results in their classrooms within the first semester of study group work. They make the study group work public and visible by displaying action plans and logs, convening IC meetings and faculty meetings to share work in progress, and using newsletters and other vehicles for recognizing and celebrating study group work. Every WFSG school ends each year with a celebration and sharing of study group work.

There are five things principals do to create an environment that produces short-term wins:

- Establish study group routines.
- Protect study group time.
- Provide timely feedback.
- Create opportunities for sharing among study groups.
- Establish an administrative study group.

Establish Routines

Study group meetings are a different way of functioning for teachers used to committee meetings and grade-level or department meetings. As Hord, Rutherford, Huling-Austin, and Hall (1987) describe in their research in the 1970s on the Concerns-Based Adoption Model for implementing innovations, groups need to progress from a mechanical use of the study group guidelines and procedures to a routine use to begin focusing on the impact of their work on their practice and on student learning. Study groups need to develop the habits of working collaboratively and following group norms; rotating leader, recorder, and IC representative responsibilities; completing and submitting their action plan and logs in a timely fashion; using protocols to examine student work; planning agendas in advance; and moving through the steps in the action research cycle.

Principals and their focus teams can increase the likelihood that groups establish productive routines before, during, and after launching study groups. During orientation and before starting the DMC, focus teams review the study group process guidelines (see Figure 5.2 in Chapter 5), provide examples of study group action plans and logs, and describe the kind of feedback principals give study groups. They also share with faculty that study group work is public and that action plans and logs will be shared and displayed.

On the day the faculty completes Steps 1–4 of the DMC and forms study groups, the Focus Team reminds faculty about next steps and distributes copies of the WFSG checklist for the first three meetings—a step-by-step guide for groups to follow. After study groups are formed, many principals send out a follow-up memo to summarize guidelines and expectations for study group work and provide a calendar for upcoming study group and IC meetings (see Chapter 5 for excerpts from a follow-up memo from Dr. Delores Bedar to faculty at the Daniel Hale Williams Preparatory School of Medicine).

Study group logs are the best evidence of whether a group has established routines around meeting regularly and effectively, rotating roles, using protocols, and engaging in action research. Principals can quickly get a sense of whether a group is developing routines by reviewing its log after a meeting and comparing this week's log to the previous log and to the group's action plan.

The Focus Team at Northside High School used walkabouts to help study groups move from the mechanical to a routine level of use. During the first month of study group meetings, members of the Focus Team visited study groups to see how they were doing and to respond to questions and concerns.

A key part of establishing routines is the process for groups submitting study group action plans and logs so that they can get feedback from the principal or other designated readers before their next meeting. The process has two key features: when to submit and how to submit.

Many schools address the "when to submit" issue by using a 24-hour rule: study group logs and action plan updates are submitted within 24 hours of the study group meeting.

"How to submit" has changed since the WFSG System began in 1987. In the early 1990s, this meant establishing a process for managing paper flow. Study groups wrote action plans and logs by hand and turned in paper copies for posting and for principal feedback. By the late 1990s, as more schools established computer networks, study groups began using computers to type their action plans and logs and e-mail copies to the principal, who could e-mail comments back to the group.

In the last few years, schools have experimented with different electronic solutions for posting and sharing study group work. Some schools, such as Western Harnett High School, have a WFSG folder on the school computer network server that all staff can access. Each study group has its own folder within this folder. Study groups post their logs and action plan updates to their group folder and the readers post their feedback to the same folder. In 2007, the Franklin County School District moved from a similar school-based system to a districtwide system, supported by Moodle, that allows anyone in the system to access any study group's folder. In the Hawthorn School District 73, study groups use a districtwide Web-based system, supported by Rubicon Atlas, to post logs and action plans and attach Web links, resources, and samples of student work. Principals can embed feedback on the Web documents or send e-mails to the group.

Protect Time

After study groups are formed, a major concern of many faculty members is that study group meeting time and IC meeting time will be usurped for other activities. For example, school leaders might schedule meetings during study group time that pull members away from their study group meetings. Administrators might ask teachers to cover another teacher's class during the period when the teacher's study group meets, or the principal might have to go to the district office and cancel an IC meeting.

When these events happen, the message faculty members perceive is that a study group meeting or an IC meeting is not as important as the activity replacing it. When it happens often, study groups lose momentum and do not achieve their intended results, which is to improve teacher practice and student learning.

The WFSG National Center recommends that school leaders develop a semester or annual calendar that specifies, in advance, study group and IC meeting times, professional development activities related to study group work, and celebration and sharing events. The calendar should then be shared with staff, parents, and the district office. Once the calendar is in place, it should be followed. The hardest task for school leaders is saying "No" to possible disruptions.

Just as school leaders have challenges in protecting study group meeting time, so do study group members. Study group members also need to protect the study group meeting time and not schedule meetings, doctors appointments, and other activities that will prevent them from attending their study group meetings. If a member is absent, the other members still meet. The work goes on.

Provide Feedback

While the "official" responsibility for reviewing study group action plans and logs and providing feedback rests with the principal of the school, principals can share or delegate this responsibility if they clearly communicate to the faculty who will be responsible. The principal is usually solely responsible for providing feedback in smaller schools where the principal is the only administrator. In schools with a principal and an assistant principal or instructional support specialist, they might meet together to review action plans and logs and provide feedback.

In larger schools with many study groups, the administrative team may serve as readers to study groups. At Western Harnett High School, members of the administrative team, comprised of the principal and four assistant principals, serve as readers to study groups. Each reader is responsible for reading and giving feedback to four or five study groups. The administrative team has its own study group and the members discuss study group work and their feedback at their meetings.

Principals and other readers need to establish their own routines to ensure that all study groups are getting regular and timely feedback. Regular feedback means study groups can count on receiving feedback on every log and action plan update. Timely feedback means that study groups can count on receiving feedback on a log or action plan update before their next meeting. This prevents study groups from feeling that they are backtracking when they receive feedback on work they did several meetings before.

The other component of the feedback routine that is important to establish right from the beginning is that the feedback is substantive and constructive, not superficial. Study groups expect their responders to read their logs and action plans carefully and to reply thoughtfully. We encourage readers to frame feedback in terms of "wows" and "wonders": "wows" for work that exemplifies quality work and indicates that the group is following the WFSG process guidelines and "wonders" for questions or comments that push the group's thinking or suggest resources that the group might explore. Feedback can also include offers of assistance and reminders about upcoming events, such as an IC meeting.

Feedback on Action Plans

In their 2005 book, Murphy and Lick describe the feedback process for study group action plans (SGAPs). This section is an expanded version of their earlier text.

> The SGAP is the single most important document that study groups produce. The action plan identifies the student needs a group will target and indicates what the group will do when it meets. If the plan is off-target, the group will be off-target. Study groups need to know immediately if their readers have questions or concerns about their SGAPs. (Murphy & Lick, 2005, pp. 186–187)

Clearly written procedures for submitting the SGAP to the principal or readers should be distributed to all staff when study groups are formed (see the example in Chapter 5 of a principal's memo to staff about expectations and procedures). We recommend the following guidelines for SGAPs:

- The first page and the needs and data source section on the second page of the SGAP is completed by the end of the second study group meeting and given to the principal (refer to the two-page action plan template in Figure 7.2).
- "SGAPs are reviewed by the principal or a designee and written feedback is given to the group BEFORE the group meets again; the written feedback is given to the leader of the next meeting or to the entire group" (Murphy & Lick, 2005, pp. 186–187).
- SGAPs are revised at the third study group meeting, copied and given to each member of the group, put in a public place, and posted electronically.
- "SGAPs are reviewed at the first Instructional Council meeting. Each study-group representative is given a set of action plans. At the next study-group meetings, the representatives will share feedback on their action plan and what the other study groups are doing" (Murphy & Lick, 2005, pp. 186–187).
- After study groups create their initial SGAPs, they update their plans to add baseline data, targets, and actual results for each need they address. They also add new resources, modify or add data sources, review and modify their norms, if necessary, and add actions. Using electronic templates, study groups have the option to add revisions to the original SGAP rather than rewriting it completely.
- Each time a study group revises its SGAP, the principal reviews the revisions against the earlier version and gives the group feedback, along with feedback on the log for the meeting when the revisions were made.
- "Feedback may be written directly on the action plan, on a post-it note and 'stuck' on the plan, in a memo on separate paper, in an email message" (Murphy & Lick, 2005, pp. 186–187), or in a dialogue box on an electronic action plan form.

The WFSG National Center has developed a checklist (see Resource B) for study group action plans that study groups and principals may use as they review an action plan.

Figure 7.2, Page 1, shows a study group action plan from a math study group at the Great Falls Middle School in Turners Falls, Massachusetts, along with feedback from the principal, Mr. Jeffrey Kenney. Group members had just created their action plan and had not posted any baseline data or targets. The form the group used is the same form we presented in Chapter 2, Figures 2.2 and 2.3.

On the first page of the action plan, this math study group identified three math learning needs they wanted to address with their students over the 2005–2006 school year, created an essential question that encompassed these needs, and indicated the main action research steps they planned to use. They also noted their group norms and their preliminary thinking on resources they might use, including the teacher's guide and textbook they were currently using. The numbers and letters beside each need refer to the corresponding standards in the Massachusetts Curriculum Framework. The principal's comment indicates he has read the action plan and is encouraging the group's efforts to demonstrate the use of math across the curriculum.

The second page of the action plan, shown in Figure 7.2, Page 2, reveals the group's preliminary thinking about the specific skills they want to address within the student needs they identified on the first page of their action plan. The first skill, "use fractions across the curriculum," relates to part of the second need they identified on Page 1, "use fractions, decimals, ratios, and percents in real-life situations." This is an example of a study group narrowing its focus, as we discussed in Chapter 4. The third skill, "explain ways in which math is used in everyday life," connects both to the second need, students using math in real-life situations, and the third need, students being able to write about their math work. The second skill, "demonstrate sequential thinking through math problems—explaining how their calculations are computed by using complete sentences," also relates to the third need. These are examples of a study group clarifying what a need means in practice.

Note that the group did not list anything on Page 2 related to the first need listed on Page 1, "Distinguish between equal, greater than, less than when using fractions, ratios, percents, and decimals." By not indicating any skills for this need on Page 2, the group is showing that it has decided to work on the other needs first.

The items listed under "data sources" are typical responses from study groups that are learning about the action research process for the first time. It is not clear from this list of five items which items relate to each of the four skills listed in the needs column. The group will need to revise these data sources to indicate for each skill what students will be expected to do to demonstrate proficiency. For example, the group will need to decide what students will be asked to do to demonstrate their current proficiency in "using fractions across the curriculum."

The principal's comments on Page 2 show a mix of encouragement, "These are much more specific and will help you focus your work;" support for the study group, "It looks like you will be looking at a lot of student work. We will spend some time looking at different protocols for doing this"; and suggestions for future thinking and action, "What do the data you have looked at indicate at this time in regards to the needs you have identified? Where do you think the students will be in December? January? How will you assess that?"

Feedback on Logs

In their 2005 book, Murphy and Lick describe the feedback process for study group action logs. This section is an expanded version of their earlier text.

Figure 7.2   Study Group Action Plan, Great Falls Middle School With Principal Feedback, Page 1

Whole-Faculty

Study Groups™

WFSG Action Plan for Group # or Name_III_

School: Great Falls Middle School   **Date:** 10-14-05

Group Members: Marie, Jessica, Nancy M. Lynn, Wendy

What is the general category of student needs the group will address? Math

---

State the specific skill within the general category the group will target. ➡️ **Check and list the specific actions the group will take when the study group meets.**

Students need to:	*Standard(s)*	*We will:*
Distinguish between equal, greater than, less than when using fractions, ratios, percents, and decimals	8.N.1	☒ Diagnose students' current levels of performance (relative to need)
		☒ Develop assessment tools
Be able to perform operations such addition, subtraction, multiplication, and division, and use fractions, decimals, ratios, and percents in real-life situations.	8.N.10 and 8.N.12	☒ Identify strategies/materials to address need
		☒ Plan lessons for how each member will use the strategy/material
		☐ Develop/design materials to address need
Be able to demonstrate this knowledge in clear concise written passages.		☐ Demonstrate/practice strategies members have used or will use
		☒ Articulate strategies we use
		☒ Examine samples of student work for evidence of student understanding
		☒ Assess results of using strategies in our classrooms
		☒ Other: Talk about ways to integrate math into all curriculums

Beside each student need, indicate the STATE STANDARD(s) that will be addressed when members target the need. Only give the code or number of the Standard.	*Comment: I am very interested in this idea to integrate math into all content areas. Please mention in your log the ideas you have. These will also be shared at the instructional council meetings.*

ESSENTIAL QUESTION that will guide the group's work:

How can we teach students to develop fraction/measurement skills and explain their work in writing?

Our resources are:	**Our norms are:**
At least one of the following resources will be used during study group meetings.	Begin and end on time.
Guest speakers	Everyone participates.
Student's work 7th–8th.	Stay focused.
Implementing math across the curriculum text.	

Source: Great Falls Middle School, Montague, MA.

Figure 7.2   Study Group Action Plan, Great Falls Middle School With Principal Feedback, Page 2

State *specific* student need that is being targeted. ***Students need to —***	**Data Sources:** What type of pre/post assessments will members give to document current performance level?	**Baseline:** What percentage of students meet, approach, or are far below performance standards **when work begins**? _____ (DATE)	**Target:** What do members **predict** will be the percentage at each performance level **after interventions**? _____ (DATE)	**Actual:** What percentage of students meet, approach, or are far below performance standards **after interventions**? _____ (DATE)
1. Use fractions across the curriculum. 2. Demonstrate sequential thinking through math problems — explaining how their calculations are computed by using complete sentences. 3. Explain ways in which math is used in everyday life. 4. Keep journals showing multi-step processes in solving problems and use of mental math strategies. *Comment: These are much more specific and will help you focus your work.*	a) MCAS scores b) outlines c) journals d) projects e) quizzes *Comment: It looks like you will be looking at a lot of student work. We will spend some time looking at different protocols for doing this.*	*Comment: What do the data you have looked at indicate at this time in regards to the needs you have identified?*	*Comment: Where do you think the students will be in December? January? How will you assess that?*	

Source: Great Falls Middle School, Montague, MA.

The study group logs (SGLs) "describe what a group does at a study-group meeting, and the log should be consistent or aligned with the group's SGAP" (Murphy & Lick, 2005, pp. 187–188). The log may be handwritten, typed, or electronic, but most study groups now are completing logs electronically. Principals use logs to communicate expectations and give support, guidance, and encouragement to study groups. Clearly written procedures for submitting study group logs to the principal should be distributed to all staff when study groups are formed.

We recommend the following guidelines for study group logs:

- "SGLs are completed at the end of every study-group meeting and copies [are] made for the principal" (Murphy & Lick, 2005, pp. 187–188), all study group members, and for public display; if the log is electronic, it would be posted or e-mailed to the principal and to others, as appropriate.
- "SGLs are given or sent to the principal or put in a designated place for the principal within 24 hours after a study group meets." (Murphy & Lick, 2005, pp. 187–188)
- "SGLs are reviewed and responded to by the principal or designee before the next study-group meeting or on a rotating schedule." (Murphy & Lick, 2005, pp. 187–188)
- In reviewing logs, the reader compares the current log with the previous one to check for leader rotation, whether the group is meeting as scheduled, and whether group members are doing what they planned, per the previous meeting. The reader also reviews the SGAP to see if the group is working on needs listed in it and if it has been revised or updated.
- SGLs have boxes at the bottom for readiness for sharing and "questions or concerns from the study group that *must* be promptly responded to if the SGL is to have any credibility." (Murphy & Lick, 2005, pp. 187–188)
- Study groups attach artifacts, such as rubrics, assessment tools, data, strategies, samples of student work, and resources, to logs that document the work of the study group during the meeting.
- Feedback may be handwritten directly on the log, on a post-it note and "stuck" on the plan, in a memo on separate paper, in an e-mail message, as a different color text directly in the electronic document, or in a dialogue box on an electronic log form. Most readers now put their comments on the electronic document or send an e-mail message.

The WFSG National Center has developed a checklist (see Resource C) for study group logs that study groups and principals may use as they review a log.

Figure 7.3 shows a study group log from the Radical Readers Study Group at Bunn Elementary School. The log is divided into two pages to show the group's responses for each section of the log. This study group was profiled in a vignette in Chapter 5. This meeting comes at the end of their action research cycle on the first student need the group addressed: cause and effect. Their action plan is shown in Figure 5.3.

The top of the log indicates that even though one member was absent, the group still met. In the left-hand column they checked the two action research steps they addressed at the meeting: diagnosing student performance and identifying strategies or materials to address their selected need.

In the right-hand column they described what they did at their meeting. They began their meeting by responding to the principal's question on their previous log. Then, they reviewed the results of the posttest on cause and effect that they gave to students and examined samples of student work from the posttest. They also looked at some Web sites with materials on cause and effect that one member had found and they filled out a progress report form that the principal asked each study group to complete.

At the bottom of the log, shown on Page 2, group members report on what they have been doing in their classrooms since their last meeting that relates to cause and effect, the student need they are currently addressing. They are doing other teaching as well, but they only record on the log their classroom work on cause and effect.

They also indicate that they are ready to share with other teachers the materials, strategies, and lessons learned about improving students' ability to identify cause and effect. Finally, they indicate their plans for their next study group meeting.

Jewel Eason, the principal of Bunn Elementary School, inserted her feedback in italics and in a different color on an electronic copy of the log and e-mailed it back to the group members before their next meeting. In her comments, she congratulates the group on their posttest results and describes a new resource group members could use to strengthen their expertise in reading skills.

Create Opportunities for Communicating and Sharing Work

"Establish a variety of communication networks and strategies" (Murphy & Lick, 2005, pp. 99–100) is the 15th WFSG process guideline. There are two main activities for communicating and sharing WFSG work as study groups start to meet: creating a public display for study group action plans and logs and holding IC meetings for study group sharing.

Public Display of Action Plans and Logs

Even with the advances in technology that enable staff to share and access electronic copies of study group work, many WFSG schools still post paper copies of study group action plans and logs in a public place in the school for students, parents, staff, and community members to see. They do this because one of the guiding principles in the WFSG approach is that the work is public, and parents, students, and community members often do not have access to the computer networks where electronic copies are kept.

Schools typically put up the study group action plans after the third study group meeting and the first IC meeting, when draft plans have been completed and revised based on feedback from the principal and other study groups. Some schools post the action plan for each study group above the clipboard or plastic pocket for study group logs and put up labels identifying each group's name or category of student needs. At Bunn Elementary School, the study group logs are copied on different colors of paper for each consecutive meeting, with the most recent meeting log on top. Many schools display study group work in the lobby of the school or entrance hallway so that parents and community members can see it. Others choose to display the work in the teacher workroom or main office.

In addition to having a display of study group action plans and logs, some WFSG schools also have bulletin boards where individual study groups can display their work. At the Arbor Hill Elementary School, study groups took turns each

Figure 7.3   Study Group Log, Bunn Elementary School With Principal Feedback, Page 1

Whole-Faculty **Study Groups™**	**WFSG Log for Group # 5 – Radical Readers**

School: Bunn Elementary Log # 6 **Date:** 11-15-06   **Leader:** M. Watts

Members Present: Beddingfield, Joyner, Murray, Watts

Members Absent: Kagarise

What specific student learning need did the group target today?   Cause and Effect

Check the steps on the WFSG action research cycle that best describe what the group did today. In Column 2, elaborate on items checked (key findings, decisions, insights).

☒ Diagnosed students' current levels of performance (relative to need)	Response to Eason's question: Within his classroom, Randy did stress reading the question first. That proved to be a very effective strategy. The group used Randy's strategy within their individual classrooms and continued to incorporate the charts and various graphic organizers.
☐ Developed assessment tools	
☒ Identified strategies/materials to address need	
☐ Planned lesson(s) for how each member will use strategy/material	We discussed the posttest results on cause and effect and looked at samples of student work. Using these strategies, listed above, and other strategies, our overall average went up. Each class showed improvement with this skill.
☐ Developed/designed materials to address need	
☐ Demonstrated/practiced strategies members have used or will use	We reviewed Beddingfield's Web sites specifically for cause and effect: www.longman.com/ae/marketing/ sfesl/tests/grade4 and www.hartcourtschool.com/ activity/trophies/rsr/build/RR_e_5_28.htm and www.quia.com (go to cause and effect). These Web sites were very useful. They had plenty of activities and games to play.
☐ Articulated strategies used last week	
☐ Examined samples of student work for evidence of student understanding	
☐ Assessed results of using strategies in our classrooms	We will update our action plan at our next meeting with our posttest results and with these new Web resources.
	We completed the yellow WFSG progress report form to return to Eason.
	Due to the holiday and lack of WFSG meeting time today, we will choose another reading skill to begin focusing on at our next meeting in December. We will continue to review and teach cause and effect within our classroom until we determine our next skill.

Did the group examine student work today? Yes   If yes, who brought? Murray, Beddingfield, Joyner, Watts

What resources/materials did members use during the meeting today? Posttest results

Source: Used with permission from Jewel Eason, Bunn Elementary School.

Figure 7.3   Study Group Log, Bunn Elementary School With Principal Feedback, Page 2

Since the last meeting, describe the specific instructional strategies members used in their classrooms that were the focus of last meeting.		
Member:	*Strategy:*	*Student Results:*
All	Graphic organizers	More organization and detailed thinking
	Questioning	Helps students understand consequences and relate cause and effect to real-life situations

What have members agreed to do in their classrooms prior to the next meeting?

We will complete the posttest and bring the results to our next meeting.

Is the group ready to share a proven strategy with the whole faculty? Yes, we are able to share the graphic organizers we are using and questioning strategies. The posttest results are also ready for review. Did the group examine student work today? Yes. If yes, who brought? Murray, Beddingfield, Joyner, Watts. What resources/ materials did members use during the meeting today? Test results.	*I reviewed your Action Plan results. Everyone made great gains. You did a good job of projecting results with your targets. I think you could call this a success!! For reading strategies, we learned of another place to receive materials that will be helpful. When we met with the Reading Plus people on the 17th we found that new elements to the program have to do with printable materials to boost these skills. See Jackie and Eddie about help with specific reading skills. I believe you will be thrilled to see what diagnostic information you will be able to get from the Reading Plus program on the students that you are sending to this program. Great job and thank you for answering my question. Jewel 11-17-06*

NEXT MEETING: Date 12-4-06 Location: Beddingfield's Room Leader: A. Joyner
Materials needed: Materials and/or strategies from each teacher; any comments/results from using these strategies. Posttest results and samples of student work.
Focus: We will review the Web sites Ms. Beddingfield gave to our group, discuss strategies used within individual classrooms, review the remainder of our posttest results and student work samples, and update our action plan.

Source: Used with permission from Jewel Eason, Bunn Elementary School.

month putting up a display of their work. Displays might include the essential question group members were addressing, specific needs on which they were working, strategies they were using, and results they were experiencing.

Sharing at IC Meetings

A key strategy for creating short-term wins is to promote communication among study groups so that groups are aware of and can learn from the work of other study groups. One vehicle to promote communication and support among study groups is the IC, which meets every four to six weeks. Figure 7.4 illustrates the composition and purposes of the IC.

The IC is composed of the principal, one or two Focus Team members, and representatives from each study group (Murphy & Lick, 2005, pp. 64–66). The principal and the Focus Team representatives attend all the IC meetings, but each study group sends a different member to represent the group at each IC meeting. The reason for rotating the study group representative at each meeting is to reinforce the WFSG guiding principles, which state that within a study group, the leadership is shared and the responsibility is equal.

The IC serves four main purposes: sharing study group work and providing feedback to study groups on their work, providing professional development, planning further implementation and professional development, and assessing the status of implementation and addressing issues and concerns.

Sharing study group work and giving feedback at IC meetings is aligned with where groups are in their cycle of action research. The first IC meeting, usually scheduled after the second or third study group meeting, when groups have completed their action plan and determined the need they will start with and the data sources they will use (see Action Plan in Figure 2.2), focuses on reviewing the purposes of the IC, establishing norms for IC meetings, and giving groups feedback on their action plans.

The second IC meeting, held four to six weeks later, is a logical time to focus study group work around collecting baseline data and setting targets. Study groups share the needs they are addressing, the assessment tools they are using, their results and insights from examining student work, and their targets.

In subsequent IC meetings, the focus shifts to the instructional strategies and concepts study groups are using in their classrooms to improve student learning, the assessment tasks they use to determine the effectiveness of strategies, their observations about using different strategies, and the impact on student learning.

We have found that this sharing is more productive when groups prepare in advance for sharing and bring materials to give to those present. Resource F in Murphy and Lick (2005, pp. 325–339) contains minutes from IC meetings and numerous examples of agendas, templates, and graphic organizers for study groups to use to prepare for the IC meeting.

In large schools with more than 20 study groups, it is impossible for 20 or more study groups to have time to share within a 60–90 minute IC meeting. These schools often cluster study groups in groups of three to five, with three to five representatives meeting together, so that sharing takes place in the smaller clusters and provides more time for each representative.

Providing professional development is a second purpose of IC meetings. We have found that trying to give faculty all of the information and skills they need to

Figure 7.4 WFSG Instructional Council

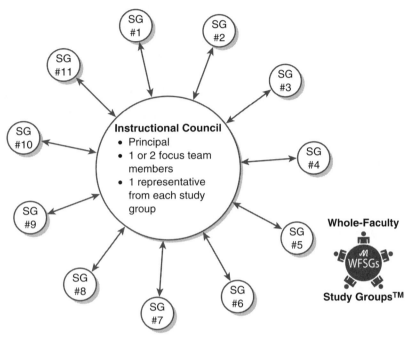

WFSG Instructional Council
A Network for Communication and Support

Instructional Council
- Principal
- 1 or 2 focus team members
- 1 representative from each study group

Whole-Faculty
WFSGs
Study Groups™

The council has several purposes

1. To keep communication open among all study groups
2. To review all action plans and revised plans
3. For study group representatives to share what the groups are doing
4. To hear problems groups are experiencing and to have joint participation in how those problems might be solved
5. To share successes and plan for dissemination of those successes
6. To determine how groups can share resources
7. To determine if the whole faculty requires common training
8. To coordinate events, speakers
9. To plan whole-faculty sharings and celebrations
10. To identify common instructional concerns
11. To set instructional goals
12. To set limits on instructional initiatives

The council meets every four to six weeks, meeting the first time immediately after all groups have met twice.

work together productively before they start working in their groups is overwhelming. Instead, we use "just-in-time" professional development, and the IC meetings are one vehicle for this.

IC meetings can be "miniworkshops" on topics such as developing baseline assessment tasks and collecting baseline data; accessing and using school or district diagnostic benchmark data; using protocols to examine student work together; and examining specific content or instructional strategies, such as concept attainment, connecting school and district initiatives to study group work, and assessing the effectiveness of teaching interventions. In these miniworkshops, study group representatives learn about the strategy or concept and then take what they learn back to their study group. At the next study group meeting, the IC representative leads his or her group through what members learned at the IC workshop.

While the Focus Team is primarily responsible for helping the school launch study groups, the IC can be responsible for planning further implementation and professional development. This might include planning how groups can share resources, determining whether the whole faculty requires common training, planning the year-end celebration and sharing event, planning the year-end reflection and evaluation activity (Step 7 of the WFSG DMC), and aligning study group work with instructional goals and initiatives.

Finally, the IC meetings are a vehicle for assessing the status of implementation and addressing issues and concerns among study groups. Many schools schedule time in each IC meeting for members to share issues and concerns and to work together to determine how best to address those issues. Other schools ask individual study groups, after a few months of work, to complete a status check on how well the groups are functioning, and then discuss the findings at an IC meeting. Most WFSG schools schedule an end-of-the-year IC meeting to review the results from the whole faculty year-end reflection and evaluation and develop plans for improvement in the system for the following school year.

Other Communication and Sharing Opportunities

WFSG schools also use newsletters and faculty meetings to share the work of study groups. At Bunn Elementary School, the principal uses her weekly newsletter to staff to highlight resources and strategies that study groups are using and their results. Franklin County puts study group news in the district newsletter to parents, and schools are doing the same in their school newsletters. Several schools feature study groups at PTA meetings. During the 2006–2007 school year, one of the countywide administrative study groups focused on how to inform the community about the work of study groups.

Principals also use their regular meetings with staff to highlight and share study group work. At Cohoes Middle School in Cohoes, New York, the principal invited study groups to share their work at the monthly faculty meetings. At Williams Elementary School in Springfield, Missouri, study groups presented "minilessons" about their work to colleagues at monthly faculty meetings. At Laurel Mill Elementary School, the principal built "Staff Connections" meetings into the study group meeting calendar so that five times a year all study groups meet together. At these meetings, one study group teaches the entire faculty how to use one of the strategies the group has found to be effective with students.

The WFSG National Center encourages every WFSG school to plan an annual year-end celebration and sharing of study group work and accomplishments. Usually the Focus Team or IC plans this culminating event. At Qualicum Beach Middle School, the Focus Team held their celebration on the last day of school, after the morning student awards celebration and dismissal. Faculty brought food for a luncheon and then each study group shared its work and lessons learned.

In the AuSable Valley School District, where all schools were implementing the WFSG System, the district leadership team organized a districtwide afternoon ice cream party and study group sharing for the study groups in all four schools. They organized the sharing like a science fair, with each study group having a table display or poster describing their group's work. Members of the group took turns at the table describing their work and answering questions while the other members visited the tables of other study groups.

Figure 7.5 is an example of a poster template groups can enlarge and use in a table display of their work.

Figure 7.5   WFSG Poster Template for Sharing Study Group Work

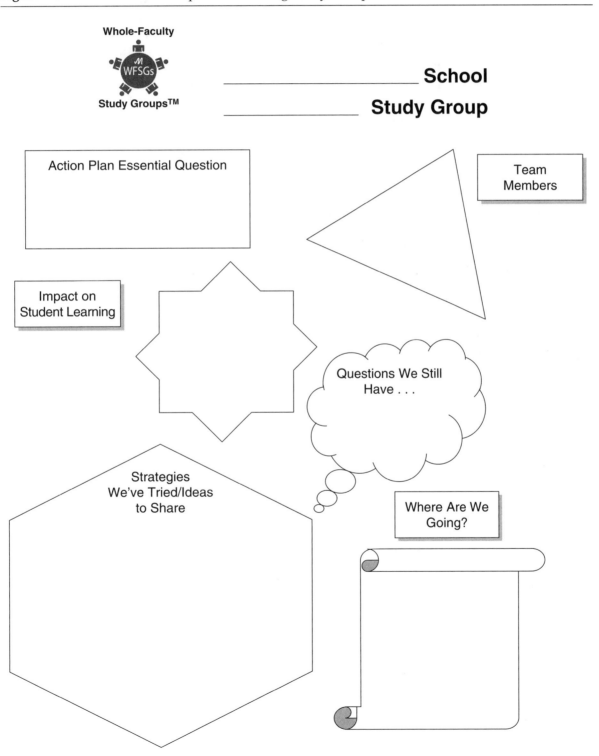

Establish an Administrative Study Group

Just as professional learning communities support teachers in strengthening their practice and improving student learning, principals and assistant principals need professional learning communities to support their work as instructional leaders. In the NSDC book, *Moving NSDC's Staff Development Standards Into Practice: Innovation Configurations,* one of the desired outcomes for principals is to participate regularly in one or more learning communities (Roy & Hord, 2003, p. 61).

In WFSG schools and districts, principals, assistant principals, and central office staff form administrative study groups that follow the same guidelines as teacher study groups. They meet weekly or biweekly in groups of three to five members, identify a set of student or teacher needs to address, create an action plan, engage in cycles of action research, and share publicly their action plan and logs. Administrators also use their study group meetings to share and examine the feedback they are giving to study groups and discuss ways to help struggling study groups.

Franklin County Schools

In the Franklin County School District, where all 14 schools have been implementing the WFSG System since January 2005, the principals and central office staff formed six cross-building and cross-level administrative study groups for the 2006–2007 school year. The focus that guides all of the countywide study groups is to strengthen and support the work of teacher study groups, or, as one group phrased it, "improving the quality of student and staff performance through the correct usage of the WFSG System." The essential questions the groups decided to address include the following: "How do you support WFSG in your school?" "How do you incorporate noncore teachers in WFSG at your school?" "How do you support WFSG in the community?" and "How do you support teachers who struggle with WFSG?" The action plans and logs from the countywide study groups are posted on the same Moodle Web site as the faculty study group action plans and logs. Principals also share their study group work at their school's IC meetings.

Western Harnett High School

The administrative study group, the "A" team, at Western Harnett High School in Lillington, North Carolina, is composed of the principal and four assistant principals. During the second semester of the 2005–2006 school year, the essential question that guided the group's work was this: "How can we help our teachers increase the active involvement of students?" And the specific needs they addressed were these: "Teachers need to increase student-centered learning" and "teachers need to work productively in collaborative study groups." As Page 1 of Figure 7.6 indicates, they added two actions to the list of action research steps their group would follow: "Discuss ways to share strategies with teachers" and "design ways to monitor effectiveness of strategies." The resources they identified were the artifacts of the teacher study groups, action plans and logs, resources about observing classrooms and designing an assessment tool to rate teachers' use of student-centered learning strategies, and resources about the actual strategies they expected teachers to use. The high school staff was trained in the Quality Teaching and Learning (QTL) instructional strategies (see Chapter 5) prior to forming study groups, and the administrative study group wanted to support teacher study groups in using these strategies as they addressed specific student needs.

Figure 7.6   The Administrative Study Group Action Plan, Western Harnett High School, Page 1

Whole-Faculty Study Groups™	**WFSG Action Plan for Group # or Name A-Team**

School: Western Harnett High School   **Date:** 3-24-06

Group Members: Terry Hinson, Roger Leggett, Raymond McCall, Frances Harrington

What is the general category of needs the group will address? Teacher Needs

State the specific skill within the general category the group will target.	**Check and list the specific actions the group will take when the study group meets.**
Teachers need to:	**We will:**
Increase student-centered learning	☒ Diagnose teachers' current levels of performance (relative to need)
	☒ Develop assessment tools
	☒ Identify strategies/materials to address need
Work productively in collaborative WFSG groups	☐ Plan lessons for how each member will use the strategy/material
	☐ Develop/design materials to address need
	☐ Demonstrate/practice strategies members have used or will use
	☒ Articulate strategies we use
	☒ Examine samples of teacher work for evidence of understanding
	☒ Assess results of using teachers using strategies in classrooms/Monitor teacher progress
	☒ Other: Discuss ways to share strategies with teachers
	☒ Other: Design ways to monitor effectiveness of strategies

ESSENTIAL QUESTION that will guide the group's work:

How can we help our teachers increase the active involvement of students?

Our resources are:	**Our norms are:**
At least one of the following resources will be used during study group meetings:	• Start and end on time • Listen to and respect each other's ideas • Be flexible and open-minded • Be present and prepared for meetings and stay focused • Put students first • Be positive
• Observation process • Teacher study group action plans • Logs • Strategies • Assessment tools • Data • Quality Teaching and Learning (QTL™) strategies	

Source: Used with permission from Terry Hinton, Western Harnett High School.

Figure 7.6   The Administrative Study Group Action Plan, Western Harnett High School, Page 2

State **specific** teacher need that is being targeted – **Teachers need to:**	**Data Sources:** What type of pre/post assessments will members give to document current performance level?	**Baseline:** What percentage of teachers meet, approach, or are far below performance standards **when work begins?** **March** (DATE)	**Target:** What do members **predict** will be the percentage at each performance level **after interventions?** **May** (DATE)	**Actual:** What percentage of teachers meet, approach, or are far below performance standards **after interventions?** **May** (DATE)
• Use prescribed strategies for student-centered learning (from Quality Teaching and Learning) or other staff development. • Assess extent teachers are proficient with each strategy. • Assess frequency of use of each strategy.	• Conduct miniobservations in classrooms. • Develop rubric or checklist to evaluate observations or work collected.	52% of teachers were using student-centered (Level 3) activities. 8% of teachers were unsuccessfully attempting to use student-centered activities (Level 2). 10% of teachers were introducing or discussing previous use of student-centered activities (Level 1). 29% of teachers were using teacher-centered activities (Level 0).	We predict that between now and May 8, 2006, we will see 65% of the teachers using student-centered activities in our miniobservations.	Even though we did not compile specific data, casual observations and conversations with teachers indicated that more teachers were using student-centered activities on a regular basis. Teachers have a heightened sense of the importance of implementing student-centered activities in the classroom.

Source: Used with permission from Terry Hinton, Western Harnett High School.

The "A" Team began meeting in late January, immediately after teacher study groups were formed. Just as the teacher study groups did, "A" Team members spent their first three meetings developing their action plan, all of Page 1 and on Page 2, the specific needs and proposed data sources. The specific needs they identified in the left-hand column speak directly to the central issue raised by Hord et al. (1987) in the Concerns-Based Adoption Model research: How proficient are teachers with the QTL strategies and how frequently do they use the strategies with students?

For the rest of February and into March, the "A" team worked on developing an assessment tool members could use in classroom observations to assess teachers' use and proficiency with student-centered learning strategies. Then, in mid-March, they did their classroom observations, compiled their baseline data, and set their targets for improvement by early May, before exams began.

To reach their target, they decided to concentrate in April on trying to help teachers at Level 1 and Level 2 increase their use and proficiency with selected strategies. They worked one-on-one with teachers and enlisted the assistance of the school's instructional specialist. They also enabled teachers to observe Level 3 teachers using the strategies in their classes. Even though they ran out of time at the end of the year and were not able to repeat the formal observation cycle, they reported on their action plan in the "Actual" column that they did see improvements in teaching practices.

Springfield Public Schools

Most of the 51 schools in the Springfield Public School District, in Springfield, Missouri, have been implementing the WFSG System for several years. Beginning in the 2003–2004 school year, the district established principal study groups as one component of the district's multifaceted leadership development program for new and experienced principals (Richardson, 2005). Principals meet in study groups facilitated by the district's instructional specialists. Each study group chooses its own focus and content and follows the same WFSG guidelines as teacher study groups. Some of the needs these principal study groups have addressed include improving mediocre teaching, improving the interviewing process by developing a common scoring rubric, and learning about Marzano's nine strategies for improving learning and what to look for on classroom walk-throughs.

In reflecting on her involvement as a facilitator for principal study groups in Springfield, Emily Weiskopf (2007a) wrote that two key lessons learned were that the frequency of meetings truly affected the quality of study group work and that principals needed to experience the study group process to appreciate its value. She found that groups that only met monthly rarely got beyond superficial sharing and never really addressed what they needed to learn and change. Even though principals had been supporting teacher study groups in their schools, going through the process of collaborative action research gave them a deeper understanding of the process and a greater appreciation of its value.

Consolidating Improvements and Producing More Change

Principals creating short-term wins is a necessary step toward establishing an innovation such as schoolwide action research in schools, but it is not sufficient to ensure that the innovation is institutionalized and becomes part of the culture, as in "the way we do things here." Kotter (1998, p. 33) identifies three additional ways to build on the short-term wins: using increased credibility to change systems, structures, and policies that don't fit the vision; hiring, promoting, and developing employees who can implement the vision; and reinvigorating the process with new projects, themes, and change agents.

We add a fourth way to consolidate improvements: improving the process by treating the creation of a system of high-quality, whole-faculty, schoolwide action research as an action research process itself. Just as teachers collect data to assess the effectiveness of their action research interventions on student learning, the principal and the Focus Team collect data from faculty about the way in which the WFSG System is being implemented and making improvements.

Change Practices

During the first year of implementing schoolwide action research, principals build on the early successes and enthusiasm to better align school schedules, structures, procedures, and operations to support the work. Often, the school schedule and calendar are already set when schools decide to launch study groups. This makes it difficult in the first year to find time for study groups to meet and time for school-based professional development to support the action research work of study groups. It is also hard for principals to make time in their own schedules for their active support and feedback for study groups.

The easiest structure for principals to change is the regularly scheduled after-school staff meeting. Most WFSG principals reconfigure staff meetings from being mostly focused on administrative matters to a focus on teaching and learning that supports looking at student work and performance data, sharing among study groups, and professional development related to the identified student learning needs. At Qualicum Beach Middle School, the principal deals with administrative issues through e-mails and Monday morning 15-minute stand-up meetings before students enter the building.

Changing the student schedule requires careful, advance planning. The Arbor Hill Community Elementary School organized study groups by teachers' common-planning periods in its first year. Based on teacher feedback during the year, the principal and faculty decided that they wanted more flexibility for forming study groups by common student needs and redesigned the student schedule to lengthen the school day four days a week and have an early release day once a week for study group meetings. They had to work out the transportation issues, and they arranged with their teachers' aides and community partners to provide activities for children who needed to stay at school during the early release time. The principal and staff at the Paul Robeson High School convinced their union, parents, and district office to support a similar shift in the student schedule to accommodate study group meetings.

A common complaint principals hear as schools begin schoolwide action research is that study group work adds to an already heavy workload. Principals use a variety of strategies to show staff that study group work connects to and replaces work that staff know they need to do. One strategy is to connect study group work to the school improvement plan so that teachers' work in study groups is the way the school will address the academic learning goals in the plan. Another strategy is to connect study group work to state recertification requirements for the development of personal professional development plans and document time spent in professional development activities. A third strategy is to streamline and reduce the number or frequency of other committee and task assignments for staff members. Often the hardest thing for educators to do is to stop doing something with some value, such as organizing a bike safety day, to start doing something with greater value, such as working with WFSG.

Principals need to reconfigure how they spend their time if they are going to move beyond creating short-term wins with schoolwide action research. Supporting and sustaining this work on improving teaching and learning is what being an instructional leader is all about, yet most principals only spend a small fraction of a typical day or week on instructional leadership. In *The MetLife Survey of the American Teacher: An Examination of School Leadership* (MetLife Foundation, 2003, p. 31), data from principal respondents indicated that they spent, on average, 35% of their time in a typical week guiding and motivating teachers, but the teacher respondents said that their principals only averaged 24% of their time on this task compared with 76% of their time on discipline, reporting and compliance, and other administrative tasks. The same survey found that time allocations for instructional leadership were lower for secondary principals compared with elementary principals.

The Massachusetts Commonwealth Leadership Project (http://www.doe .mass.edu/cslp/leadership/dlp.html) sees the primary responsibility of principals being educational leadership, which encompasses curricular and instructional leadership, strategic planning, strategic partnerships and public relations, data-based decision making, organizational development and change, and supervision, evaluation, and motivation of staff. The organization estimates that principals currently spend 10% to 20% of their time on these tasks, but should be spending 55% to 65% of their time on educational leadership tasks.

Strengthen Staff

Collins, in *Good to Great* (2001), argues that one of the keys to transforming organizations is ensuring that the right people are on the bus and in the right seats to drive the bus (p. 41). This reinforces Kotter's assertion (1998, p. 33) that leaders can consolidate improvements through hiring, promoting, and developing employees who can implement the vision.

As schools start to implement schoolwide action research, principals can actively recruit new staff with an interest and experience in working collaboratively with colleagues and with engaging in action research with colleagues to improve their practice and student learning. Principals can also reinforce the importance of schoolwide action research by linking this work to classroom walk-throughs and observations, both by principals and teachers. This means scheduling walk-throughs and observations to look for evidence of study group work in classroom interactions with students and discussing observations with teachers after the visits.

Even when the whole school commits to implementing schoolwide action research, there are usually some staff who resist the changes. Robert Evans, in *The Human Side of Change* (1996, p. 21), sees resistance to change by those who must implement it as a natural, human response when the change engenders feelings of loss, incompetence, confusion, and conflict. This resistance might stem from not wanting to change and grow, not being comfortable working collaboratively in a study group but being willing to talk about and change practices that are not effective, or from participating in a study group that is stuck on one step of the action research process, or is not building its expertise or experimenting with new content and strategies in its classes, or is not seeing any changes in student learning. The challenge for every principal and Focus Team in the first year of implementing schoolwide action research is to help each study group experience success—success at working collaboratively, building their expertise, trying out new content and strategies in their classes, and improving student learning.

Unfortunately, there is no magic wand for principals to use to make resistance disappear. Evans (1996) states that a truly collaborative culture develops over time through sustained effort under a strong leader that "nurtures higher levels of mutual support and permits people to develop truly meaningful relationships" (p. 241).

Improve the Process

There are three ways principals can use data to improve the schoolwide action research process: improve the quality of feedback to study groups, improve the quality of study group work, and improve the implementation of the WFSG System by treating the creation of a system of high-quality, whole-faculty, schoolwide action research as an action research process itself.

Improving the Quality of Feedback

Just as teachers need feedback on their action plans and logs to strengthen their study group work, principals, assistant principals, and others who give feedback to study groups need feedback on their feedback to improve the quality of their feedback.

One source of feedback is from the study groups themselves. Readers can ask study groups about timeliness, format, tone, and substance. Timeliness is about whether groups are getting the feedback with enough lead time before their next study group meeting. Format is about whether the form of the feedback, such as a separate written note or e-mail message, a post-it note on a hard copy, comments added directly to the bottom of the electronic log or action plan, or comments inserted into sections of the electronic action plan or log, is helpful. Tone is about whether the recipients feel that the feedback is supportive, encouraging, and respectful, or negative, demeaning, and prescriptive. Substance is about whether the feedback indicates that the reader has carefully read the study group's work and compared it to previous work and the action plan and offers suggestions and resources to help the group, and poses questions that push the group's thinking and understanding, or whether the feedback is simplistic or mechanical and shows little evidence that the study group's work has been read.

Readers can collect feedback from individual groups, at an IC meeting, and at the end of the school year as part of the year-end evaluation. We recommend collecting initial feedback after responding to logs from three or four study group meetings and then checking with groups every few months to see if perceptions have improved.

A second source of feedback is from colleagues in one's administrative study group. Members of an administrative study group can use a "Looking at Student Work" protocol, such as the "Wows and Wonders" protocol presented in Chapter 4, Figure 4.2, or the Tuning protocol (Blythe, Allen, & Powell, 1999) to examine a study group's action plan or log and the reader's feedback, and discuss both strengths of the feedback and questions or suggestions about improving the feedback. Members can take turns bringing feedback to the group for examination.

Sometimes readers aren't sure how to respond to a study group, particularly if the study group seems stuck on one aspect of the action research cycle. Readers can use a problem-solving protocol, such as the Consultancy protocol, developed by the Coalition of Essential Schools (Turning Points, 2001), to help them analyze the dilemma concerning the study group's work and explore suggestions.

A third source of feedback is external, and consists of people who are helping to support the school in implementing schoolwide action research. In Springfield, Missouri, the district-level instructional specialists, who facilitate principal study groups, also work with individual principals to model the feedback process and to review and offer constructive feedback on principals' feedback to their study groups. WFSG consultants play the same role for schools that have asked the WFSG National Center for assistance in launching and implementing the WFSG System. The Centers for Quality Teaching and Learning and ATLAS Learning Communities, organizations that have incorporated the WFSG action research process into their school improvement designs, have trained their staff to provide feedback and support for principals and other study group readers.

Improving the Quality of Study Groups' Work

Study groups typically need assistance in five areas to improve the quality of their work together: identifying or creating classroom assessment tools and collecting data, building content expertise, identifying and building expertise in research-based instructional strategies, looking at student work collaboratively, and assessing the effectiveness of classroom interventions. The challenge for principals is helping all study group members, who often have different levels of expertise in each of these areas, develop their comfort, knowledge, and skills.

One of the first challenges confronting study groups is identifying or creating classroom assessment tools and collecting baseline data. While teachers have lots of experience identifying or creating tests, they often are not used to developing a classroom assessment task for a specific student learning need or a task that will help them pinpoint exactly where students are having difficulties and why they are having difficulties. Other teachers may not be familiar with creating scoring rubrics for the assessment task or resolving differences in how members interpret and use a rubric.

In our work with study groups, we find that it is helpful to provide guidelines and examples up front as groups prepare to start working on their first student learning need and then offer coaching support as they start to identify or develop their own tools. One way to provide this support is through miniworkshops, such as the ones QTL staff offer to study groups in their schools. These miniworkshops can be held on a professional development day, after school, or during study group meeting time.

We also encourage teachers to examine assessments from textbooks, supplementary materials, and state and district tests to find tasks and questions that they can modify and improve and to look for different levels of performance by different student subgroups, rather than just determining classroom averages.

To build expertise in diagnostic assessment, the Hawthorn District 73 is offering districtwide professional development in designing and developing standards-based performance assessments and creating common assessments. At the Daniel Hale Williams Preparatory School of Medicine, the principal is also providing professional development for teachers in developing standards-based performance assessments.

A second challenge is building content expertise in the student learning needs study groups have chosen to address. Regardless of whether study groups are composed of teachers from the same grade level or content area or different grades and areas, everyone in the same study group may not have the same level of knowledge about the content related to a specific student need, such as reading comprehension or problem solving. Study groups should have access to content experts and resources that can help them understand what teachers and students need to know and what kinds of difficulties students tend to have in learning the content. Some groups have the resources or the expertise to locate what they require; other groups must have assistance. Often the resource section of the action plan and the notes in the logs provide clues about a group's level of expertise.

Building content expertise is an important link between the WFSG process and school and district content initiatives. In Louisiana, most of the Learning-Intensive Networking Communities for Success (LINCS) schools (see Chapter 5) are focused on improving student achievement in mathematics and science. Each school sent teams of staff to summer institutes that focused on developing teachers' knowledge in mathematics and English language arts. Content leaders and coaches in each school work with other teachers to help them apply knowledge and skills in their study group work and in their classrooms.

The Springfield, Missouri, school district has districtwide initiatives in reading (Reader's Workshop, Guided Reading, Comprehension Strategies) and writing ("6 + 1 Traits of Writing" and Writer's Workshop) and offers ongoing professional development for teachers and has district specialists who provide resources for study groups. In Franklin County, each school has a Curriculum Resource Teacher who works with individual teachers, study groups, grade-level teams, and content-area teams to assist faculty with instructional strategies and specific content information.

Another component of building expertise, and a bridge between content knowledge and instructional strategies, is building knowledge about how the brain functions, how students learn, and how to design lessons and units that reflect these principles. Hawthorn District 73 expects teachers to create units using the Understanding by Design framework (Wiggins & McTighe, 1998) and provides ongoing professional development for teachers. The Centers for Quality Teaching and Learning Capacity First program provides professional development for teachers in how the brain functions and how students learn as a basis for understanding the value of using research-based instructional strategies that promote active student learning.

Expanding teachers' repertoire of research-based instructional strategies is another way that schools and districts can help improve the quality of study group work. Teachers at the Daniel Hale Williams Preparatory School of Medicine are strengthening their expertise in strategies for differentiating instruction and are using these strategies in their study group work. The QTL and Learning-Focused Schools programs, both described in Chapter 5, were specifically designed to expand teachers' repertoire of strategies that they can then use in their study group work. The LINCS program in Louisiana connects content expertise with instructional strategies through the summer institutes and the work of a school-based coach.

While teachers have lots of experience examining student work to give grades, many have had little experience looking deeply at student work collaboratively. "Looking at Student Work" is the process of

> focusing on small samples of student work, looking together at student work with colleagues, reflecting on important questions about teaching and learning, and using agreed upon structures and guidelines ("protocols") for looking and talking about student work. . . . Some of the protocols emphasize evaluation—analyzing effectiveness of curriculum, instruction or assessment practices; others emphasize description to heighten teachers' understanding of individual children and hence affect teacher practice. . . . Protocols are vehicles for building the skills and culture necessary for collaborative work. Thus, using protocols often allows groups to build trust by actually doing substantive work together. (National School Reform Faculty, n.d.)

Consultants from the WFSG National Center offer workshops and training in using protocols for looking at student work on-site for schools and districts and at the WFSG institutes and conference. See Figure 4.2 for one protocol for looking at student work.

A final area component to improving the quality of study group work relates to assessing the effectiveness of classroom interventions. This is the heart of the schoolwide action research process—Are the classroom interventions initiated by study groups effective in improving student learning? Most teachers approach assessing the effectiveness of strategies or interventions they try out in classrooms informally by seeking evidence to respond to questions such as the following: Did students like the strategy? Did they do well on tasks related to the strategy? Did their performance on chapter or unit tests improve?

Through miniworkshops, we encourage study groups to be more rigorous in their assessment of strategies and interventions. We demonstrate and provide examples of using similar preassessment and postassessment tasks to look for changes in students' thinking and understanding. We ask study group members to monitor how they introduce and teach a strategy and to monitor student reactions to the strategy and the tasks. We help study groups think about determining whether students have mastered the strategy, such as using a graphic organizer, in a teacher-directed situation and when they use it independently without teacher direction. And we help study groups look for evidence that students can transfer the understanding they have gained through using the strategy to other contexts, such as district or state tests.

Evaluate the Schoolwide Action Research System

Step 7 in the annual WFSG DMC is assessment of study group work. While the primary focus of the year-end evaluation is the impact of study group work on student learning, the school also assesses the impact of study groups on changing teacher practices, the extent to which study groups have followed the WFSG process guidelines, and how well the implementation of the WFSG System, including school, district, and external support, has enhanced the work of individual study groups.

There are two levels to the year-end evaluation: individual study groups and the school as a whole. Individual study groups are asked to assess and report on the types of activities the group engaged in, the perceived benefits of the study group's work to its members and to students, changes in student learning on the needs it addressed, changes in teacher practice, and how well it has implemented the WFSG process guidelines (see Resource D for a sample set of forms). Study groups also review and update their action plans to ensure that the plans accurately reflect their work during the school year.

The second level of evaluation is schoolwide. Three sets of data support schoolwide evaluation of the WFSG System: data from individual study groups, staff feedback on implementation of the system, and status on the WFSG rubric.

Assessment data from individual study groups is aggregated and shared with the entire staff and discussed at an IC meeting or a staff meeting. Data from study groups on student performance on specific student learning needs can be used the following fall as schools begin anew with Step 1, Analyze Data, in the WFSG DMC.

Staff feedback on implementation of the WFSG System is the second set of data for evaluating the system. One source of feedback is the feedback to readers during the year on the quality of their feedback and support for study groups. A second source is the feedback on issues and concerns voiced at IC meetings. A third source is a year-end survey that asks staff to provide feedback on various aspects of the system, including support from the district and external organizations (see Resource D for an example).

Status on the WFSG rubric (see Resource A) is a third set of data for evaluating the system. For schools in the first year of implementing the schoolwide action research system, the level of implementation, from "not yet" to "advanced," on each indicator in the three domains of context, process, and content, becomes the school's baseline data. Schools in later years of implementation can compare their progress from year to year and use the rubric to target specific areas for improvement that are then incorporated into the school improvement plan.

Schools have used different strategies for completing the rubric. Some schools ask each study group to rate themselves on the indicators using a copy of the rubric. Then the school's leadership team aggregates the results to develop a schoolwide picture. Other schools enlarge the rubric pages, post them on a wall, and ask members of each study group to place a colored sticky dot on each indicator to mark where they think their group or the school is currently in terms of their level of implementation. The position of the sticky dots provides a visual image of where groups are in implementation for all of the indicators.

Reinvigorate the Process

Schools that have been implementing the schoolwide action research system for several years can reinvigorate the process with new projects, themes, and change agents. For example, after reviewing student performance data, the faculty at the Edward Best and Royal Elementary Schools decided that all study groups in each school needed to focus on improving writing during the 2006–2007 school year. In previous years, study groups chose different categories of student needs to address.

Introducing new professional development is another strategy to reinvigorate the process. At the Daniel Hale Williams Preparatory School of Medicine, each year's professional development focus is linked to study group work where teachers are expected to connect their learning in professional development to the interventions they develop in their study groups. During the 2006–2007 school year, professional development focused on strategies for differentiating instruction and creating standards-based classroom assessments.

Institutionalizing New Approaches

It often takes three to five years to establish a major innovation so that it becomes an integral part of the way a school operates and the regular routines of staff and leaders. As Murphy and Lick (2005, p. 183) indicate, schoolwide action research is a complex innovation involving new relationships, new roles and behaviors, new expectations and accountability, new visibility, and new knowledge, skills, and teaching strategies. Resource E provides an illustrative, step-by-step, three-year implementation plan that schools can use to guide the development of their school-wide action research system.

The challenge of institutionalization for a school's staff is to embed study groups practically and inspirationally in the school's culture. Embedding study groups practically means dealing with issues of time, budget, staff turnover, accountability, school improvement plans, and district priorities. Embedding study groups inspirationally means connecting to core values, the school's vision and mission, and to stories, legends, and rituals. John Kotter and Dan Cohen, in their book *The Heart of Change* (2002), see the major challenge in large-scale change as changing people's behavior and that changing behavior is not just a matter of influencing thinking but more importantly influencing feelings, because our feelings are our truths.

Build Inspirational Connections

Connecting to Core Values and School Vision

For schoolwide action research to continue beyond the enthusiasm of the first few years, it needs to be seen as a logical outgrowth of the school's vision, mission, and core values as they relate to beliefs about good teaching and learning and how people work together. Often, these connections are discussed in the initiation phase, when school staff are learning about study groups and deciding whether to begin, but then they are overlooked as implementation proceeds. While part of leading change is creating a vision that provides meaning for the innovation being implemented, Kotter (1998) points out that it is equally important to relentlessly communicate that vision, using every possible vehicle. He also emphasizes the importance of linking the innovation to organizational successes. This is why the WFSG System emphasizes sharing study group results and successes during the year through study group logs, IC meetings, newsletters, bulletin boards, and faculty meetings. It also emphasizes the importance of year-end reflections and sharing and celebration events.

Connecting to Successes

At the end of the 2005–2006 school year, the principal at Bunn Elementary School asked each study group to reflect on three questions: What specific needs did you address and what were the outcomes? When you reflect on the work you have done this year as a study group, what do you know now that you didn't know before? Where do you see your group going next year? She created a booklet with each study group's reflections and action plans to share with staff and district leaders. This booklet documented study group successes and reinforced the link between study group work and successes in improving teaching and learning.

Creating Rituals

At many WFSG schools, the Focus Teams purposefully hold the launch session at the beginning of the year, when the whole faculty meet together to go through Steps 1–4 of the WFSG DMC. The sharing and celebration session at the end of the year is a colorful and exciting event, with music, food, and table and room decorations. Their goal is to signal that these sessions are special and not just "business as usual."

Build Practical Connections

The institutionalization of schoolwide action research also depends on taking care of the details that embed the system in regular school operations.

Time

As we have said before, time is one of the biggest issues because most school and district schedules and calendars were created before educators realized the value of teachers working together collaboratively to improve student learning. Time for study group meetings, IC meetings, and related professional development must be built into the school calendar and the weekly student and staff schedules. Most principals find that it is easier to secure time after the first year of implementation when they have positive results to show from the investment in time for study groups.

Budget

Embedding financial support for schoolwide action research into the regular operating budget is another key factor for institutionalization. After the first year of implementation, the maintenance costs associated with schoolwide action research are costs for resource materials for individual study groups; materials for orienting new staff to the system of schoolwide action research; refreshments for the launch, sharing, and celebration events; and ongoing professional development, including conference travel, which is related to student learning needs and strengthening the study group system.

Schools should not pay teachers stipends to meet in study groups. Time for study group work should be on contract time, not personal time, because working collaboratively to improve student learning is part of being a professional teacher. Clauset worked with a rural district that launched the WFSG System with funding from a comprehensive school-reform grant. Rather than change the schedule so that study groups met during the school day, the district decided to allow teachers to meet in study groups before or after school and receive a stipend. When the grant ended, the district could no longer afford stipends and teachers stopped meeting except on the districtwide, early-release days. These early-release days were too far apart for groups to maintain momentum and the system fell apart.

Turnover

Staff and leader turnover is inevitable in schools. New teachers need to be oriented by the Focus Team or principal to study groups and the schoolwide action research process before they join a study group. If they join the school midyear, new teachers should be invited to join existing study groups with fewer than five members and student needs that the new teachers can address in the classes they teach, or if there are at least three new teachers, they can form a new study group.

At the beginning of each school year, faculty meet to review new student data, revise their list of student learning needs, and form study groups based on these needs. Faculty who were in study groups have three options for the next year, if the schedule permits:

- Stay in the same study group and work on the same needs or category of needs.
- Stay in the same study group and work on a different category of needs.
- Disband and join new groups.

New principals, assistant principals, and other school staff who are part of the school's administrative study group also need orientation to the system and to their responsibilities for supporting the faculty study groups. Those recruiting new school leaders need to ensure that candidates know about and support the leadership responsibilities for schoolwide action research. In Springfield, Missouri, the district developed a leadership program for new and experienced principals that makes district expectations explicit and helps principals achieve them.

Accountability

Philip Schlechty, in his book *Schools for the 21st Century: Leadership Imperatives for Educational Reform* (1990, p. 101), says the following: "People know what is expected by what is inspected and respected." Linking schoolwide action research to faculty and principal accountability is one component of institutionalizing the system. Principals need to see leadership and support for schoolwide action research as an integral part of their work as principals and instructional leaders, and their supervisors need to "inspect" this work as part of their supervision and evaluation of principals. In Franklin County, the superintendent makes regular visits to schools to talk with principals about study group work and their support for study groups.

Similarly, when a school faculty decides to launch schoolwide action research, the shared expectation is that every certificated faculty member will participate in study group work as part of their professional responsibilities. Principals "inspect" this work as part of their supervision of faculty through reviewing and responding to study group action plans and logs, IC meetings, and classroom walk-throughs, where they look for study group strategies being used in the classroom.

School Improvement Plans

One of the loudest complaints about embarking on schoolwide action research is, "We have too much to do already." Savvy principals and Focus Teams create ways to demonstrate to faculty that study groups provide a vehicle to do the work we know we need to do and show that it is not just another program. One important way to do this is to embed study groups and action research in the school's improvement plan. Whether it is an annual or multiyear plan, study groups should be explicitly included in the detailed plans and timelines as a key vehicle for changing teacher practices and improving student learning. At Bunn Elementary School, the school improvement team included study groups in their implementation plans for their academic goals in reading, writing, and mathematics.

District Priorities

Aligning school-based innovations with district goals and priorities is one way to ensure their survival. It is much easier to connect schoolwide action research to district-goal priorities when a set of schools in a district or the entire district is implementing the same system. But even a single school can create connections by demonstrating how study groups and the schoolwide action research process are using district curriculum and instructional initiatives and are helping the district reach its goals for improving student learning.

CONCLUSIONS

The principal's role in leading and supporting schoolwide action research has two phases: leading the launch and after the launch. This chapter uses John Kotter's principles for leading large-scale change to organize our description of specific responsibilities for each phase. These principles establish a sense of urgency, form a powerful guiding coalition, create and communicate a vision, empower others to act on the vision and eliminate obstacles to change, plan for and create short-term wins, consolidate improvements and produce more changes, and institutionalize new approaches.

For each of the aforementioned principles, we describe how it connects to launching, establishing, and maintaining a system of schoolwide action research and offer examples from schools implementing a study group system.

There are several key points to remember about the principal's role in leading and supporting schoolwide action research:

- *Success with schoolwide action research requires the principal's active commitment and leadership.*

    Engaging in schoolwide action research requires the principal's active involvement both as an advocate, cheerleader, and spokesperson for the work and as a servant leader supporting individual study groups through regular, timely, constructive feedback to their work and through orchestrating cross-study group communication, learning, and problem solving. Even when the school has an active Focus Team of teachers helping to guide implementation and a team of readers to assist in reviewing and responding to study group action plans and logs, the principal needs to be visibly and actively involved. Most of the "failures" to implement the system beyond the first year are a direct result of lack of principal commitment and leadership.

    Carlene Murphy describes the principal's role toward leading schoolwide action research as one combining the right mix of support and pressure. The support are the tasks described in the preceding paragraph and elsewhere in this chapter: regular, timely, constructive feedback to study group work and cross-study group communication, learning, and problem solving. The pressure is about high expectations—the expectations that all teachers and children can learn, all study groups can be successful within the current school year at improving their teaching practices and their students' performance on the needs they address, and study group work will lead to improvements in student performance on school, district, and state assessments.

    With all of the ups and downs in daily school life and in leading any initiative, it is important to remember the advice Bruce Joyce gave Carlene when they were first implementing the WFSG System in Augusta, Georgia: "Smile. Be kind. Don't stop" (Murphy & Lick, 2005, p. 199).

- *Being in an administrative study group is "walking the talk."*

    Principals who are members of their own administrative study group experience the schoolwide action research process firsthand. This deepens their understanding of the process and helps them give better feedback to teacher study groups. It is also a public symbol of "walking the talk"—that everyone in the school needs to be engaged in action research to improve teaching and learning. Being in an administrative study group is another way for principals to demonstrate their instructional leadership.

- *Once study groups are formed, ensure that each study group experiences success.*

    The saying, "success breeds success," applies to implementing schoolwide action research. Our experience has shown that the single most important factor in building faculty commitment to schoolwide action research is experiencing success in the first semester or year in each person's personal study group. Study groups achieve success when (1) all group members feel that they are working on student needs that are important to their students and that they can address in the curriculum they teach, and (2) they choose one specific need to address and identify and use at least one strategy that leads to improvements in student learning that they see in their classroom assessments. Success also comes from teachers developing proficiency with the new content and instructional practices that they are learning in their study groups and other professional development opportunities.

The principal's role, with support from the administrative study group, is to ensure that every study group member achieves this success.

- *Schoolwide action research changes the school's culture.*

Implementing a system of schoolwide action research is hard work because it is fundamentally about changing the school's culture. Consistent with Kotter's principles for leading change, the WFSG System assumes that school culture changes last, not first. What changes first are assumptions about how to change student learning, then attitudes and beliefs, and finally, administration, faculty, and student behaviors relating to approaches for increasing student learning. The structure of the WFSG System, as embodied in the set of WFSG principles and guidelines developed in schools since 1987, importantly helps change assumptions, attitudes and beliefs, and behaviors.

It is important to keep in mind the long-term goal, institutionalization and sustainment over time of schoolwide action research, as one tries to lead and support launching and implementing a study group system through day-to-day activities and decisions. How one makes decisions and implements activities can enhance or impede sustainability as much as the content of the decisions or activities. Such a system must be built on assumptions about (1) the importance of inquiry and sharing knowledge and information, (2) transparency in decision making, (3) operation on the basis of mutual respect, and (4) the view that study groups are self-governing groups of professionals who shape their own work and make informed choices. If a principal does not support these assumptions, then schoolwide action research is not going to work in that school.

Chapter 8 recognizes that no school operates in a vacuum and focuses on how districts and external organizations can support principals and their schools as they engage in schoolwide action research.

Supporting Schools in Schoolwide Action Research

Guiding Questions

■ How do district leaders support schoolwide action research in district schools?

■ What resources are available to help schools and districts conduct schoolwide action research?

Most of the rhetoric and most of the federal and state initiatives to improve student achievement have focused on the school as the unit of analysis and change. Only recently are policy makers realizing that schools operate within districts and the district context may enhance or inhibit the efforts of principals and their faculty to improve student learning.

In a 2004 review of more than 80 research reports and articles from the past 15 years, Shannon and Bylsma (2004) identified 13 factors associated with school districts making substantial progress in improving student learning. They cluster these into four categories: effective leadership, quality teaching and learning, support for systemwide improvement, and clear and collaborative relationships. Following are the 13 factors they identified (Shannon & Bylsma, 2004, p. 8):

Effective Leadership

1. Focus intentionally on student learning.

2. Have dynamic and distributed leadership.

3. Sustain their improvement efforts over time.

Quality Teaching and Learning

4. Hold high expectations for adults.

5. Have a coordinated and aligned curriculum and assessment system.

6. Provide coordinated and embedded professional development.

7. Ensure quality classroom instruction.

Support for Systemwide Improvement

8. Rely heavily on data to make decisions.

9. Have a high degree of policy and program coherence across the district.

10. Allocate resources strategically.

Clear and Collaborative Relationships

11. Exhibit a professional culture and collaborative relationships.

12. Maintain clear and effective district and school roles and responsibilities.

13. Interpret and manage the external environment effectively.

Shannon and Bylsma (2004) view these 4 categories and 13 factors as interrelated elements that all districts need to address to continually improve student learning. Figure 8.1, reproduced from Shannon and Bylsma, p. 10, illustrates these relationships.

We use the Shannon and Bylsma (2004) framework in the next section of this chapter to organize our discussion of the ways districts support schoolwide action research when all schools in the district are implementing it and when only one or two schools are implementing it. Concrete examples are drawn from districts in North Carolina, Georgia, Massachusetts, Missouri, and Illinois that are engaged in promoting schoolwide action research in their schools.

A second section of this chapter provides a description of the resources currently available to help schools and districts support schoolwide action research. This section includes a discussion of the services provided by the WFSG National Center and other action research resources.

HOW DISTRICTS SUPPORT SCHOOLWIDE ACTION RESEARCH

Superintendents and district office staff can lead, enhance, and support school-based efforts to implement WFSG schoolwide action research by providing effective

Figure 8.1   A Conceptual Framework for Districts Improving Student Learning

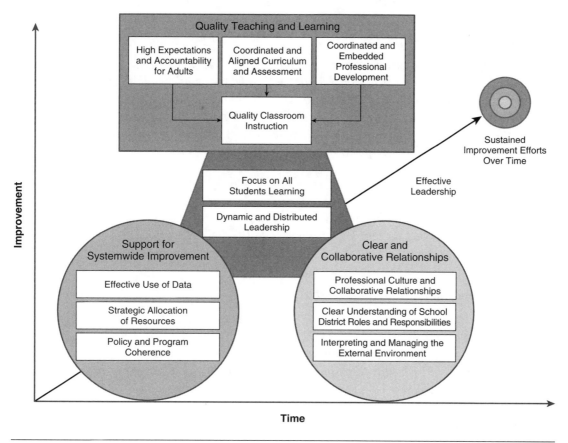

Source: Used with permission of the Washington State Office of Superintendent of Public Instruction. Authors: G. Sue Shannon and Pete Bylsma.

leadership, promoting quality teaching and learning, supporting systemwide improvement, and fostering clear and collaborative relationships.

Effective Leadership

Focus on Improving Student Learning

Districts that focus intentionally on improving student learning and communicate that this is every staff member's responsibility help create a culture where engaging in schoolwide action research through study groups is an essential part of one's job. District vision statements and strategic plans signal this focus.

Franklin County Schools

All 14 schools in the district have implemented the WFSG System. The banner on the district's Web site and in all district publications is as follows: "Our Future, Our Commitment, Our Students." The first priority in the district's Strategic Plan adopted in

2003 is continuous student achievement. The goals of the district continue to include read-ing proficiency by Grade 3 and closing achievement gaps at all grade levels.

Hawthorn School District 73

All 6 schools in the district have implemented the WFSG System. "Learning for All, Whatever It Takes" is the banner on the district's Web site and in all district publications. Higher student achievement is the top priority in the school board goals and the superinten-dent, Dr. Yomtoob, stated in remarks to staff in August 2006 on "creating a world-class school district" that "student achievement is the most important thing we do" (see http://www.hawthorn73.0rg/superintendent/).

Springfield Public Schools

Fifty of fifty-two schools in the district have implemented the WFSG System. The No. 1 district goal is to improve student achievement, and the district motto is as follows: "We exist for the academic excellence of all students."

Gill-Montague Regional School District

All 6 schools in the district have implemented the WFSG System. In her August 2006 Superintendent's Education Plan, Dr. Gee states the following: "The School Committee's vision is to provide a quality education for all students, with equity—no excuses, no excep-tions" and that "the best education plan is a simple plan for continuous improvement in student achievement."

Dynamic and Distributed Leadership

Based on their review of research on improving districts, Shannon and Bylsma (2004, p. 16) define dynamic and distributed leadership as follows:

> Leaders in improved school districts are described as dynamic, united in purpose, involved, visible in schools, and interested in instruction. Leaders provide encouragement, recognition, and support for improving student learning. Instructional leadership is expanded to encompass the superinten-dent, principals, teacher leaders, and other administrators at district and school levels. The ethical and moral nature of effective leadership is demon-strated when leaders move beyond talking about the belief that students can learn to taking concrete action to change instruction so students *do* learn.

In the four WFSG districts, the superintendents and central office staff see instructional leadership as an integral part of their role and have gone well beyond just talking about the belief that all children can learn.

In Franklin County, the superintendent, the senior administrators, and department directors joined with the 14 principals to form six countywide study groups that meet monthly. Each countywide study group develops and implements an action plan, just as do the teacher study groups. Some of the essential questions guiding the groups' work are as fol-lows: (a) How do you support study groups in your school? (b) How do you support study groups in the community? (c) How do you support teachers who struggle with study groups? (d) How do you incorporate noncore teachers in study groups at your school?

In Hawthorn, Springfield, and Franklin County, the districts have embraced distributed leadership and identified teacher leaders to serve as resources to other teachers to improve teaching and learning. In Hawthorn, they are called teaching and learning coaches; in Springfield, instructional support specialists; and in Franklin County, curriculum resource teachers. In all three districts, these teacher leaders either participate in teacher study groups or serve as resources to the teacher study groups in the schools they serve.

Sustained Improvement Efforts Over Time

As Shannon and Bylsma (2004, p. 19) found, "The task of improving student learning is difficult; changing practice—which involves changing people's minds about teaching and learning—requires steady and persistent work." Many teachers and principals are skeptical about district initiatives because of many years experience with changing initiatives every year or two or three. Teachers need time to develop new skills and create new materials to support changes in practice. The reality is that schools, like students and adults, progress at different rates through levels of understanding and implementation. In Franklin County during the 2006–2007 school year, where schools were in their third year of study group implementation, and in Springfield, where many schools have been implementing study groups for six years, there are differences in the quality of implementation among schools. Both districts need still more time to bring all schools up to the advanced level of implementation in the WFSG rubric.

Quality Teaching and Learning

High Expectations and Accountability for Adults

Holding high expectations for adults is also about holding adults accountable for producing results. High expectations are at the heart of the schoolwide action research process. Study groups can improve student learning and change practice for their students in the areas they target. However, principals must continually communicate these expectations to their faculties and rely on district staff to reinforce the message, even if all of the schools in the district are not implementing study groups. In Franklin County, the superintendent, the executive director for curriculum and instruction, and the directors of elementary and secondary education continually reinforce the importance of study group work for improving student achievement.

Districts support accountability for high expectations by encouraging or requiring schools to include study groups in their school improvement plans as a key vehicle for improving student learning. They also reinforce the message when central office staff visit schools for walk throughs and look for evidence of study group work in posted action plans and logs, instructional practices in classrooms, student work samples and conversations with students, and improvements in student performance.

Coordinated and Aligned Curriculum and Assessment System

School districts throughout the United States are concerned with aligning curricula with state standards and state tests. Shannon and Bylsma (2004, p. 25) found that many districts identified as successful in improving student achievement were taking a centralized approach to developing districtwide curricula aligned vertically and horizontally. Districts were developing pacing guides and internal assessment systems to monitor student progress during the school year and make improvements rather than waiting for state assessment data that often was not received until after the close of the school year.

Franklin County Schools

Teams of teachers developed pacing guides for core content areas for Grades K–8. These pacing guides were revised annually, based on feedback from teachers and analysis of student performance on the state end-of-grade tests. As noted in Chapter 5, the district has formed curriculum study groups that meet monthly and are composed of Curriculum Resource Teachers (CRTs) and teacher volunteers from different schools. At the elementary level, the writing group during the 2006–2007 school year used data from the previous year's writing assessments to identify areas to address in writer's workshops in each school and identify strategies to model for teachers. The reading group worked on lesson plans for leveled books (guided reading) and matched the leveled books to other content areas. The math group used data from the previous year's state tests and district benchmarks to identify key concepts to address and developed investigative math lessons for all teachers to use.

Franklin County study groups used data from district assessments to determine which student needs to address and whether students were making progress. To monitor student writing in Grades 3–8, the district gave mock writing assessments every nine weeks that mirrored the state writing assessment.

In 2005, the district began to administer benchmark assessments for students in Grades 3–12 in subjects assessed by the state. These benchmark assessments were given in reading and math for Grades 3 through 8 and in core high school subjects. To develop the Grade 3–8 benchmark tests, the school-based CRTs met by level with the director of elementary education and used the state course of study, district pacing guides, and results from the previous year's state tests to decide which concepts were to be assessed in the fall and spring. The high school CRTs and department chairs followed a similar process to create the benchmark assessments for the core high school subjects with state End-of-Course tests. The types of questions on all of the benchmark assessments were similar to the questions on the state tests.

Hawthorn School District 73

Curriculum mapping in all subjects and all grades (K–8) has been a priority for a number of years. Each year, under the leadership of the assistant superintendent of student achievement and staff development and the school-based Teaching and Learning Coaches, teams of teachers refine and revise the district curriculum guide (Hawthorn School District 73, 2006a). While the curriculum maps in core content areas had been aligned with state standards, Hawthorn began, for the 2005–2006 school year, to identify, for each grade and subject, the "power" standards that were essential for every student to master before moving to the next grade. The 2006–2007 curriculum guide includes power standards and specific performance indicators for the four core academic subjects—language arts, math, social studies, and science, and power standards for the other content areas—fine arts, physical education and health, foreign language, and technology. The district's next steps for further improving the curriculum guides include developing performance indicators for all subjects at each grade level and developing meaningful common classroom, school, and district assessments to provide evidence of student progress in attaining the power standards.

Hawthorn study groups also use data from district assessments to guide their work. Hawthorn uses the Northwest Evaluation Association's Measures of Academic Progress computer-based achievement tests in math, reading, and language usage to monitor growth in student learning during the year and from year to year. Students in Grades 2–7 are tested in the fall and in the spring each year. Students in Grade 1 are tested in the spring only.

Students in all grades, K-8, are assessed in writing twice a year, to identify strengths and weaknesses, and to evaluate growth over time. The districtwide writing assessment is based on the "6 + 1 Trait Writing" that all schools use and it provides data for teachers and study groups on each component of writing: integration, ideas, organization, voice, word choice, sentence fluency, and conventions. As in Franklin County, all Hawthorn students in Grades 3–8 have access to the Study Island Web-based state assessment preparation program in the subjects tested on the Illinois Standards Achievement Test, which are mathematics, reading, writing, science, and social studies.

Springfield Public Schools

In communication arts, Springfield has developed K–5 curriculum guides with major instructional goals and performance standards for each grade, recommended instructional materials to be used for each content strand, a Grade 1–8 midyear communication arts benchmark assessment, a middle school and high school writing assessment, and common high school final exams in communication arts. The district provided professional development for teachers in "6 + 1 Trait Writing," writer's and reader's workshops, guided reading, and reading comprehension strategies.

Over the last several years, Springfield has implemented the Everyday Mathematics program districtwide in Grades PreK–6, a Grade 1–8 midyear math benchmark assessment, and common high school exams in algebra and geometry. The district also provides extended learning opportunities and tutoring for students in Grades 1–8 who are at risk for not reaching proficiency in reading and math. Results from the midyear benchmark assessments are analyzed, shared publicly, and used to improve instruction.

A primary focus for the system is increasing the percentage of students who graduate. The district strategies include providing more alternative school options, increasing reading interventions, and reducing the achievement gap within subgroups.

Coordinated and Embedded Professional Development

Districts have learned that offering a smorgasbord of unrelated workshops on release days does not lead to sustained improvements in teacher practice or in student learning. Instead, districts are aligning professional development to district priorities for improving student learning and providing school-based, job-embedded opportunities for learning, practicing, and modeling best practices and content knowledge. The purpose of professional development is to ensure quality classroom instruction. This was the same purpose of the professional development program that Bruce Joyce and Beverly Showers created around Models of Teaching in the Richmond County Schools in 1987 with Carlene Murphy, the initial program for the creation of the WFSG approach. Twenty years later we are still working to ensure quality classroom instruction.

Hawthorn School District 73

The mission of Hawthorn's professional development work is improving student achievement by building the knowledge and skills of educators and school leaders.

For the 2006–2007 school year, improving literacy, and specifically improving reading and writing across the curricula, was the main focus with an emphasis on teachers introducing, implementing, and practicing strategies to make all students better readers, writers, and thinkers. Staff development focused on the best practices and strategies to improve literacy, with an emphasis on "6-Traits Writing, examining students' work and consistent assessment of students' work using rubrics" (Hawthorn School District 73, 2006a, p. 6). It also included ongoing support for Understanding by Design (Wiggins & McTighe, 1998) and the Leonard Bernstein Center's Artful Learning® model and new support for creating common assessments.

Teaching and learning coaches in every school help study groups and teachers connect professional development to classroom practice. Such coaches share and model best practices, teach teams, help teachers and study groups plan units, and provide follow-up support for districtwide initiatives.

Franklin County Schools

Franklin County also invests in coordinated professional development to support the implementation of the WFSG System. During the 2004–2005 school year, the district sent teams of teachers and administrators to Augusta, Georgia, to attend the WFSG Level I Institute to learn about the WFSG System and how to launch it. They invited Carlene Murphy, the founder of the system, to make follow-up trips to Franklin County to visit each school to meet with the focus teams and representatives from every study group in all 14 schools, and then to meet with the district leadership team to plan next steps in supporting schools. Each visit had a different focus, based on where the study groups were in their action research cycle. During the 2005–2006 school year, Carlene made five visits to the district, again visiting each school to work with study groups and build leadership. In addition, Lynn Baber, another WFSG consultant, went to the district to lead a two-day workshop on looking at student work collaboratively using protocols for representatives from each study group in the district. Carlene asked principals to collect action plans with baseline data and final results, and samples of pretests and posttests from every study group, and then compiled a booklet with summary data from all groups. During the 2006–2007 school year, Carlene made three return visits but focused her consultation and assistance on building leadership in central office staff and their countywide study groups.

Springfield Public Schools

In Springfield, the focus of the district's professional development plan is to improve student performance. The plan, developed in 2005 by the district's professional development committee after reviewing data about teaching and learning, focuses on literacy (reading and writing), math, assessment, mentoring, cooperative learning, differentiated instruction, and teacher support. Professional development opportunities for Springfield teachers are aligned with these identified areas of emphasis and school improvement plans.

One of the challenges in supporting study groups with coordinated and job-embedded professional development is timing. Study groups often need assistance with designing classroom assessments at the beginning of the semester as they collect baseline data. They need support in identifying research-based instructional strategies and developing proficiency with these strategies within three or four weeks of forming study groups in the fall. These are examples of the need for "Just-In-Time" (JIT) demand-driven professional development.

Another challenge relates to the range of student learning needs that study groups choose to address. In some schools, the faculty may have chosen a common focus for their study group work, as the Edward Best Elementary School in Franklin County did in choosing writing as a focus for their study group work for the 2006–2007 school year. Other schools, such as Qualicum Beach Middle School, may have study groups working on very different needs in different content areas. Districts cannot provide JIT professional development on every student need, but they can begin to develop a resource database that identifies people within the district with particular areas of expertise, such as the CRT in Franklin County who had expertise in the "Empowering Writers" program.

Quality Classroom Instruction

Improved student achievement depends on what is taught and how it is taught. This is the underlying premise behind the schoolwide action research system and a premise that guides district improvement efforts. Shannon and Bylsma (2004) found in their research review that districts improving student learning

> pay close attention to classroom practice and provide guidance and oversight for improving teaching and learning. Districts emphasize principles of good instruction and communicate clear expectations for what to teach. Districts develop a common vision and understanding of quality teaching and learning. They monitor instruction, curriculum, and changes in instructional practice. Their guidance and improvement efforts require actions such as systemwide approval, interventions and corrective instruction, tutoring, and alignment. (p. 31)

> Districts differ in their visions and philosophies regarding coordinating and monitoring instruction. While some districts offer guidance, others mandate given practices. Some districts adopt textbooks that are quite prescriptive with lesson plans and pacing guides and monitor teacher adherence to these in implementing the curriculum. Some emphasize the need for particular instructional processes, such as organizing instruction to allow for assessing skills regularly before students move on, providing tutoring or extra help for students who fail to master the skills and enrichment activities for those who have, and frequent practice throughout the year to help students remember what they have learned. Other districts provide explicit expectations for instructional practice and then use "walkthroughs" or other processes to look at classroom instruction. (Shannon & Bylsma, 2004, p. 32)

The three WFSG districts, Springfield, Hawthorn, and Franklin County, have all taken steps to ensure that quality classroom instruction is the focus for all of their schools and study groups:

- Identifying research-based instructional strategies to jump-start study groups and provide professional development in using these strategies.
- Deepening teachers' content knowledge and supporting curriculum articulation and alignment.
- Providing assistance in designing classroom assessments.

Franklin County Schools

The district began its efforts to ensure quality classroom instruction by engaging all district staff members in a book study of Philip Schlechty's (2002) *Working on the Work,* which emphasizes authentic student engagement in work that is intellectually challenging and demanding.

Over the past three years, the district has been working on the work in a variety of ways. At the elementary level, all teachers have been trained in balanced literacy and guided reading, and cross-school math study groups worked on investigative math lessons and posted them online for teachers to use. Empowering writers is a districtwide initiative in Grades K–8, and the district is beginning training and support for writers workshops. Elementary schools formed cross-school reading study groups in 2006 to work on lessons and correlate benchmark bookrooms to other areas. Middle schools have been trained in "reading apprenticeship" programs, which are strategies to use cross-curriculum, and all high school teachers have been trained in vocabulary, note taking, and study skills strategies based on Marzano, Pickering, and Pollock's (2001) *Classroom Instruction That Works.*

In 2006, Franklin County strengthened its focus on effective instruction for study groups with support from the Centers for Quality Teaching and Learning (QTL). During the 2006–2007 school year, teams in all 14 schools participated in the five-day QTL professional development program described in Chapter 5. The district also piloted regular, on-site assistance from a QTL coach at two elementary schools in the Spring 2006 semester to support the link between QTL teaching tools and strategies and teachers using them in their study group work. The district is developing a multiyear plan to enable all teachers to develop expertise in QTL.

Springfield Public Schools

Springfield has several programs that support teachers in providing quality classroom instruction. Beginning in the 2004–2005 school year, the district started a five-year induction program for new teachers called STEP-UP (Supporting Teachers, Examining Practices & Uncovering Potential). STEP-UP is divided into three tiers of development over a period of five years. Tier I is for first-year teachers, Tier II is for second-year teachers, and Tier III is for teachers in their third through fifth year teachers.

Relative to classroom instruction, Instructional Specialists for School Improvement (ISSIs) are a cadre of teacher leaders who support teachers and study groups in improving the quality of instruction. Each ISSI is responsible for a set of schools and for helping schools align instruction with curriculum to meet the needs of students. ISSIs serve as resource providers, data coaches, curriculum specialists, classroom supporters, mentors, learning facilitators, school leaders, change agents, and models for continuous learning.

One of Springfield's staff development goals was to enable all teachers in the district to use cooperative learning strategies to increase student achievement by enhancing student engagement and accountability in the learning process and increasing students' communication, thinking, and problem-solving skills. Training in cooperative learning strategies is included in their five-year teacher-induction program for new teachers and is provided to veteran teachers through ongoing professional development workshops and on-site coaching by the ISSIs.

Beginning in the 2006–2007 school year, Springfield began a multiyear initiative in continuous quality improvement (CQI) in classrooms with pilot programs in several of their schools. The CQI initiative had two goals: increasing student engagement and improving student achievement.

The CQI process involved a weekly Plan-Do-Study-Act cycle that mirrored the schoolwide action research cycle. Teachers and students set weekly learning goals, and teachers guided students through learning activities and diagnostic assessments Monday through Thursday after preassessing their levels of proficiency and understanding. On Fridays, students completed postassessments, discussed with the teacher what worked during the week and what didn't, and set goals for the coming week. All students were expected to meet weekly targets. At McBride Elementary, one of the pilot schools, several study groups focused on improving student engagement in conjunction with their CQI work.

Hawthorn School District 73

Providing quality classroom instruction is a logical extension of the district's curriculum-mapping process. All teachers are expected to use the three-stage Hawthorn Learning System for planning instruction. In Stage 1, teachers specify what they want students to learn. Stage 2 focuses on how teachers will measure and assess progress. Stage 3 concentrates on the activities, resources, programs, and materials teachers used to accomplish their goals (Hawthorn School District 73, 2004).

At the elementary level, teachers are expected to use the Understanding by Design (UbD) framework to design units and principles of differentiated instruction to differentiate content, process, product, and learning environment. Each teacher is expected to create one new UbD unit per year, and all of the units created are archived electronically and on paper so that any teacher in the district can access them. Teachers are expected to update units on reuse. The district provides a template for UbD units. Three levels of UbD training and a six-hour course on differentiating instruction (DI) were to be completed by all teachers prior to the 2007–2008 school year. The teaching and learning coaches assist individual teachers and study groups in designing lessons and units that use the UbD and DI framework. They also do classroom walk-throughs to monitor progress on the use of differentiated instruction strategies (Hawthorn School District 73, 2006b).

At the middle school level, teachers are also expected to use the UbD and DI framework that elementary teachers use, add the use of "6 + 1 Trait Writing," rubrics to assess writing, and incorporate Marzano strategies for teaching, note taking, summarizing, and comparing and contrasting. Teachers work in grade-level groups to create UbD units, in departments to analyze writing using the "6 + 1 Trait Writing" rubric, and in study groups to address specific student learning needs. As in the elementary schools, the middle school teaching and learning coaches assist individual teachers and study groups in designing lessons and units and conduct walk-throughs to monitor progress in using differentiated instruction and Marzano strategies (Hawthorn School District 73, 2006b).

In math, the goal of the K–8 curriculum is to have all students leave eighth grade prepared to take at least Algebra I in high school. The district eliminated basic math classes from the middle schools' schedules and are using flexible groups extensively in the elementary buildings to better meet the needs of all students. Study groups working on student needs in math focused on the content and instructional strategies that would help students reach proficiency in the math power standards.

Study groups working on student needs in reading and writing had been able to build on professional development on "6 + 1 Trait Writing" and in strategies to enhance reading comprehension in the content areas to improve instruction. The teaching and learning coaches in every school play a key role in supporting quality instruction. They work with individual teachers and study groups to plan interventions to address student needs, identify and model best practices, and provide informal feedback when observing lessons.

Support for Systemwide Improvement

Effective Use of Data

A PowerPoint presentation to staff members in Springfield sums up the position on data in districts focused on improving student achievement: "In God we trust. All others bring data."

Shannon and Bylsma (2004, p. 36) found that "improved districts use data as evidence to monitor results, for making instructional and resource allocation decisions, and for accountability. District staff provides time and training in the use of data and helps schools in gathering and interpreting data. The evidence is used to monitor equity, make decisions about alignment, and target professional development efforts."

Schools engaged in schoolwide action research use four levels of data about student learning as they implement the seven-step WFSG Decision-Making Cycle (DMC).

Level 1 Data

The first level of data is data from state and district assessments that show performance of student subgroups over time in core content areas, such as reading, writing, and math. Schools use Level 1 data to identify achievement gaps for student subgroups and patterns in performance over time.

Level 2 Data

The second level of data is data from state and district assessments that show strengths and weaknesses within a content area in specific skills, standards, and content strands by student subgroups. Using the second-level data, the whole faculty develops a master list of student learning needs that guides the action research of individual study groups.

Level 3 Data

The third level of data is data from state and district assessments that show strengths and weaknesses within a content area for the specific skills and standards that individual study groups are addressing. Study groups want to examine the data from past assessments on their specific student learning needs for their current students and student subgroups.

Level 4 Data

The fourth level of data is data from classroom assessments or computer and Web-based supplementary programs such as Study Island or STAR Math for the performance of current students on the specific skills and standards that individual study groups are addressing. Study groups use this data to determine their students' baseline performance, monitor improvements, and assess the effectiveness of specific instructional strategies.

Districts help schools access, understand, and use data at each of these levels.

Hawthorn School District 73

To help schools access data from Illinois state assessments and the district Measures of Academic Progress]assessments, Hawthorn School District 73 has created a data warehouse accessed through the Just5Clicks data management software. The district provides training for administrators, teaching and learning coaches, and teachers, to access, interpret, and use the Level 1, 2, and 3 data. The data-management system can also be used by study groups to input and track data from classroom assessments. The district also provides teachers with training in creating common standards-based assessments that study groups can use to generate Level 4 data about student learning.

Franklin County Schools

The district helps each school create an annual data book of relevant state and district data for schools to use in developing or updating their school improvement plans and for identifying areas of strength and weakness for study group work. Teachers can also access the state's electronic database, NC WISE, for information about student test scores and demographics. The district also supports the creation of reports on district benchmark assessments in reading and mathematics in Grades 3 through 8 and in high school core courses to provide Level 3 data for schools and study groups.

Springfield Public Schools

The district provides Levels 1, 2, and 3 state and district data for schools from the state assessments and the district midyear assessments in communication arts, math, and writing and has trained school staff to do "data autopsies" to pinpoint specific student learning needs. The CQI process that the district began to implement systemwide during the 2006–2007 school year includes a component on using weekly classroom assessments to monitor progress in student learning.

Policy and Program Coherence

Finding districts that have a high degree of policy and program coherence focused on improving student achievement is a rarity. More often, as Clauset and Nelsen (2004, p. 1) note,

central office departments operate as separate fiefdoms with little or no coordination among departments or in their interactions with schools for information or action. Rarely are schools and their staff, students, and parents seen as customers to be served. Many policies and procedures have been developed over decades and reflect a factory model of schooling with limited opportunities for collaborative work among staff and expect principals to be managers, not instructional leaders.

Shannon and Bylsma (2004, p. 42) describe the following:

Improved districts develop and implement policies and strategies that promote equity and excellence, and they review and revise those policies and strategies to ensure coherence among programs and practices linked to district goals. Student learning is central to roles, budget, operating procedures, and personnel practices—all are redefined as needed. All district systems are explicitly included in reinforcing common goals and efforts to attain the goals. The central office monitors coherence of actions and programs to the focus and vision of the district.

Districts with schools implementing study groups align district policies, practices, and accountability systems to value and support schoolwide action research.

Springfield Public Schools

The district has revamped its teacher induction policies and programs to provide support and training for teachers in their first five years in the district to build the experience and expertise necessary for teachers to work together in study groups and provide high-quality instruction in their classrooms. Experienced teachers use their study group work toward fulfilling district and state requirements for annual professional development.

The district also revised its support for principals (Richardson, 2005). Missouri State University, in partnership with the district, offers workshops for aspiring leaders. All new leaders, principals, assistant principals, and program leaders participate in a two-year Evolving Leaders Induction Program. The induction program includes structured sessions that focus on leadership skills, school and program improvement, performance results, policy and practices, and human resources. All first-year leaders have a trained mentor, a practicing principal or other leader in the district, who provides weekly support, and all principals and assistant principals participate in study groups that meet monthly.

Improvement plans focused on the district's two long-standing goals, improving student achievement and reducing dropout rates at the district and school levels, drive planning and budgeting in Springfield. The human resources department has retooled its recruiting practices to ensure Springfield attracts the type of teachers and leaders who want to work in a system focused on learning.

Franklin County Schools

The district has built coherence by starting with direct support for study groups and then expanding to other areas and by "walking the talk." Since launching study groups in 2005, the district has invested in training in study group approaches off-site and within the district, with school teams attending the annual National WFSG Conference and on-site technical assistance by WFSG consultants.

In 2006, it established countywide administrative study groups, described in Chapter 7, to support schools in their implementation of the study group process, and developed guidelines for schools on holding regular IC meetings. The central office curriculum and instruction team reviews principals' minutes from the IC meetings and gives personal feedback to each principal. To further strengthen the work of study groups and the infusion of research-based teaching strategies into classrooms, the district launched, in 2006, a districtwide initiative to train and support all teachers in QTL strategies, in collaboration with the Centers for Quality Teaching and Learning.

The superintendent includes instructional leadership and active support for study groups as key elements in his supervision and evaluation of principals and his visits to schools. During the 2006–2007 school year, the district revised its recruiting process to make participation in the study group process an explicit expectation for new teachers and principals.

Hawthorn School District 73

In Hawthorn, the focus on improving instruction permeates policies and programs. As stated in the school board policy manual, principals are the chief administrators and instructional leaders of their schools and are evaluated on their instructional leadership ability and their ability to maintain a positive educational and learning environment.

Strategic Allocation of Resources

Shannon and Bylsma (2004, p. 30) found that districts with improved student achievement "provide, allocate, reallocate, and find resources to ensure quality instruction" and "provide additional resources—financial as well as human and social capital—to support low performers." Time is also a resource to allocate. Another part of the resource challenge is ensuring that schools and the district have the in-house capacity, both human and material, to sustain the work of improving student learning over a number of years.

WFSG districts use resources strategically to support schoolwide action research, quality instruction, targeted professional development, a technology infrastructure to support collaboration, and the development of in-house capacity to sustain the work.

All three WFSG districts

- Have invested in training and support for teacher leaders—the curriculum resource teachers in Franklin County, the teaching and learning coaches in Hawthorn, and the instructional specialists for school improvement in Springfield
- Are engaged in multiyear efforts to infuse schools with research-based teaching strategies and curricular programs that support student learning and update and strengthen curriculum guides and internal diagnostic assessment systems for monitoring student progress and improving instruction
- Are investing people, time, and funds to support the schoolwide action research in their schools and building the internal capacity to sustain the work

Another way in which WFSG districts strategically allocate resources to schools to support schoolwide action research is through giving schools flexibility with time—time within contract parameters for study group and IC meetings and time on professional development days for building-based professional development that supports the school's action research process.

Clear and Collaborative Relationships

Professional Culture and Collaborative Relationships

WFSG districts embody the findings in the literature that Shannon and Bylsma (2004) surveyed for building a professional culture and collaborative relationships. They found that districts with improved student achievement

> build a culture of commitment, collegiality, mutual respect, and stability. Professional norms include peer support, collaboration, trust, shared responsibility, and continuous learning for the adults in the system. Districts support school communities of practice and also develop central offices as professional learning communities. (p. 46)

The WFSG System is an approach explicitly designed to create professional learning communities to improve student learning. It expects study group members to continually develop their knowledge and expertise, and all three of the aforementioned districts emphasize the importance of continuous learning for staff as well as students. In Springfield, for example, teachers also can meet their district and state recertification requirements for continuing professional development through their study group work.

In Hawthorn, the Hawthorn Planning Council, composed of teachers, teaching and learning coaches and administrators from each school, central office staff from all departments, and the union, lead the focus on teaching and learning for the district. In Franklin County, central office staff from all departments meet monthly with principals in countywide study groups to support the study group system. In Springfield, principals meet monthly for principal study group meetings and work collaboratively to address common needs. Both Hawthorn and Franklin County invested in technology to support collaboration. Hawthorn used RubiconAtlas to support sharing among study groups and Just5Clicks to support accessing and sharing data and teachers' unit designs. Franklin County used Blackboard to support cross-school and cross-study group collaboration.

Clear and Effective Roles and Responsibilities

Districts that focus on improving student learning redefine the role of the central office, shifting from top-down, command, and control departments operating independently to central services working collaboratively to support principals and teachers in improving teaching and learning. Karl Weick (1976) described school districts as "loosely coupled systems" where people in different roles, departments, schools, and levels operate relatively independently. Many districts are now trying to create "tightly coupled" teaching and learning systems:

> Improved districts set expectations, decentralize responsibility and support to schools, and serve as change agents enabling schools to improve. Districts restructure central offices to support learning, serve critical roles as mentors, and help seek solutions. Districts balance district authority and school autonomy; they simultaneously empower and control. The central office has responsibility for defining goals and standards; schools have latitude in the use of resources and influence over issues important to school staff. (Shannon & Bylsma, 2004, p. 49)

All three WFSG districts are engaged in multiyear efforts to create tightly coupled systems focused on teaching and learning. In Springfield, the entire district is guided by the district's five-year, comprehensive, school improvement plan and the associated plans for the board, cabinet, central office, departments, and schools. Plans at each level establish expectations and standards and include an accountability system with measurable objectives for each goal. The district's leadership development program is explicitly designed to ensure that school and district leaders understand and implement their role in enhancing teaching and learning. In Hawthorn and Franklin County, central office staff, who are responsible for departments not directly focused on teaching and learning, are still expected to understand how their departments and functions impact teaching and learning and how they can support district goals for improving student achievement.

Interpreting, Managing, and Engaging the External Environment

Leadership in any organization has dual responsibilities to support improved teaching and learning—leading and supporting the internal organization and interpreting, managing, and engaging the external environment. Shannon and Bylsma (2004) identify in the literature several common characteristics of districts that effectively interpret, manage, and engage the external environment:

> Improved districts access, analyze, interpret, and mediate state and federal policy with local policy. Districts buffer schools against external disturbances and distractions, mobilize and manage community and business support, and involve family and community as partners. (p. 52)

Each WFSG district has taken the external pressure for greater performance and accountability and turned it into an opportunity to focus all parts of the district on improving teaching and learning performance and accountability of all stakeholders, including parents and the community, for helping students achieve high standards.

The WFSG System for schoolwide action research was initially developed in 1987, four years after the National Commission on Excellence in Education (1983) published *A Nation at Risk.* It also turned pressures from the external environment for greater performance and accountability into opportunities by expecting every study group in a school to build expertise, improve practice, and increase student learning, and by providing a structure to achieve these goals. But, it also built on needs within schools for greater collaboration, focus, and professional responsibility.

One of the challenges to districts sustaining improvements over time is the lure of the external educational "fad du jour." Teachers are justly cynical about a constant call for new initiatives and programs.

All three of the WFSG districts accept the responsibility for helping schools make thoughtful choices about strategies and programs that could help improve teaching and learning. All three have partnered with the WFSG National Center to support schoolwide action research. Hawthorn is also partnering with the Center for Performance Assessment to shape district work in standards-based instruction and assessment. Springfield is partnering with Jim Shipley & Associates to support continuous classroom improvement in every school. Franklin County is partnering with the Centers for Quality Teaching and Learning to infuse quality teaching strategies into every study group and every classroom.

RESOURCES FOR SCHOOLS AND DISTRICTS DOING SCHOOLWIDE ACTION RESEARCH

Context, process, and content are the three dimensions of the National Staff Development Council's Standards for Staff Development and are the three dimensions describing the WFSG System for schoolwide action research. Schools and districts may need external assistance in one or more of these dimensions as they launch and implement schoolwide action research.

The National WFSG Center

The National WFSG Center assists schools and districts with context and process: how to plan, launch, implement, support, and evaluate schoolwide action research. Entities such as the Centers for Quality Teaching and Learning, Learner Focused Schools, the Louisiana LINCS program, and ATLAS Learning Communities assist schools and districts with content: what study group members teach and how they teach to improve student learning. The Centers for Quality Teaching and Learning and ATLAS Learning Communities also offer support in all three dimensions for schools and districts that want comprehensive programs.

The National WFSG Center was formed in 2004 with a mission "to ensure student achievement through the authentic application of the WFSG System in schools worldwide." The Center founder and executive director is Carlene Murphy, the creator of the WFSG System, and it is located in Augusta, Georgia. The current Center staff is composed of four WFSG consultants who live in different sections of the country and work full or part time for the Center. Karl Clauset, the lead author for this book, is the Center director and one of the WFSG consultants.

The Center supports schools and districts in planning, launching, implementing, supporting, and evaluating schoolwide action research through programs, technical assistance and consultation, and implementation tools.

Support for planning and launching a schoolwide action research system is provided by the Center through a training institute, technical assistance, and implementation tools. The WFSG Level I Institute, "The ABCs of Getting Started," is a two-and-a-half-day interactive workshop to help participants learn about the WFSG System and how to launch it. School focus teams go step-by-step through the WFSG DMC so that they can learn how to lead their faculty through an orientation to study groups and the DMC. Participants receive a copy of Murphy and Lick's 2005 WFSG book and a binder with implementation materials. The institute is offered in Augusta, Georgia, in February, June, and July, and can be offered on-site in a district. Institute objectives are listed in Resource F.

The Center staff can also assist schools and districts on-site with planning, launching, implementing, and evaluating the application of their study group system. They can work collaboratively with school focus teams or lead the orientation and launch themselves. As described in the illustrative three-year implementation plan (Resource E) and Center services (Resource F), Center consultants provide follow-up support to schools and districts during the first three years of implementation.

For schools and districts that have begun implementing schoolwide action research, the Center offers an annual conference in Augusta in February for teams from different schools and districts to share their work and deepen their understanding of the WFSG System and its network. The Center also offers a two-day Level II institute, "Continuing and Deepening the Work of the Whole-Faculty Study Groups and Focusing on Impact," in February, June, and July in Augusta. This institute for school and district teams is designed to address specific implementation challenges they are experiencing and to strengthen their understanding of the WFSG System and of leading change.

Murphy (2007b) describes the National WFSG Center in more detail in Chapter 30, "Establishing a Support Network: The National Whole-Faculty Study Groups Center," in Lick and Murphy's (2007) *The Whole-Faculty Study Groups Fieldbook*.

Other Helpful Organizations

In Chapter 5, we described how organizations such as the Centers for Quality Teaching and Learning, Learner Focused Schools, the Louisiana Learning-Intensive Networking Communities for Success (LINCS) program, and ATLAS Learning Communities help teachers build knowledge and expertise in the content and pedagogy they use to address specific student learning needs.

To briefly recapitulate, the Centers for Quality Teaching and Learning works with a number of schools in North Carolina, Virginia, and Georgia to provide the teachers in the school with a repertoire of research-based instructional strategies that they can use to address specific student needs. QTL training addresses learning styles, brain-based and cooperative learning, diversity and differentiation, multiple intelligences and inquiry and problem-based learning, direct instruction and cooperative grouping, a field study using a constructivist approach to instruction, and culminating group presentations. Each strategy is presented, modeled, and practiced, and teachers are able to apply them immediately to their own classroom instruction.

Many WFSG schools in Georgia use instructional strategies and the lesson- and unit-planning model from Learning-Focused Schools. The model guides teachers in designing learning units that preview the unit with a student learning map and key vocabulary and offers concept and skill acquisition lessons with essential questions and activities to motivate and activate prior knowledge. It also trains teachers to use specific teaching strategies such as collaborative pairs, mnemonics and graphic organizers, and summarization, and creates, extends, and refines lessons and tasks that emphasize critical thinking skills activities.

ATLAS Learning Communities, one of the original New American Schools designs and now a national Comprehensive School Reform design, helps teachers build expertise in using techniques, methods, and strategies that develop deep understanding and incorporate authentic assessment. ATLAS offers an annual summer institute, Pathways for Understanding, that focuses on helping teachers and administrators identify the dimensions of understanding and visible thinking routines and apply them to designing curriculum, instruction, and assessment for understanding.

The Louisiana LINCS program has a professional development process for low-performing schools that provides a LINCS coach, who works alongside classroom teachers, modeling lessons and coaching, to support study groups and the implementation of standards-based teaching and learning strategies. LINCS also provides for teams from each school summer programs at universities on content and pedagogy in math and language arts.

CONCLUSIONS

Chapter 8 explored how district context and support are fundamental to the success of schoolwide action research to improve student learning. The chapter also described the roles that external organizations are playing in supporting districts and schools in implementing the WFSG System for schoolwide action research.

There are several key points to remember about enabling schools to be successful with schoolwide action research that improve teacher practice and student learning. The astute reader will recognize that some of these key points are the same as key points we made in earlier chapters. This is because district staff and external organizations have the same responsibility to support principals and schools as principals have to support study groups within their schools.

- *District professional development becomes "data- and demand-driven."*

  If the guiding question for a school's professional development program is "What do our study groups need to help them more effectively address our students' learning needs?" then the guiding question for districts is "What do our schools need to help them to more effectively meet the professional development needs of their study groups?" It is data-driven because study group learning needs are based on the student learning needs that are derived from student learning data.

  It is demand-driven because what professional development to offer and when to offer it depends on the specific needs and timing for each school. As we noted in Chapter 5, a principal knows his or her study groups' learning needs within three or four weeks of forming study groups in the fall.

- *Each school and each principal have different needs and different areas of expertise.*

  Both Springfield Public Schools and the Franklin County Schools created administrative study groups to provide opportunities for support and collaboration for principals. Both districts provide schools with support through curriculum or instructional specialists. Springfield has a formal induction and mentoring program to help new principals become successful instructional leaders.

- *Both pressure and support are important.*

  Just as principals provide pressure and support for study groups, district leaders must provide both pressure and support for principals and their faculties. The first two points listed earlier emphasize support, so we focus on the pressure part here.

  The old adage, "what's inspected gets respected," holds true in the WFSG System at both the school level, principal to study groups, and at the district level, district leaders to principals. One key to institutionalization of the WFSG System is aligning the human resource system to support collaborative schoolwide action research. This means aligning teacher contracts, recruitment, retention, reward, and supervision practices to support study group work and continual improvements in teacher practice and student learning. It also means aligning the principal contracts, recruitment, retention, reward, and supervision practices to support creating a collaborative climate in each school for study group work and continual improvements in teacher practice and student learning.

- *This work is about changing the district culture.*

  If the WFSG approach to schoolwide action research is about changing the culture of the school to embody distributive leadership, a culture of collaboration and shared responsibility for the success of all students, experimentation and risk taking, and continuous improvement of each adult's knowledge and expertise for addressing specific student needs and improving student performance, then district leaders need to align policies and practices to support these same attributes in every school and within the district office.

- *Success with schoolwide action research requires the active commitment and leadership of district leaders and staff.*

     School districts, like most organizations, have developed policies and procedures to maintain the status quo. Implementing schoolwide action research in one school or all the schools in a district is not maintaining the status quo. Its implementation and institutionalization demands changing the culture. Without the active, daily, commitment of district leaders, principals will not be able to sustain the work. In Franklin County, every central office department head is a member of an administrative study group and is expected to support the study group work in schools. This ultimately requires redefining the role of central office from command and control to that of "central services."

In Chapter 9, we focus on next steps for schoolwide action research. We step back to reflect on what we have written about the WFSG approach to schoolwide action research and the examples we have provided and to think about the challenges ahead for refining, extending, and supporting this approach to creating professional learning communities that improve teacher practice and student learning.

Taking Schoolwide Action Research to the Next Level

Guiding Question

■ What are the challenges for taking the WFSG approach to schoolwide action research to the next level?

We believe the challenges of taking schoolwide action research and support for this approach to the next level revolves around the answers to four sets of questions. These sets of questions are directed at those who support teachers in districts—principals, assistant principals, school-based coaches, instructional specialists, curriculum resource teachers, central office staff, superintendents, and school boards—and outside supporters such as Quality Teaching and Learning (QTL) and Whole-Faculty Study Group (WFSG) consultants, Learning-Intensive Networking Communities for Success (LINCS) regional coordinators, teachers' unions, state departments of education, institutions of higher education, foundations, and federal regional laboratories and technical assistance centers. In this chapter, we explore the four challenges and the following sets of questions:

1. Understand the essence of the WFSG System as a bundle of innovations.

   How can we help others understand that the essence of the WFSG System is a bundle of innovations that include different types of, or approaches to, staff development? When should we introduce the concept of the "bundle" and, after the introduction, highlight or underscore the components of the bundle, knowing that several of the components or approaches will need to be taught?

2. Transfer and use—content and pedagogy.

How can we design our work with faculties so teachers will transfer training in skills, content, and teaching strategies to their study group work and use these new skills, content, and strategies consistently and appropriately in their classrooms?

3. Support study groups.

How do we use our tools (e.g., forms, procedures, and processes) to support and direct or redirect study groups?

4. Sustain change.

How well do we understand the complexities of the change process, and what do we need to know and understand about it to be able to support others as they are experiencing the anxieties, frustrations, doubts, resistance, and excitement of new materials, processes, and relationships?

UNDERSTAND THE WFSG SYSTEM AS A BUNDLE OF INNOVATIONS

How can we help others understand that the essence of the WFSG is a bundle of innovations that include different types of, or approaches to, staff development? When should we introduce the concept of the "bundle" and, after the introduction, highlight or underscore the components of the bundle, knowing that several of the components or approaches will need to be taught? For example, we have to teach groups how to conduct action research, how to do a lesson study, and how to coach colleagues.

When fully executed, the WFSG System contains the following approaches to professional development:

- Theory and knowledge development—Study groups read, share, discuss, and use professional materials to strengthen their understanding of content and curriculum, pedagogy, assessment, and their students so that they can design and implement classroom interventions to improve student learning. Some study groups use a common text to guide their work.
- Action research—Study groups engage in cycles of action research described in Chapter 4 to address specific student learning needs: assess students' current levels of proficiency, identify or design interventions, monitor implementation, assess impact, and revise the interventions.
- Coaching and mentoring—As we discussed in Chapter 3, study group members, by being part of a synergistic team and comentoring each other by sharing expertise and offering support and encouragement, expand individual and group understanding and improve the group's effectiveness and productivity. In many WFSG schools, instructional coaches assist and support study

groups. They suggest appropriate instructional strategies to use for specific student learning needs, demonstrate how to use the strategies, help the group plan how to use strategies, observe members as they use strategies, and help debrief and improve implementation.

- Lesson study—As part of improving instruction for a student learning need, a study group uses the Japanese lesson-study process for in-depth work on one or more lessons—researching lesson content, developing a lesson, teaching the lesson, and debriefing the lesson.
- Training—An "expert" works with a study group at one or more study group meetings to strengthen members' understanding of content and curriculum, pedagogy, assessment, and their students. Members also might attend workshops or participate in online courses.
- Practicing, modeling, and demonstrating teaching and learning skills and strategies—This is what study group members do with each other to build their expertise and understand the instructional strategies and interventions they are using with their students. This is the process of "transferring learning to action" in the classroom.
- Looking at student work—Study groups regularly examine samples of student work together to look for evidence of student thinking and understanding, explore possibilities for improving the work, and assess the effectiveness of an instructional strategy or an assessment task. Study groups use a variety of protocols to guide their review of student work, choosing protocols based on what they want to learn about the work.

Leaders know that any major whole-school initiative, no matter what the focus, is complex and multifaceted. We wonder if, in our attempts to enlist schools in a particular initiative, leaders present initiatives too simplistically. Later, when teachers are expected to take certain actions, teachers feel they have been misled and that they did not "sign up" for what we are suggesting they do. On the other hand, "telling all" could create fear and make the faculty hesitant to begin.

We currently give faculties a complete description of the WFSG System, although we may not cover all aspects in our presentations. We give focus teams notebooks that include a section on strategies for study groups to use, for example, lesson study, mentoring and coaching, and training. There is also a chapter in the Murphy and Lick (2005) book on strategies for collaborative work in WFSG. The procedures for using the strategies during study group meetings are also described. We do spend time in our training sessions to demonstrate how to review and use student work. A whole-faculty meeting to review the notebook section or the book chapter is time well spent.

At one time, knowing that the essence of the WFSG System is a bundle of innovations with each having its own set of processes and procedures, Murphy shied away from being too explicit, even to the point of not calling a process what it is. For example, when talking about Step 6 on the Decision-Making Cycle (DMC), she described what groups do but did not use the term *action research*. Her fear was that individuals would say, "You mean we are going to do WFSG and action research (stressing the "and")?" Then, at a school where she was working, teachers indicated that they would be leaving early to go to a workshop. When she inquired about the content of the workshop, one said, "We are going to learn how to do action research." She responded, "You are currently doing action research." She took the experience as a lesson learned. We are now explicit in calling a process the commonly used name for the process.

Letting faculties know that a lesson study can be accomplished in their study group is positive as teachers realize that many processes described in professional journals can be accomplished through WFSG-type processes. As we have become more explicit, we find that teachers actually appreciate the rolling together of different effective working strategies. We hear the following: "It's good to know we can have advanced training in the new math program when our study group meets." If school leaders are not clear on the various strategies that study groups can use to make study group work more meaningful for group members and more beneficial for students, WFSG and other consultants can provide assistance.

This book has focused on one of the approaches to professional development, action research, but within the action research cycle, study groups are usually engaged in theory and knowledge development, training, mentoring, practicing strategies, and reviewing student work. More and more frequently, schools and districts are hiring instructional and content coaches who can coach study groups as well as individual teachers.

There are several challenges that can be better understood and appreciated by viewing the essence of the WFSG System as a bundle of innovations.

1. Helping teachers, school administrators, and district staff recognize the different approaches to professional development within the WFSG bundle

   Sometimes we do not realize we are doing something unless it is named. If the approach isn't named and recognized as a discrete set of actions and activities, how can study groups be reflective about their use of the approach? In the action research cycle, most study groups develop implicit action hypotheses but rarely articulate them. Instead, they tend to jump immediately into a search for strategies to use in class. By naming the step, creating an action hypothesis, study groups can be encouraged to articulate their hypotheses and examine them, both for their robustness and for their implications, before starting the search for interventions. How do we help teachers and administrators name the parts of the WFSG bundle without feeling overwhelmed by complexity?

2. Building the capacity, willingness, and ability of staff to use these approaches in authentic, not imitative, ways

   This is the challenge of building expertise and putting it into use in the study group and the classroom. For example, developing expertise in looking at student work is more than downloading a protocol from the Internet and using it once. It requires using a range of protocols multiple times with different samples of student work and taking time to reflect on both the process and the quality and depth of the discourse. How do we help study groups develop this expertise while keeping in mind that the goal of study groups is to improve student learning?

3. Recognizing that the sense of urgency for gains in student learning within the current school year may lead study groups to not use some of these approaches or only use them superficially

We often tell schools to think about study group work as a spiral, spiraling deeper and deeper into content, instruction, assessment, and professional development over the course of a school year and from year to year, but at the same time, ensuring that the focus remains on trying to achieve measurable gains in student learning in the current year. Should we expect both depth and impact? Can this tension be managed?

The problem-solving study group at Daniel Hale Williams Preparatory School of Medicine in Chicago spent most of a semester using the "Quiet Conversation" strategy with students to help them improve their problem-solving ability. They tried the strategy, assessed results, made modifications, used the strategy again, assessed again, made more modifications, and repeated the cycle. By the end of the semester, they had a much better understanding of how to use the strategy with their students and the impact they had on students' problem-solving ability. They might have had more impact on problem solving if they had tried several strategies during the semester. Should they have been encouraged to move on?

4. Making connections in our efforts to integrate and bring coherence to the professional development initiatives in schools as we work with faculties

Too often district and school leaders initiate new staff development programs that duplicate or minimize a component of study groups. For example, most schools now have "instructional coaches" that function outside of the WFSG System, but could be connected to the study group work, as LINCS, Springfield, Franklin County, and Hawthorn have done. When parallel initiatives are being planned and introduced, how can we build "making connections and links" into school and district training and implementation programs?

Springfield, in the 2006–2007 school year, piloted the Continuous Quality Improvement (CQI) process in several schools that had also been implementing study groups for three to five years. As we described in Chapter 5, this process asks teachers to work with students in a weekly Plan-Do-Study-Act (PDSA) process to set instructional goals and provide instruction and cooperative learning activities that build student proficiency and engagement. Some of the schools immediately saw the connections between the schoolwide action research cycle and the CQI- PDSA cycle and realized that teachers could work together in study groups to support their CQI work. How can the district, as it continues to spread CQI throughout the district, build in connections and links with the WFSG System that schools are already using?

TRANSFER AND USE—CONTENT AND PEDAGOGY

How can we design our work with faculties so that teachers will transfer training in skills, content, and teaching strategies to their study group work and use these new skills, content, and strategies consistently and appropriately in their classrooms?

The expected outcome of the work of study groups for students is a measurable increase in student learning in the need or skill targeted by a study group. Joyce and Showers (2002) emphasize that the classroom

is the place where the interface between staff development and student achievement exists. The learning environment of the students changes, and those changes are of a quality and amount that enable increased learning to take place. (p. 71, italics in the original)

If we equate professional learning communities with other types of training and development experiences, Joyce and Showers (2002) describe the expected outcomes of study groups for teachers as the following:

- Knowledge or awareness of educational theories and practices, new curricula, and academic content
- Positive changes in attitudes toward self (role perception changes), children (poor, minorities, handicapped, gifted), and academic content (science, reading, math)
- Development of skill (the ability to perform discrete behaviors, such as designing and delivering questions of various cognitive levels, or teaching an instructional strategy, such as mnemonics)
- Transfer of training to the classroom with the consistent and appropriate use of new skills and strategies for classroom instruction

How easy it is for teachers to achieve these outcomes depends on the relationship of the new knowledge, skills, and strategies to teachers' existing repertoire and to the complexity of the new learning (Joyce & Showers, 2002). If teachers in a study group have experience using math manipulatives, it will be easier for them to learn to use a new manipulative than if they have no experience.

Joyce and Showers (2002) state that transfer of training to the classroom with the consistent and appropriate use of new skills and strategies for classroom instruction is the highest level of transfer, what they call Level 5 or "executive use" (p. 102). The other four levels are as follows: Level 1—imitative use, Level 2—mechanical use, Level 3—routine use, and Level 4—integrated use. These are similar to the levels of use in the Concerns-Based Adoption Model (Hall et al., 1975).

They also concluded from a review of the research on transfer that transfer of skills and strategies to the classroom requires the components of formal training (study of theory, demonstrations, and practice) and peer coaching during application in the classroom (Joyce & Showers, 2002, p. 77).

If the expected outcomes of study groups are supported and expanded through formal training activities, such as workshops, courses, and conferences, and reinforced through coaching, peer coaching, and mentoring, how do we create these opportunities for every study group to attain executive use of the skills and strategies they use?

This question pinpoints what initially captured Murphy's interest in working with Bruce Joyce and Beverly Showers. Having been a district staff developer since 1977, in the early 1980s, Murphy began to question the impact district staff development efforts were having on student learning in schools. As she visited schools, she saw little evidence of sustained, appropriate use of techniques and strategies that were the focus of workshops and courses.

The concerns Murphy felt in the 1980s continue to nag at us today. As expressed earlier, if teachers are expected to use new practices in the classroom, trainers need to know how to build theory-practice-demonstration into their skill-building training designs, or school leaders need to help study groups build the training components into study group work through the feedback they give.

When Murphy meets with a study group focusing on a specific instructional skill or strategy, she asks the following: "Do you understand why this skill works? "Have you seen a demonstration of this skill (trainer, colleague, video)?" "Have you built into your work opportunities for members to practice the skill during a study group meeting?"

It is not unusual for teachers to become frustrated and put a proven teaching practice aside because they are unsure or uncomfortable with its use. Spending a faculty meeting on understanding the importance of the levels of use of an innovation (Hall et al., 1975) is time well spent.

A concern about study groups with members who have not attended formal training in teaching strategies they want to use in their classrooms is that the teachers might go through action research cycles without developing deep understanding and proficiency. For example, if a study group is going to use the district's new math program to address student learning needs in math, WFSG consultants do not know if the teachers understand the theory that supports the new math program, have had opportunities to practice using new materials and strategies in the training, or saw multiple demonstrations of appropriate use of the new materials and strategies. If these opportunities were not provided, members of a study group may misuse the materials and strategies and students may not get maximum benefit from the new math program, which would reduce the group's impact on student learning.

In Franklin County, curriculum resource teachers provide resources, modeling, and support for groups to help build their expertise. In the QTL implementation of WFSG, the QTL expert consultants coach and support study groups in the strategies and serve as WFSG consultants. Usually, school leaders are in the best position to know the training conditions of new initiatives, be in contact with the trainers and, through feedback, provide direction to groups.

SUPPORT STUDY GROUPS

How do we use our tools (forms, procedures, processes) to support and direct or redirect study groups?

The tools of our trade are the study group action plan and log forms and checklists we use and give faculties to use, the procedures we ask faculties to follow, and the protocols and processes we train faculties to use in decision making and looking at student work. Tools are artifacts we ask study groups to save, such as prestudent and poststudent assessments, scoring rubrics, instructional strategies they use, and articles and resources they find. Tools are the journaling, or videotaping, or classroom visits that study groups do as they observe students responding to new strategies or learning new skills. Tools are also training and evaluation materials, such as the Faculty Workbook for the DMC (Murphy & Lick, 2005) and the WFSG rubric (see Resource A). Tools are the strategies and guidelines we have developed for working with "stuck" study groups that may be stuck because of context, process, or content concerns (Murphy & Lick, 2005, Chapter 10).

Just as carpenters need tools to build high-quality cabinets, we need adequate and appropriate tools to help study groups do high-quality work. But carpenters also need to know how to use their tools correctly, and so do we. If we expect teachers in study groups to achieve Level 5, executive use of the strategies they use with students, shouldn't we, the people who support study groups, have Level 5 use of the tools and strategies in the study group "toolbox"?

A corollary question is whether we have the right tools, or too many or too few, to support and direct or redirect study groups. For example, we have revised the forms for study group action plans and logs several times over the last 10 years. Are the new forms better than the old ones at helping study groups do quality work and document that work, or do groups perceive completing these forms as "busy" work?

Supporting WFSG work can come in many forms and be delivered by individuals on-site or off-site, by reading publications, and by watching videos. The most effective support comes from building and district leaders. There is no long-term substitute for knowledgeable, skillful, local leaders.

SUSTAIN CHANGE

How well do we understand the complexities of the change process and what do we need to know and understand about it to be able to support others as they are experiencing the anxieties, frustrations, doubts, resistance, and excitement of new materials, processes, and relationships?

Often we become frustrated with others and ourselves because we may not appreciate and understand the complexity of feelings that individuals experience when they encounter new materials, beliefs, expectations, relationships, and processes. Usually, our first tendency is to blame others or ourselves for not attaining the level of success we desire.

We argued in Chapter 3 that most innovations in schools fail because leaders and others involved had

- Not reframed their own thinking from reactive change management to proactive change creation
- Implemented an incomplete and inadequate strategic-planning approach that failed to build understanding and commitment
- Failed to prepare their school for the important transformations that major change requires, including not adequately implementing the universal change principle, *learning must precede change*
- Not provided and implemented a detailed plan that would transition people, processes, and the culture from the old paradigm to the new one

We wonder to what extent we have created our own problems by being reluctant to tell faculties that implementing schoolwide action research, with its bundle of imbedded approaches to professional development, represents a major cultural transformation for most schools. As Joyce and Showers observed, it represents the type of innovation that is both complex and far from a faculty's existing repertoire of skills and knowledge. The WFSG System and its study groups are like the Trojan Horse, deceptively simple and unthreatening on the outside, but full of complexity and transformational demands of teachers and leaders on the inside.

When schools have started implementing the WFSG System, how do we help leaders and their faculty see that study groups really are a vehicle to improve student learning rather than "just another program or fad"? We say that the only way to convince people of this is for them to follow faithfully the WFSG process and experience success as a study group. For this to occur, we need to help every study group be successful, which means the groups are functioning as genuine, synergistic, learning teams.

We do know that without some form of support through the initiation and implementation stages, institutionalization is unlikely. The pitfalls along the way are too easy to fall into. However, support without pressure to use resources provided often results in waste or misuse of the resources. Through the research on change, we know the value of support and pressure (Murphy & Lick, 2005, p. 186).

Supports for WFSG in Franklin County Schools

District and school administrators in Franklin County Schools give both support and pressure. Most of the support strategies were not initiated because the district is implementing WFSG. Once the WFSG System was put into place, the question became as follows: "What do we already have in place that will support WFSG? Or, as new technology was purchased for instructional use, the question was as follows: "How can we also use the technology to support WFSG?

In support of WFSG, Franklin County

- *Provides early release time for study group meetings*
- *Has Carlene Murphy and other consultants returning to the district*
- *Has all district and school administrations meet regularly in countywide study groups*
- *Assigns district-level staff to schools to guide WFSG implementation*
- *Has district-level study groups in math and reading with members from elementary and middle schools provide support to school-based reading and math study groups*
- *Provides opportunities for teachers from each school to attend the annual National WFSG Conference in Augusta, Georgia*
- *Provides video conferencing capability in all schools so study groups across the district can communicate without having to travel*
- *Provides instructional strategies specialists from Centers for Quality Teaching and Learning to train and work with teachers to use WFSG to practice and further develop new teaching practices*
- *Provides a Web-based electronic system for cross-school communication and collaboration among schools*
- *Provides teachers with interactive classroom technology with the expectation that study groups would be the place to learn and practice appropriate use*
- *Includes information about WFSG in interviews with prospective new teachers so that participation is an expectation on being hired*
- *Puts dates for school Instructional Council meetings on the district calendar*
- *Provides benchmark assessments so teachers would have current data regarding student progress*
- *Communicates with the community and board members about study group work*
- *Assigns a Curriculum Resource Teacher to each school whose job description includes the support of WFSG*

Pressure is often felt through support channels. Providing release time means principals and teachers are accountable for time spent in study group meetings. District level administrators and support staff "circulate" during early release time. Making presentations to the Board of Education and placing articles in school and community newsletters about the status of implementation and results of WFSG indicate the importance of staying true to the design. New technology systems mean posting WFSG action plans and logs on school Web sites is an expectation.

Making public study group work is one of the guiding principles of WFSG. Benchmark assessments make public what students are doing and the impact WFSG are making on specific skills being targeted. These assessments make accountability a top priority. Establishing dates for school Instructional Councils to meet means that the sharing of study group work is public and that this important aspect of the WFSG System is not ignored. Minutes of council meetings are sent to designated district administrators who give feedback to schools.

One of the most effective support-pressure strategies is the routine practice of the Franklin County School District's superintendent of visiting schools and, at such times, making inquires about WFSG work with principals and teachers. These regular visits reinforce the superintendent's public commitment to the innovation.

All of the support and pressure mechanisms being used in Franklin County were not put into place overnight or for the sole purpose of supporting WFSG. Each mechanism or strategy took careful, thoughtful, and deliberate planning and execution from many people. For a major innovation to be sustained, it takes many people working together through various programs and initiatives for any single initiative to impact student performance. Often, sustainability is only possible through the integration of a school district's instructional initiatives so that teachers do not see each initiative as separate or another thing to do.

How important is internal and external support to sustaining an innovation over time? The answer is the same as the answer to the following question: "How important is breathing to living?" Support can come from a mixture of individuals and materials. For school leaders, external support can come from district leaders, individuals from other district schools, and individuals from outside the district.

Those at the National WFSG Center have devoted considerable energy to helping schools and districts launch and implement the WFSG System and implement effective schoolwide action research. Usually the focus is on the first three to five years of implementation.

During this period the goal is twofold: (1) to enable study groups to become learning teams doing extensive, focused, self-directed collaborative action research, and to enable the school and its entire staff to become a learning community with an overarching goal and schoolwide vision, mission, and implementation plan integrating effective teaching and learning practices into school programs to improve student learning; and (2) to embed the work in the institutional fabric of budgets, calendars, contracts, professional development, recruiting, supervising, and evaluating staff and leaders, so that engaging in study groups and schoolwide action research becomes "the way we do things."

We have found that the biggest challenges to institutionalization of study groups and schoolwide action research are new district initiatives and leadership transitions at the school and district level.

Hargreaves and Fink (2006, pp. 8–9) cite the change-management expert Eric Abrahamson's repetitive change syndrome that encompasses initiative overload from too many initiatives and change-related chaos from constant upheaval as the modus operandi in many school systems. No wonder that many teachers are distrustful and cynical when study groups and schoolwide action research, or the WFSG System, are first presented to them by their colleagues.

The second challenge to institutionalization is frequent leadership turnover coupled with the belief that every new leader has to take the school or district in an entirely different direction. Many schools and districts resemble sailboats on a sunny day, tacking aimlessly around and going nowhere at all. Springfield, now in its sixth year with the WFSG System in 2006 and 2007, has instituted a leadership development program to ensure that new principals maintain the course and sustain a superintendent transition with the new superintendent maintaining the WFSG System.

This book has used examples ranging from single schools implementing study groups and schoolwide action research to districts where all schools in the district are implementing these. One question to consider about institutionalization is this: Can study groups and schoolwide action research become institutionalized in a single school in a district?

Before answering this question, let us describe two districts that have institutionalized WFSG with two different approaches to supporting schools: Springfield Public Schools in Missouri and Franklin County Schools in North Carolina.

Springfield Public Schools

Springfield, Missouri, is a large, urban district of 51 schools. In the spring of 2003, Murphy traveled to Springfield once to introduce school and district administrators and district support staff to WFSG in a two-day session. Members of the district's instructional staff attended training in Augusta, Georgia, during the summers of 2003, 2004, 2005, and 2006. As new staff members were hired, individuals committed to the summer training. Representatives from the district's instructional staff and from schools attended the National WFSG Conferences from 2004–2007.

During the 2004–2005 school year, a consultant from the WFSG National Center visited the district once a month to meet with principals. Principal study groups were organized and continue to meet. The job description of instructional staff was revised to include supporting WFSG work in schools. The district built the expectations for supporting WFSG into the evaluation process for administrators. The district built in the expectation for teachers to participate in WFSG in personnel policies and hiring practices. A new superintendent was hired by the board of education at the beginning of the 2006–2007 school year. Because of the existing commitment to WFSG, the new superintendent continued to support the WFSG work in schools.

Franklin County Schools

Franklin County is a small, rural district in North Carolina with 13 schools. The district purchased 25 days of Murphy's time during its first year of implementation, the 2004–2005 school year; 20 days the second year; and 15 days the third year. Representatives from every school have attended the 2005, 2006, and 2007 National WFSG Conferences. In 2007, a study group from each school made a presentation at the conference, describing its work. Administrative study groups met twice a month and the groups included all principals and district staff. Minutes from the schools' Instructional Council meetings were sent to the superintendent and feedback was given to the schools. The district calendar reflected 13 early release days for WFSG to meet. During the 2006–2007 school year, the district contracted with the Centers for Quality Teaching and Learning to train faculties on effective teaching strategies. During the 2007–2008 school year, the individual who did the training is returning to the district to coach teachers through the process of integrating the teaching strategies into their WFSG work. All teachers in the district are members of WFSG. A district staff member now has support of WFSG as part of her job description.

Springfield used an approach that included a limited use of on-site external consultants. Franklin County used an approach that maximized on-site consultation. Both districts used a variety of funding sources to support the work, including local funds, state funds, title funds, and special project or grant funds. Both districts, after selecting WFSG as its major school improvement design, earmarked resources and personnel to ensure that the system would be implemented with integrity.

Both are examples of school districts that, through their leaders' actions, have set high expectations for teachers to use WFSG as the structure to work on the work of teaching and learning.

We have not seen that a single school, without the support of the district, can over time sustain a whole school initiative. Schools can begin an initiative with limited support from the district but institutionalization is unlikely. Murphy, Clauset, and the other WFSG consultants have worked with hundreds of faculties that tried to "go it alone." Most did a Herculean job of implementation and saw results. However, after three or four years, the demands to implement programs initiated by district leaders who did not take into consideration what the schools are already doing, make continuation very difficult and create a sense of overload that completely demoralizes teachers. There are single schools that have successfully institutionalized WFSG in districts where district leaders essentially leave the school alone. Placing in a school a new principal who does not understand or want to understand what the faculty is already doing is death to a schoolwide structure that requires administrative support.

Even getting to the institutionalization stage does not mean that the WFSG System is sustainable in schools and districts over time. Fullan (2005) defines educational sustainability as "the capacity of a system to engage in the complexities of continuous improvement consistent with deep values of human purpose" (p. ix). Hargreaves and Fink (2006) suggest that "sustainable educational leadership and improvement preserves and develops deep learning for all that spreads and lasts, in ways that do no harm to and indeed create positive benefits for others around us, now and in the future"(p. 17).

Despite the fact that schools have been implementing study groups since the early 1990s, we still don't know much about their sustainability. So, the real challenge for us is to assess whether the study groups and schoolwide action research have the capacity for being sustainable and what we need to do to increase the likelihood of their sustainability.

As we noted in Chapter 6, there has been very little formal research done on the WFSG System. There have only been six dissertations on WFSG and no funded research. None of the research has addressed the impact of WFSG schoolwide action research on student learning, an in-depth analysis of changes in teacher practice, or the challenges and success in long-term institutionalization. We would love to have a cadre of doctoral students or funded researchers address the issues we have described.

We do expect, though, that the WFSG learning community, composed of study groups, schools, districts, and external organizations, will generate responses to these questions that enable us to create a sustainable future for study groups and schoolwide action research.

It is only fitting that Carlene Murphy, the founder and chief architect of the WFSG System, shares in the Epilogue that follows, her vision of the past and future for the WFSG System for schoolwide action research, the building of professional learning communities, and the improvement of student learning and teacher practices.

Epilogue

Carlene U. Murphy

REFLECTIONS

As I reflect on the contents of this book, I am again struck by the courage of the district staff, principals, and teachers in Augusta, Georgia, in 1987, when we began implementing an undocumented school improvement strategy. We determined to figure out, in the school district where I was the director of staff development, how to redesign the workplace of teaching so that students would learn more.

To be asked by teachers, "Where else are they doing what you are asking us to do?" and not have an answer was scary. Today, to begin an initiative, most faculties will not begin unless they have multiple sources of evidence that show the initiative is "tried and true." Leaders wisely want evidence of success and, when given data collected from other schools, question the data in its application to their school.

Trailblazers cut the path for others to follow. In 1987, three Augusta schools were the trailblazers at a time when much of what we hear about today, such as professional learning communities, wasn't even a blip on the staff development radar screen. To begin a major school improvement effort, committing most of a district's staff development resources without evidence of prior success was heroic.

We had evidence that the different components worked independently. Joyce and Showers (1983) had a proven training design. Working with individuals enrolled in a training program, they had also shown the effectiveness of peer support in the workplace. We did not have documentation of what would happen in terms of student results if we integrated the proven training design with workplace support for a whole faculty.

Without the trailblazers in education, technology, medicine, and other fields of science, we would not have the advanced society we have today. Few have the will and the skill to be true trailblazers, to go where no one has gone. Often, trailblazers do not know they are venturing into the unknown. Such was the case in Augusta.

Without the genius of Bruce Joyce and his mentoring of me from 1987 through 1992, this book and all references to whole-faculty study groups would not exist. Bruce Joyce, with Beverly Showers, mentored me every step of the way through a massive school improvement effort when I was director of staff development in the Richmond County, Augusta, Georgia, School District (Murphy, J. A., Murphy, C. U., Joyce, & Showers, 1988).

Bruce Joyce taught me the basics and inspired me to learn more about how to think about the change process; how to work with others through the change process; how to design training; how to support faculties in the initiation, implementation, and institutionalization stages of the change process; the importance of data analysis and collection; how to use several models of teaching with adult learners and with students at all grade levels; and the mechanics and logistics for redesigning the workplace. His greatest gift was to encourage me to be kind to individuals as they struggle with change. As of this writing, I have not worked with Bruce in 16 years. Yet his influence on my thinking and actions is fundamental to all I do professionally.

As I reflect on the three schools in the project in Augusta where the whole faculty were involved and on other schools where groundbreaking work has been done, I am reminded of a statement attributed to Ron Edmonds (1979): "If you have seen one, how many more do you need to see to believe?" Fifteen years later, we have other WFSG schools where synergistic teaching and learning environments are being created, and I ask the same question: How many more do you need to see to believe?

CONNECTING THE PAST TO THE PRESENT AND FUTURE

What does the work we did over 20 years ago have to do with this book and with current and future WFSG work?

It has everything to do with what we do today and what we do tomorrow. The past leads us to where we are today and, when shaped by the present, takes us to where we will be tomorrow.

As I review current work being led by the brightest minds in education today, I see the same goal we established two decades ago: determining how to redesign the workplace of teaching so that students will learn more. Even though many of us have made great strides in the right direction, I use as my measuring stick what Bruce Joyce and Beverly Showers wrote in 1983 in an Association for Supervision and Curriculum Development publication, *Power in Staff Development Through Research on Training:*

> We would build a synergistic environment where collective enterprises are both normal and sustaining and where continuous training and study both of academic substance and the craft of teaching are woven into the fabric of the school, bringing satisfaction by virtue of an increasing sense of growth and competence. Thus, we envision a major change in the ecology of professional life. (p. 1)

It is 2008; are we there yet?

As a profession, we are not there yet; but, we are not as far away as we were.

Currently, collaborative enterprises are becoming more the norm. Expectations are higher for teacher collaboration as demonstrated by the National Staff Development Council staff development standards for learning communities (NSDC, 2001). But how that collaboration looks in practice still varies greatly. While we would expect variation in the sense that teachers and students in schools have different needs, the challenge is that we still see wide variation in the degree to which *"continuous training and study both of academic substance and the craft of teaching are woven into the fabric of the school"* (Joyce & Showers, 1983, p. 1, emphasis added).

The future holds many opportunities and challenges for the WFSG System.

NEW OPPORTUNITIES FOR WFSG

State Networks

The State of Nebraska is building on its commitment to local standards and assessments to introduce the WFSG System statewide. During the 2006–2007 school year, staff at the Nebraska Department of Education's Office of Professional Development invited me to present an overview of the WFSG System at the Excellence in Education Conference for schools, districts, and the regional Educational Service Units (ESUs). Department staff also attended a WFSG training institute to learn more about WFSG. Building on the interest generated at the conference, the department organized a summer WFSG training institute in Nebraska. More than 100 people from schools, district offices, and ESUs attended the training institute. As a result of the institute, two districts launched WFSG in September 2007, two other districts are planning to launch during the 2007–2008 school year, and a fifth district is planning to launch during the 2008–2009 school year. Plans for the 2007–2008 school year include on-site and remote support from the National WFSG Center and two training institutes in the summer of 2008: a Level 1 institute for new schools and districts and a Level 2 institute for schools and districts that have already launched WFSG. The Department of Education has set up a Web site for the initiative: http://www.nde.state.ne.us/WFSG/index.htm.

Since much of Nebraska is rural, the goal for the Nebraska initiative in the coming years is to use distance learning technology and the ESUs to build local capacity to support WFSG and to infuse into the state's preservice teacher and administrator preparation programs the principles of professional learning communities engaged in schoolwide action research to improve teacher practice and student learning.

WFSG Design Schools

Most schools that launch WFSG are public schools that are incorporating the WFSG design into existing structures and cultures. To our knowledge, the only school that was designed from Day 1 to implement WFSG is the Daniel Hale Williams Preparatory School of Medicine in Chicago. The Grade 7–12 school is one of Chicago's Renaissance 2010 schools that began in September 2005.

The WFSG design holds particular promise for reconstituted public schools or new charter schools that wish to build a school culture and structure around professional learning communities engaged in schoolwide action research to improve student learning.

Field Research

While we know that every component of the WFSG System is built on a solid research base and hundreds of schools have implemented it since 1993, there has been no funded research of the WFSG System and only six doctoral dissertations on WFSG have been published. WFSG is a national school improvement design that is not adequately visible on the educational research radar screen.

There are many research opportunities within the WFSG System for understanding the process and its impact. For example, since study groups work autonomously, we have little firsthand information about how study groups actually become synergistic learning teams and what impact context and external support play in enhancing or inhibiting the process. We also have little information about the complexity of institutionalizing WFSG in a school or district. Neither we nor our colleagues in schools and districts have the time or resources to document and analyze their efforts to sustain WFSG, which hampers our ability to distill and share the lessons learned with others.

Saying that WFSG study groups impact student learning is easier than proving it. As the North Carolina example in Chapter 6 illustrates, it is difficult to separate from other factors the effects of WFSG study groups on student performance on district and state assessments. We also do not have any studies on whether WFSG leads to sustained changes in teacher practice and proficiency. Do teachers really develop proficiency with new strategies through the WFSG process?

These areas for field research are both potential dissertation topics and opportunities for projects by education students that relate to their courses.

Building Connections With Colleges and Universities

Shouldn't aspiring teachers and administrators learn about and experience working in professional learning communities that improve teacher practice and student learning as part of their preservice training program, rather than after they start their jobs?

It would be exciting to build on college and university partnerships with districts in preservice education to include WFSG as part of the program design so that student teachers and administrative interns experience the WFSG approach during their training.

Building connections with colleges and universities not only builds understanding about the value of focused collaboration, it also could help with two of our other wishes—promoting more research on WFSG and raising the bar.

THE CHALLENGES FOR WFSG

Raising the Bar

In describing the role of school and district leaders in supporting WFSG in Chapters 3, 5 , 6, 7 , 8, and 9, we were focused on how they can act to "raise the bar" on the quality of study group work and the way their WFSG System operates. The National WFSG Center team also needs to raise the bar both on the services we provide to WFSG schools and districts and on the WFSG System.

How can we use technology to support distance coaching and WFSG professional development? Services such as PD 360 provide ways for teachers to assess high-quality content and teaching strategies on demand. Similarly, the WFSG Center could offer WFSG professional development video modules on demand.

How can we improve the quality of the WFSG institutes and conferences so that schools and districts continue to see their value and relevance as they move from launch to institutionalization? This summer, we redesigned the Level 2 institute to respond to the needs of the schools attending. We also changed the structure of the annual conference to emphasize study group sharing. What else do we need to change?

We also need to think about how to improve the WFSG System. Over the past five years we have worked to improve the action research and data components of the system and have become much more explicit about the value of using protocols for looking at student work. We think the next five years should focus on creating structures that help study groups and the leaders who support them to understand the value of developing real proficiency in content and a repertoire of instructional strategies. This is a challenge of instilling the rigor of Models of Teaching, where WFSG started 20 years ago, without prescribing Models of Teaching as the design.

Creating a Global Community of WFSG

We need a low-cost, easily accessible "MySpace" or "Facebook" page for WFSG study groups. The National WFSG Center team members are human bumblebees flying from one WFSG "field" to another to cross-pollinate study groups by telling them about what another study group in a different city, state, or country is doing with the same set of student needs. Why can't study groups use the Internet to build their own virtual professional learning community of study groups working on similar student needs, where they could share their plans and logs, resources found and used, and their triumphs and failures? Our colleagues at RubiconAtlas in Portland, Oregon, have generously created a WFSG Web environment to support this collaboration, but only a few WFSG schools are using it, often because their district is using different technology.

Collaborating Among National Leaders and Consultants in Professional Learning Communities (PLC)

Those of us who provide consultation to faculties in structures or systems to support professional learning communities seldom collaborate with each other. We read and get secondhand information about each others' work. From a business perspective, we seem to see each other as competition. When I work with leaders in state departments, districts, and schools, I am often asked to compare my work with another consultant's work. I resist doing so and try to focus on how the work is the same but with different strategies. A network for sharing "what we learned today" would keep PLC consultants from reinventing the wheel and help us integrate the very best of our designs.

Passing the Baton

A final challenge for us is engaging a new generation of people in the work of the National WFSG Center. It is our hope and plan to build a new leadership cadre for the Center from among those in schools, districts, and external organizations who are working with WFSG and see both the value and potential of the WFSG System.

FUTURE ECOLOGY OF PROFESSIONAL LIFE

Our understanding of how to build systems in schools that target increases in student learning is growing. The future is bright as educators learn from each other and hold each other accountable for the time, energy, and resources allocated for teacher collaboration.

As I look into the future of the schools that my great-grandchildren and their children will attend, I see schools that are learning communities and learning laboratories for everyone. Teachers and leaders view themselves as students, always learning, experimenting, and exploring in collaboration with their colleagues. Students view themselves in the same ways with confidence and self-reliance, with success, and with an eagerness to know and understand their worlds and the people in them.

What more could we wish for future generations than to have schools where the work of adults and children, as Joyce and Showers said, *"bring satisfaction by virtue of an increasing sense of growth and competence"* (1983, p. 1, emphasis added).

Resources

Resource A

WFSG RUBRIC OR INNOVATION CONFIGURATION

- A rubric is an innovation configuration in that it identifies or describes the different components of an innovation. Going deeper into each component, it describes the practices or behaviors within each component. Rubrics represent the patterns of innovation use, usually on a scale using specific descriptors of behavior, and are ways to precisely define quality and measure fidelity.
- The components of the Whole-Faculty Study Groups (WFSG) System are context, process, and content.
- Every faculty member should have a copy of the WFSG rubric.
- At predetermined intervals during the school year, as individuals, each teacher completes the rubric, placing his or her study group where he or she perceives the group is in its implementation of the WFSG System. This is done prior to a study group meeting. When the study groups meet, members share how they scored the rubric and discuss differences in perception. A consensus is reached and one marked rubric will represent one study group.
- Study groups also determine what members need to do to move from one implementation level to the next level.
- The whole faculty (all of the study groups) will have a strategy for sharing how all of the groups are moving to higher levels of implementation.

There are two sections to the rubric. The first section is a summary of the key behaviors within each component—context, process, and content—that represent an advanced level of implementation. In parentheses beside each behavior we have placed the name of the indicator for the corresponding row in the matrix in the second section to the rubric.

The second section is the innovation configuration matrix that specifies for each indicator under each component the expected behaviors at four levels of implementation—not yet, beginning implementation, developing implementation, advanced implementation. The activity described earlier is using this matrix.

Whole-Faculty

Study Groups™

WFSG RUBRIC OR INNOVATION CONFIGURATION

Key Behaviors at the Advanced Level of Implementation

The CONTEXT *component* of the WFSG rubric describes the range of behaviors that impact the context of the school and the study group itself; these behaviors are as follows:

- WFSG are formed by following the steps on the WFSG Decision-Making Cycle (DMC; Forming WFSG).
- The group uses feedback from the principal (Principal Feedback).
- The group uses feedback from other sources (Feedback From Others).
- The group communicates through its action plan and logs (Communication).
- The group collaborates with other study groups (Collaboration).
- The Instructional Council is an important component of the system (The Council).
- There are multiple communication networks in place (Networks).
- The group connects its work to the School Improvement Plan (Connections).
- Decisions are made based on data (Data-Based Decisions).

The PROCESS *component* of the WFSG rubric describes the range of behaviors that apply to the procedural guidelines and to the functioning of groups; these behaviors are as follows:

- Leadership is rotated (Leadership).
- Norms are followed (Norms).
- The action plan guides the group's work (Action Plan).
- Logs describe the work of the group (Logs).
- Members reflect on what they do and what their students do (Reflection).
- Members interact effectively (Interaction).
- WFSG are synergistic teams (Synergy).
- The size of the group allows all members to be engaged in the work (Group Size).
- Time spent in study group meetings during a month is three to four hours (Time).
- All members are equally respected (Equality).
- Assessment of results is part of every meeting (Assessment of Results).
- Everyone is responsible for the work (Shared Responsibility).
- Mechanics of group work are considered to be secondary to what the group does (Mechanics).
- Members are willing to do whatever is needed (Willingness).
- Members commit to the work of the group (Commitment).
- Members have open classrooms to each other (Openness).

The CONTENT *component* of the WFSG rubric describes the range of behaviors that apply to what study groups do when members meet; these are as follows:

- Students are the focus (Students).
- Action research cycles are used to describe how the group works (Action Research).
- The actions taken when the group meets indicate highly engaged members (Actions).
- Implementation or use of new strategies and materials in the classroom is the ultimate purpose of WFSG (Implementation).
- Members investigate a few issues deeply (Depth of Work).
- Looking at student work is central to the group's work (Student Work).
- Members use information from expert voices (Expert Voices).
- Members focus on what they teach and how they teach (Instructional Focus).
- Members take deliberate action to make different initiatives coherent (Coherence).
- Members do joint work (Joint Work).
- Members value the work they do (Valuing the Work).
- Members have a high awareness of the consequences of the group's actions (Consequences).
- Members feel comfortable experimenting with new strategies and materials (Experimentation).

WFSG Rubric or Innovation Configuration

CONTEXT	Not Yet	Beginning Implementation	Developing Implementation	Advanced Implementation
Forming WFSG	• WFSG DMC not followed to identify student needs or to form groups.	• Steps 1–3 of DMC were followed; but groups are formed based on teacher needs, availability, existing groups, or personal friendships.	• Steps 1–4 on DMC followed to identify student needs and to form study groups.	1. Study groups are formed each year around student learning needs using Steps 1–4 of the DMC.
Principal Feedback	• Members disregard, resent, or do not receive feedback from the principal.	• Members review principal's feedback with no action.	• Members discuss feedback, making attempts to comply with principal's suggestions.	2. Members often refer to principal's helpfulness and seek additional input.
Feedback From Others	• Members do not utilize feedback given to the group by anyone external to the group, e.g., IC.	• Members pose few questions for feedback and are unsure of what to do with the feedback received.	• Members appreciate the feedback received, sometimes acting on it, sometimes not.	• Members engage in a rich dialogue with those giving them feedback, evaluating all input for its value and usability.
Communication	• Study group action plans (SGAP) and logs are not posted or have a number of logs missing.	• SGAP and logs are posted but not immediately on completion; members often have to be reminded.	• SGAP and its revisions during the school year and all of the group's logs are posted in a timely manner.	• Items promptly posted, members show evidence of reviewing and using the feedback from other groups.
Collaboration	• Members show no awareness of and no interest in what other study groups are doing.	• Members indicate some interest in learning about what others are doing.	• There is evidence in logs that the study group is discussing the work of other groups.	• Members frequently seek out and use work from other study groups at the school.
Instructional Council (IC)	• There is no IC for members to attend.	• Same member of study group attends every meeting of the IC.	• Members rotate attending IC but little, if any, time is spent at the next study group meeting, sharing what took place.	• Members rotate attending the IC, discuss and use information from IC, and tie what the study group is doing to what other groups are doing.
Communication Networks	• The only way groups know what other groups are doing is by "word of mouth."	• Action plans and logs are posted.	• In addition to reports from IC meetings and posting plans and logs, little else is done to highlight the work of groups.	• In addition to IC and posting materials, groups make presentations, place items in the school newsletter, and hold celebrations.

(Continued)

Whole-Faculty
Study Groups™

WFSG Rubric or Innovation Configuration (Continued)

CONTEXT	Not Yet	Beginning Implementation	Developing Implementation	Advanced Implementation
Connections	• Members do not connect their work to others in the group and to whole school improvement.	• Members connect to each other but not to whole-school improvement.	• Members talk about "whole school" but no evidence of tying their work to the School Improvement Plan.	• Members continually refer to the School Improvement Plan and their role in meeting schoolwide goals.
Data-Based Decisions	• Members are uncomfortable with routinely examining data and prefer reviewing data in faculty meetings using computer printouts supplied by the district of which they have little understanding or interest.	• Members are transitioning from having state test data presented in grade level or department meetings to using classroom assessment data in study group meetings.	• Members are becoming more comfortable in study group meetings with making data-based decisions, looking at results together, and taking ownership of how each other's students perform on a range of assessments.	• In study group meetings and other settings, staff value working collaboratively using qualitative and quantitative data from several sources for diagnosing their students' instructional needs, setting improvement targets, evaluating effectiveness of instructional strategies, and monitoring progress toward targets.

CONTEXT: The organization or culture in which the study groups exist.

WFSG Rubric or Innovation Configuration

PROCESS	Not Yet	Beginning Implementation	Developing Implementation	Advanced Implementation
Leadership	• The same person leads the group each time it meets.	• Leadership is rotated.	• Leadership is rotated and group members feel comfortable with this.	• Each member willingly takes his or her turn leading the group.
Norms	• The group has not agreed on a set of norms.	• Norms are written but not honored.	• Group norms are written and mostly honored.	• All feel responsible for the success of the group and hold themselves accountable for the group's norms.
Action Plan	• The action plan is not complete or recommended revisions have not been made.	• The action plan is complete. Occasionally the group reviews it and makes minor revisions.	• The action plan is complete and revised, with additions and deletions as work progresses.	• The action plan is complete and often referred to during meetings, is a living document, and is kept in front of the group at all times.
Logs	• Logs are not turned in, not complete, or do not accurately describe what the group did.	• Logs are turned in but group members do not use them as a point of reference for future work.	• Logs are helpful reminders of the work of the group.	• Logs tell a rich story of dialogue and action around student learning.
Reflection	• The group does not show evidence of reflecting on student work or their own learning and teaching.	• Reflection on learning and teaching is practiced as debriefing.	• Members look at student work but without it generating reflection on practice.	• Looking at student work is the basis of reflection on learning and teaching and guides actions.
Interaction	• Members are confused and feel alienated because of misunderstandings.	• Members are beginning to trust each other and build credibility with each other.	• Members are effectively communicating with each other and actively listening to each other but continue to be too judgmental.	• Members respect and appreciate differences, empathize with each other, and consider all input.
Synergy	• Members feel they have nothing of value to contribute and what they have to offer will have no bearing on the final outcome.	• Members feel valued but are not sure they can depend on other members.	• Members feel empowered but continue to hold back and not openly and fully share their skills, knowledge, and ideas.	• Members feel they have something to contribute and what they offer will have a bearing on the final outcome and are genuinely cooperative and mutually dependent.

(Continued)

Whole-Faculty Study Groups™

WFSG Rubric or Innovation Configuration (Continued)

PROCESS	Not Yet	Beginning Implementation	Developing Implementation	Advanced Implementation
Group Size	• Group size is not within guideline of three to five in a group.	• Group size is five or fewer but one member dominates.	• Group size is five or fewer but several members are not fully engaged.	• Group size is five or fewer and all members are equally and fully engaged.
Time	• The group meets once a month or for about one or two hours a month.	• The group meets for an hour every other week or for about two hours a month.	• The group meets two or three times a month for a total of three to four hours a month.	• The group meets weekly for at least an hour or for four hours a month.
Equality	• There is a hierarchy within the group.	• Some members have more influence than others.	• Members espouse equality but it is not always evident in practice.	• Equality is evident in all behaviors and actions.
Assessment of Results	• The group uses annual district and state assessments to measure changes in student performance on their student learning needs.	• Some members use a classroom assessment to assess student results at the end of the year on the study group's targeted student learning needs.	• The group uses a common classroom assessment to collect baseline data and assess student results at the end of the year on the group's chosen student learning needs.	• The study group uses a common classroom assessment to collect baseline data, monitor student progress every 6–12 weeks, and assess results at the end of the year on the study group's chosen student learning needs.
Shared Responsibility	• Members act as if the study group is a committee with one person primarily responsible for the work.	• Members claim to be equally responsible but still depend on one or two members.	• All members take responsibility but do not always follow through.	• All members do what they agree to do.
Mechanics	• Members are trying to figure out what a study group does, focusing on the mechanics of group work.	• Members have established a routine for their meetings, but remain overly conscious of the question, "are we doing this right?"	• Members are focused on their work with little energy being spent on logistics and more attention being given to the impact the work is having on students.	• Members function in such a way that the operational system is invisible, all of the group's energy is focused on the task, and the work is stimulating and impacting their students' learning.

Whole-Faculty Study Groups™

WFSG Rubric or Innovation Configuration

PROCESS	Not Yet	Beginning Implementation	Developing Implementation	Advanced Implementation
Willingness	• Members do not show evidence of their willingness to be vulnerable within the group.	• Members are hesitant but will share what is not working.	• Members accept suggestions and share the results of the revisions.	• Members are genuinely open with one another about their strengths and weaknesses and willing to give to each other whatever support is needed.
Commitment	• Members rarely, if ever, buy in and commit to decisions.	• Members feign agreement during meetings.	• Members are cautious yet show willingness to confront and be confronted on expected behaviors and actions.	• Members openly remind each other of behaviors and actions that aren't consistent with agreed on behaviors and receive reminders without resentment.
Openness	• Members seem to have no interest in observing in each other's classrooms.	• Members have invited other members to observe in their classrooms, but there is no action.	• Members are observing in each other's classrooms, but not debriefing within the group.	• Members routinely observe in each other's classrooms and preconference and postconference within the group.

(Continued)

PROCESS: The means for the acquisition of new knowledge and skills, how change happens, how study groups function.

WFSG Rubric or Innovation Configuration (Continued)

Whole-Faculty Study Groups™

CONTENT	Not Yet	Beginning Implementation	Developing Implementation	Advanced Implementation
Students	• Members are focused on teacher needs, not on student needs.	• While student needs guide the group's work, considerable time is spent on hearing opinions of group members that are not grounded in data.	• Members use classroom data to understand student learning needs and research strategies to try, spending little energy rehashing opinions.	• Members are focused on the learning needs of the students in their classrooms and engage in cycles of action research in their group.
Action Research	• Members spend many meetings examining standardized tests and trying to establish a baseline for current work.	• Members give prompt attention to current assessments in establishing a baseline, but get stalled on researching strategies for addressing needs.	• Members develop lessons using new strategies and materials, but do not show evidence of using the lessons in their classrooms.	• Members establish a baseline and targets, identify best practices, develop lessons, use lessons in classrooms, and reflect on results within repeated cycles of inquiry (one cycle equals about four weeks).
Actions	• Logs reflect few, if any, differences in types of actions taken from one meeting to the next, indicating members spend most of their time talking about behaviors of students.	• Planning to take action is the primary work of the study group.	• Members actively practice or demonstrate strategies routinely, teaching each other what works.	• All members are active in planning, teaching each other, and examining student results from all the members' classes.
Implementation	• Members are not open to doing anything different in their classrooms.	• Members identify and discuss strategies they think will work in their classrooms, but show no evidence of using the strategies.	• Members design lessons to teach and share results of what happened when the lessons were taught.	• Members incorporate new content and strategies into their repertoire for continued use and revise curriculum units accordingly.
Depth	• Members only address what is in their comfort zone and what is of interest to them.	• Members identify key issues related to student learning needs and their teaching, but only skim the surface.	• Members work together to learn and experiment with best practices, actively engaging their students in work emanating from their study group.	• Members examine key issues deeply and challenge each other's assumptions, evaluating all input for its value and usability.

238

WFSG Rubric or Innovation Configuration

CONTENT	Not Yet	Beginning Implementation	Developing Implementation	Advanced Implementation
Student Work	• Members seldom bring student work to collaboratively examine using a protocol.	• Members share examples of their best students' work from a culminating lesson, meaning there is no obvious intention to reteach the material.	• Members share examples of a range of student work and discuss how to improve it, always using the same protocol.	• Looking at student work together using protocols is the heart of group work. It is used routinely on varying levels and content and leads to further changes in teachers' practice.
Expert Voices	• Members rely on what they already know.	• Members bring some types of literature into the meetings, only discussing material superficially.	• External content "experts" are invited to group meetings, books are used as resources, and videos are viewed, but members do not hold each other accountable for using the expert knowledge.	• Members actively seek multiple sources to push themselves to higher levels of understanding of academic content and effective pedagogy.
Instructional Focus	• Logs indicate that members spend a lot of time on administrative and managerial issues.	• Members focus on designing instructional projects for others to implement.	• Focus is on improving members' teaching, but not on improving their students' learning in their classes this school year.	• Members have internalized the following: "What do students we are teaching now need for us to do?"
Coherence	• Members do not use materials and strategies from any of the school's current instructional initiatives.	• Members refer to new programs at the school, but there is no deliberate effort to connect the initiatives to the study group's work.	• Members investigate strategies for connecting the group's work to new instructional programs at the school.	• Members incorporate materials and strategies from several initiatives and existing programs into the group's work for coherence and assimilation.

(Continued)

WFSG Rubric or Innovation Configuration (Continued)

CONTENT	Not Yet	Beginning Implementation	Developing Implementation	Advanced Implementation
Joint Work	• Members share lessons they developed in the past and tell about their classrooms.	• Members develop lessons separately and sometimes share what they are going to do or have done.	• Members develop lessons separately but accept input from the group and share classroom results.	• Members routinely do joint work, meaning that group members work as one in the development of lesson components and use each other's results in modifying their work.
Valuing the Work	• Members complain about study groups being a waste of time and what they are to do is not clear.	• Members indicate that study group work seems more like busy work than real work.	• Members are trying to "do the work they have to do anyway" but find that expectation hard to actualize (do).	• Members value their work and indicate that study group work is meaningful and saves them individual preparation time.
Consequence	• Members are not focused on improving student performance in specific learning needs for their current students.	• Members are easily distracted and express doubt that results are possible.	• Members refer to data and express concern and desire to attain results.	• Members are confident that the work of the group will impact student learning and hold themselves accountable for attaining results.
Experimentation	• Members seem to have no interest in trying new strategies and materials.	• Members are hesitant to try new strategies and materials.	• Members develop lessons that incorporate new strategies and materials in classrooms.	• Members share results from using new strategies and materials in classrooms.

CONTENT: The actual skills and knowledge educators want to possess or acquire; what study groups do to become more skillful and knowledgeable.

Adapted from Lick, D. and Murphy, C. (2007). *Whole-Faculty Study Groups Fieldbook: Lessons Learned and Best Practices from Classrooms, Districts, and Schools.* Thousand Oaks, CA: Corwin Press.

Resource B

Whole-Faculty

Study Groups™

Study Group Action Plan Checklist

The checklist may be used by members of study groups in the development of the Study Group Action Plan and by the person reviewing action plans. A check in front of an indicator means "Yes, the indicator is present."

Part I: Student Needs

(Completed in the first two study group meetings; may be revised during the year)

_____ Needs describe what students should do to be more successful academically.

_____ Needs are concrete and specific, e.g., improve ability to make inferences vs. improve reading.

_____ Needs begin with a verb.

_____ Needs are student needs (e.g., "improve ability to make inferences") rather than needs of teachers (e.g., "provide more time for reading workshops").

_____ Needs can be seen in work students do, e.g., members can bring to study group meetings samples of student work that targets the need.

_____ Needs fit the category the group selected and are chosen from the master list of student needs developed by the staff in Step 2 of the Decision-Making Cycle.

_____ Needs can be addressed through what teachers teach and how they teach. For non-teaching staff, needs can be addressed through what staff members do with students.

_____ Needs are within the control of study group members to change.

_____ Appropriate number of needs for the amount of time members will have to address the needs (1–4 needs).

_____ Beside each need, the code or number for the appropriate state standard is indicated.

Part II: Actions Taken When Group Meets

(Completed in the first two study group meetings; may be revised during the year)

____ The group has checked most or all of the action research steps, indicating that group members understand that these are the steps their group will take as they address their chosen student learning needs.

____ Actions are aligned with the listed student needs.

____ Actions indicate that the group will be examining student work.

____ Actions indicate that the group will go beyond what they already know.

____ Actions reflect the cycle of action research.

Part III: Essential Question

(Completed in the first two study group meetings; may be revised during the year)

____ Essential question encompass the student needs listed.

____ Essential question focuses on what students should do and what members will do to address those needs.

Part IV: Resources

(Completed in the first two study group meetings; may be revised during the year)

____ Primary resources are textbooks, accompanying supplementary materials provided by textbook publishers, and teaching materials from special instructional programs.

____ Resources include materials from school, district, and state workshops, e.g., Differentiated Instruction, Quality Teaching and Learning strategies, Learning-Focused Strategies.

____ Resources listed are aligned with the group's student needs and study, group actions.

____ Resources are likely to help study group members develop deeper understanding of the needs being addressed and will expand their instructional repertoire of teaching strategies.

____ Resources represent a variety of "expert voices" from outside the study group, e.g., books, articles, videos/DVDs, Internet resources, and school/district/regional/state/national consultants.

____ Resources are specific, not vague and general.

Part V: Norms

(Completed in the first two study group meetings; may be revised during the year)

_____ Norms listed are standards of behavior that all members agree to uphold.

_____ Norms relate to the work that study groups do and how members interact with each other.

_____ Norms listed are likely to help the group be productive and effective.

Part VI: Assess Impact of the Group's Work

First Column: Specific Student Needs

(Completed in the first two study group meetings; may be revised during the year)

_____ Needs listed are the same as in the upper left box on Page 1 of the Study Group Action Plan.

_____ If the need is complex, the group has listed specific skills or concepts group members plan to target within the need.

Second Column: Data Sources (Tools or types of assessments)

(Completed in the first two study group meetings; may be revised during the year)

_____ Tool or assessment for each need is given, e.g., teacher checklist, pretest designed by teacher or publisher of textbook.

_____ Tools and assessments given can be used throughout the year by the study group to collect data about changes in students' level of performance relative to the targeted needs.

_____ Tools and assessments are ones that teachers can use in their classes to collect data (rather than a once-a-year state or district test).

_____ Tools and assessments are specific enough to give the reader a clear idea of what the group will be doing. For example, to assess reading comprehension, a study group might adapt a task from a state test where students read a passage and respond to multiple-choice questions about the passage.

Third Column: Baseline

(Completed usually within the third to fifth study group meetings; note: study groups may choose to collect baseline data on all of their student needs as they begin their work or they may choose to focus on only one need at a time. The study group logs should clarify this.)

_____ In column heading, date given for when the baseline data will be collected.

_____ Data show performance for all students in the study group members' classes. (Study groups should present data class by class _or_ teacher by teacher.)

_____ Data are quantitative.

_____ The standard for proficiency is defined.

_____ Data tell how many of the students (number and percentage) are proficient, almost proficient, and far below proficient with regard to each need.

_____ If more than one need is listed in the first column ("Specific student needs"), it is clear in the "Baseline" column the need for which the data are presented.

_____ Student performance is disaggregated by student subgroup if there are achievement gaps among subgroups.

Fourth Column: Target

(Completed for each need at the same or following meeting as the baseline data for which the need is entered. Study groups may choose to set targets on all of their student needs as they begin their work or they may choose to set targets on only one need at a time. The logs should clarify this.)

Note: The Study Group Action Plan has a page with two sections on data. Study groups may use sections differently. Groups may add sections if they want more.

Option 1. Yearlong Target—In all three sections, the baseline and targets are the same—baseline for the beginning of the year, the targets for the end of the year. Actuals would represent students' progress at two intermediate points and at the end of the year.

Option 2. Short-Term Targets—In the first section, the Baseline, Target, and Actual would represent a three-month block, with Baseline in September, the Target set for December, and Actual data collected in December. Then in the second section, the Baseline is the same as the December Actual (from the first section), a new Target is set for March, and Actual data is collected in March. The third section repeats the process with Baseline the same as March Actuals, a new Target set for June, and Actual data collected in June.

Under either option, the three data sections could contain data for more than one need.

Another way study groups could use the two data sections is if they are working on different needs at different times of the year. In this situation, the group could use each section for a different need—each with different dates for Baseline, Target, and Actual.

_____ In column heading, target date for each need is given.

_____ Targets are specific and quantifiable.

_____ Targets are described in the same way as the baseline data.

_____ Actual progress against the targets can be measured using the same assessments used to collect baseline data.

_____ Targets are a "stretch," challenging but attainable. (Targets can't be achieved with just "business as usual.")

_____ Targets differentiated for different groups of students within the teachers' classes.

Fifth Column: Actual

(Completed during the month indicated as the Target date)

_____ In column heading, actual date is given.

_____ Actual results in the same format as the Baseline data, with the same proficiency standards.

_____ Data show performance for all students in the study group members' classes. (Study groups should present data class by class *or* teacher by teacher.)

_____ Data are quantitative.

_____ Data tell how many of the students (number and percentage) are proficient, almost proficient, and far below proficient with regard to each need.

_____ For each need listed in first column ("Specific student needs") it is clear in the "Actual" column for which need the data are presented.

Resource C

Whole-Faculty

Study Groups™

Study Group Log Checklist

The checklist may be used all or in part by members of study groups in completing and reviewing their Study Group Logs and by the person reviewing logs. A check in front of an indicator means "Yes, the indicator is present."

Process

Top part of log

_____ The study group has accurately completed the top portion of the log indicating log number, date, study group name, leader, and members present.

_____ The log was publicly posted and given/e-mailed to the principal within 24 hours of the meeting.

_____ Members are not repeatedly absent (comparing current log with previous logs).

_____ The group is meeting regularly (comparing current log with previous logs).

_____ The leader is the person designated in the previous log.

_____ The group is rotating leadership (comparing current log with previous logs).

Bottom part of the log

_____ The group indicated the date, time, location, leader, and recorder for the next meeting.

_____ The next meeting date is aligned with school expectations about how often study groups will meet.

_____ The leader and recorder for the next meeting is different than the leader and recorder of today's meeting, or follows the group's rotation schedule.

_____ The group is sharing responsibility for preparing for future meetings (comparing current log with previous logs).

Content

What specific student-learning need did the group target today?

_____ The group indicates the need it is addressing at the meeting and the need is on the group's latest action plan.

What happened today? *(the list of tasks on the left and the narrative space on the right)*

_____ Work described in this section of the log is connected to the student needs and study group actions listed on the study group's action plan.

_____ Recorder has checked the step or steps of the action research cycle that indicate which step(s) the group is working on.

_____ Study group is doing what they said they would do in the previous log.

_____ If the group examined student work ("Did the group examine student work today?"), they described what they learned from the work—either in the "What happened today" section or in a separate attachment, such as the LASW report.

_____ Description of what happened today in the space for narrative gives the reader a clear sense of what happened and where the group is heading.

_____ Description suggests that the group used its meeting time productively.

_____ The verbs used indicate active involvement, e.g., modeling, demonstrating, constructing, and practicing, rather than more passive verbs, e.g., shared, discussed, and explained.

Did the group examine student work today?

_____ Group is frequently looking at student work (compare current log with previous logs).

_____ Responsibility for bringing student work is shared by all group members (compare current log with previous logs).

What resources/materials did members use during the meeting today?

_____ Specific resources/materials are listed.

_____ Resources/materials listed are also added to the action plan.

_____ Resources listed are appropriate to the need and will help build the group's expertise.

Describe the specific instructional strategies members used in their classrooms since the last meeting.

_____ Evidence that action has happened in each study group member's classroom(s) as a result of the group's work at prior group meetings.

_____ Evidence of changes in what students are doing and learning in each study group member's classroom(s) as a result of the group's work at prior group meetings.

_____ Group frequently reports classroom applications (comparing current log with previous logs).

_____ Members did, in their classrooms, what they said they would do in their previous log.

What have members agreed to do in their classrooms prior to the next group meeting?

_____ Actions that group members have agreed to do in their classrooms before the next meeting reflect the work and decisions of the study group described in this log.

_____ Actions that group members have agreed to do in their classrooms relate to the student need the group is addressing.

Is the group ready to share a proven strategy with the whole faculty?
(Note: Comments about items to share usually require a response on logs about the process for sharing.)

_____ Group frequently reports items to share (comparing current log with previous logs).

Questions, Concerns, Comments (Note: These require an immediate response before the next study group meeting.)

_____ Comments or questions indicate that the group is functioning effectively.

_____ Comments or questions indicate that the group is being reflective about the WFSG process and their work together.

Next meeting (agenda items, work to prepare, materials needed)

_____ Description gives the reader a clear image of what the group will be doing at its next meeting and what each member will do to prepare for the meeting.

_____ Agenda items for the next meeting follow logically from the description of what happened in the current meeting.

_____ Agenda items for the next meeting are connected to the student needs and study group actions listed on the group's action plan.

_____ Agenda items for the next meeting suggest a productive use of the group's meeting time.

Resource D

WFSG Assessment Forms

This resource contains assessment forms that schools implementing schoolwide action research may use for a year-end assessment of study group work and the implementation of the action research system.

The forms included are as follows:

1. Checklist for WFSG Process Guidelines
2. Assessment of WFSG Work—I—Study Group Benefits
3. Assessment of WFSG Work—II—Study Group Activities
4. Assessment of WFSG Work—III—Impact on Teacher Practice
5. Assessment of WFSG Work—IV—Impact on Student Learning
6. Improving the WFSG System

Whole-Faculty

WFSGs

Study Groups™

Checklist for WFSG Process Guidelines

Directions: As a group, rate your study group using the following symbols:

* = We're there!

> = We're developing!

< = We're struggling!

_____ Size of our group is between three and five members and allows for participation from all group members.

_____ Meet on a regular schedule and have established a regular meeting time.

_____ Have established group norms.

_____ We adhere to our established norms.

_____ Have established a schedule for rotating responsibilities for leader, recorder, and IC representative.

_____ Have an Action Plan and keep it updated.

_____ Keep our Action Plan updated.

_____ Our Study Group Action Plan has been posted in a public place.

_____ Complete a log after each meeting and follow procedures for posting it.

_____ Maintain an instructional focus during meetings.

_____ Work is impacting our instructional practices in the classroom.

_____ Routinely examine student work when we meet.

_____ Group works well together and shares responsibilities.

_____ Are sharing our work with other study groups.

Assessment of WFSG Work—I

Whole-Faculty

WFSGs

Study Groups™

Name: _____ Study Group: _____

This page is completed by individual study group members.

To respond to the questions on this page, individuals should refer to their Study Group Action Plan and Logs for indicators of frequency.

During your study group time, how often does your group engage in the following?

Activity Engaged In	Almost Every Time	Most of the Time	Sometimes	Rarely
Addressing issues of curriculum				
Focusing on instructional strategies				
Designing and/or redesigning lessons and units to develop deeper understanding				
Looking at student work to improve teacher practice				
Looking at student work to deepen student understanding				
Looking at teacher work to improve teacher practice				
Looking at teacher work to deepen student understanding				
Bringing in references to research regarding teaching practices				
Focusing on reaching students with learning differences				
Engaging in reflective dialogue				
Working on authentic assessments				

Whole-Faculty

WFSGs

Study Groups™

Assessment of WFSG Work—II

Name: _____ Study Group: _____

This page is completed by individual study group members.

In what ways have you personally benefited from being in a Study Group?

Benefits to Me	Definitely Yes	Somewhat	Little or None
Greater sense of collegiality with other teachers			
I use more varied instructional practices			
I feel more effective in my teaching			
I have fewer classroom management problems			
I am able to reach my students better			

In what ways have your students benefited from your participation in a Study Group?

Benefits to Students	Almost Every Time	Most of the Time	Sometimes	Rarely
More actively engaged in their work				
Demonstrating better performance in the learning needs you have been working on				
Demonstrating deeper understanding of key concepts and ideas				
Taking more responsibility for their learning				
More reflective on their own learning				
Other:				

The items on this assessment are from a survey prepared by Rosenblum Brigham Associates for ATLAS Communities.

Whole-Faculty

WFSGs

Study Groups™

Assessment of WFSG Work—III

Study Group: _____ **Date:** _____

As a Study Group

Examine the artifacts from the work the study group did this year.

In the following spaces, share what evidence you have that teaching practices have changed as a result of the work of the study group. For example, what were common teaching strategies, assessment tools, types of teaching materials, or lesson formats that have now been changed, revised, or discarded?

BEFORE the study group began its work:	AT THE END of the study group's work:

Whole-Faculty

WFSGs

Study Groups™

Assessment of WFSG Work—IV

Study Group: _____

What evidence does the group have that student performance changed in each of the student needs listed on your Action Plan?

Specific **Student Needs** listed on Action Plan. Students need to:	Data **Sources** that document need and is evidence of impact of group's work	**Baseline**— what data indicate when work began in _____	**Target**—what study group projected would be the results of the work in _____	**Actual**—what data indicate in _____

Column 1: List two or three of the SPECIFIC student needs on the SGAP.

Column 2: List data sources you used to track progress, e.g., teacher made tests, teacher observations, six-week averages, textbook checklists, benchmark tests.

Column 3: What the data indicated when you began meeting (Aug.–Oct.).

Column 4: What you wanted the data to indicate at the end of the year.

Column 5: What the data indicates at the end of the year.

Columns 3, 4, & 5: Give the percentage of students in each member's classes that meet different performance levels. For example: 25% meet expectations, 30% almost meet, and 45% struggling or far below. Performance levels are defined by study group members. The same rubric or other rating system is used by all members.

Whole-Faculty

WFSGs

Study Groups™

Improving the WFSG System

Study Group: _____

As a group, discuss and identify suggestions for improvement for each element listed below. If you have other suggestions for improvement, please put them on the bottom or back of this form.

1. The data we use to identify student needs.
   - *Types of data (should we use the same data sets, drop some, add others?), amount of data, ease of understanding.*

2. The feedback and support your reader gives to your study group.
   - *Frequency and timeliness of reader feedback on action plans and logs, quality of feedback, amount of feedback (just right, too much, too little), follow-up on questions, concerns, requests.*
   - *Suggestions for improvements next year.*

3. Ways to improve cross-study group sharing and communication.
   - *Such as improving the WFSG bulletin board and IC meetings, creating a WFSG resource area/library, sharing WFSG work at staff meetings, moving ideas/strategies from WFSG to schoolwide, and communicating study groups' work to parents and students.*

4. Support provided by our WFSG Focus Team.
   - *Did support from our WFSG Focus Team help your study group deepen its work or help improve WFSG at your school?*
   - *What type of support would be helpful next year?*

5. Support and feedback provided by district staff or outside consultants.
   - *What support and feedback did you receive? Did the support and feedback help your study group deepen its work or help improve WFSG at your school?*
   - *What type of support would be helpful next year?*

6. Time for study group and method for forming study groups.
   - *Was the way we organize study groups this year a productive strategy?*
   - *What would you recommend for next year—same process or a different process?*
   - *Do you feel that study group meeting times were too long or too short? Did the frequency of meetings scheduled enable your group to achieve results?*

7. Other Suggestions.

Resource E

Whole-Faculty

Study Groups™

Three-Year Implementation Plan
for WFSG Schoolwide Action Research

The purpose of this resource is to share the possibilities for implementing the WFSG schoolwide action research system over a three-year period and to suggest appropriate points where a school might utilize the services of the WFSG National Center or other consultants.

Schools have several options for launching WFSG schoolwide action research:

1. Form a Focus Team to orient faculty and launch WFSG schoolwide action research, using the resources in the Murphy and Lick 2005 book on Whole-Faculty Study Groups and the Video Journal's video on WFSG.

2. Form a Focus Team, train the Focus Team at a WFSG Level I Institute offered by the WFSG National Center on-site, in Augusta, or at a national conference, and then the Focus Team leads the school faculty through the orientation and launch. The school may contract with the WFSG National Center for follow-up on-site support services and/or send teams to the annual WFSG conference or to a Level II Institute. This scenario is presented as Option One on the next page.

   Some schools following this scenario chose to invite a WFSG Consultant to assist the Focus Team with the faculty orientation and/or the launch.

3. Invite a WFSG Consultant from the WFSG National Center to orient faculty, lead the WFSG launch, and provide follow-up on-site support. This scenario is presented as Option Two on the next page.

Whole-Faculty

Study Groups™

WFSG Continuation: Year One

	Option One	Option Two
Activities	Focus Team Conducts WFSG Launch With Its Faculty: 1. Faculty is provided an orientation (Feb.–Aug. prior to Year One). 2. Consensus for participation reached. 3. Focus Team members identified. 4. Focus Team attends WFSG Level I Institute at regional, state, or national level, or WFSG Consultant conducts WFSG Level I Institute for several Focus Teams within a district (June–Sept.). 5. Focus Team schedules and plans meeting with faculty, selecting student data to be reviewed. 6. IC meetings put on school calendars. 7. Focus Team leads faculty through Steps 1–4 of DMC, study groups formed. 8. Action Plans completed by end of second meeting. 9. Action Plans sent to WFSG Consultant for feedback to principals. 10. WFSG Consultant visits district/ schools (Sept.–Nov.) to give feedback on WFSG work, to continue training, and to conduct LASW training for Focus Teams or at schools (Sept.–Nov.). 11. Action Plans posted and logs being posted on Web site by 11/1. 12. WFSG Consultant visits district/ schools (Dec.–Feb.) to give feedback on WFSG work and continue training, to include Action Research.	WFSG Consultant Conducts WFSG Launch With a Faculty: 1. Faculty is provided an orientation (Feb.–Aug. prior to Year One). 2. Consensus for participation reached. 3. Principal or his/her designee attends WFSG Level I Institute at the district, state, regional, or national level. 4. IC meetings put on school calendar. 5. Data the whole faculty will review are selected. 6. WFSG Consultant visits to consult with district leaders and to lead one or more faculties through Steps 1–4 of DMC, study groups formed (Aug.–Oct.). 7. Action Plans completed (Sept.–Oct.). 8. Action Plans sent to WFSG Consultant for feedback to principals. 9. WFSG Consultant visits to give feedback on WFSG work, to continue WFSG training, and to conduct training in LASW with whole faculty, through the IC, and/or with individual study groups (Oct.–Nov.). 10. Study group logs reflect authentic work.

(Continued)

(Continued)

	Option One	Option Two
Activities	13. National WFSG conference (February) is attended by at least one person from each WFSG school. 14. Study group logs reflect authentic work. 15. WFSG Consultant visits district/schools (Mar.–May). 16. SIP includes strategies from WFSG. 17. Study group work assessed and celebrated (May). 18. Results/reports sent to WFSG Nat. Center. 19. Options available for attendance at Summer Institutes.	11. Action Plans posted and logs being posted on Web site by 11/1. 12. WFSG Consultant visits to give feedback on WFSG work and continue training (Feb.–March), to include LASW and Action Research. 13. National WFSG Conference (February) is attended by at least one person from each WFSG school. 14. WFSG Consultant visits district/schools to give feedback on WFSG work and continue training (April–June). 15. SIP includes strategies from WFSG. 16. Study group work assessed and celebrated. 17. Results/reports sent to WFSG National Center. 18. Options available for attendance at Summer Institutes conducted at the National WFSG Center, i.e. Level II Institute, LASW Institute.
Time	• 4 days for Focus Team to be trained and to plan. • ½ day for whole faculty to DMC. • Average of 1 hr. per week for study group meetings or 2 hr. every 2 wks. • ½ day for introducing LASW and other protocols. • ½ day for celebration. 3 visits from WFSG Consultant.	• ½ day for whole faculty to do DMC. • Average of 1 hr. per week for SG meetings or 2 hr. every 2 wks. • ½ day for introducing LASW and other protocols. • ½ day for celebration. 4 visits from WFSG Consultant.

Whole-Faculty

Study Groups™

WFSG Continuation: Year Two

	Options One & Two

Activities	By the end of Year One, faculties that launched with a Focus Team and faculties that launched with WFSG Consultant are at the same point. At the beginning of Year Two, the activities are generally the same. However, the WFSG Consultant will do some customizing during Year Two.
	
	• At the end of Year One, study groups had three choices:
	  1. Stay together, continue addressing same student needs;
	  2. Stay together, select different student needs;
	  3. Disband, regroup.
	• At beginning of Year Two, the whole faculty revisits Steps 1–3 of the DMC to confirm student needs.
	• Groups that chose to disband regroup around student needs.
	• WFSG Consultant visits to give feedback on WFSG work and continue training (Aug.–Sept).
	• Action Plans completed by mid-September.
	• Action Plans posted and logs being posted on Web site by 11/1.
	• Study group work deepened and extended to reflect shared understanding of school instructional foci.
	• Study group work includes connecting classroom strategies to measurable learning goals linked to district and state standards.
	• WFSG Consultant visits to give feedback on WFSG work. (Oct.–Feb.).
	• WFSG National Conference is attended by at least one person from each WFSG school.
	• District-wide sharing through newsletters and WFSG special events.
	• WFSG Consultant visits to give feedback on WFSG work and to set goals for next school year (Feb.–June).
	• Study group work assessed and celebrated.
	• School Improvement Plan includes strategies from WFSG.
	• Results and reports sent to WFSG National Center.
	• Options available for attending Summer Institutes at National WFSG Center, e.g., Level II Institute, LASW Institute.

Time	• ½ day to establish WFSGs (Aug./Sept.) • ½ day for LASW and Action Research training • Average 1 hr. per week for study group meetings (could be 2 hours every 2 weeks) • ½ day for celebration 3 visits from WFSG Consultant

Whole-Faculty

Study Groups™

WFSG Continuation: Year Three

	Options One & Two
Activities	By the end of Year Two, regardless of how WFSGs were launched, faculties have been exposed to similar WFSG strategies. Differences will be in the depth of the experiences. • At the end of Year Two, study groups had the same three choices they had at the end of Year One. • At the beginning of Year Three, the whole faculty revisits Steps 1–3 on the DMC to confirm student needs. • Groups that chose to disband, regroup around the student needs. • Action Plans completed by mid-September. • WFSG Consultant visits to give feedback on WFSG work and continue training (Aug.–Sept.). • Action Plans posted and logs being posted on Web site by 11/1. • WFSGs continue to be the vehicle for implementing instructional initiatives, i.e., new curriculums, textbooks, strategies. • All study groups are using protocols to LASW and following the Action Research cycle. • LASW is a routine practice. • Instructional decisions based on data. • WFSG Consultant visits to give feedback on WFSG work (Oct.–Feb.). • Multiple assessments used to assess student learning. • WFSG National Conference is attended by at least one person from each WFSG school. • WFSG Consultant visits to give feedback on WFSG work and to continue training (Feb.–June). • District fair held for faculties to share WFSG work. • Study group work assessed and celebrated. • School Improvement Plan is generated primarily from the WFSG. • Results and reports sent to WFSG National Center. • Options available for attending Summer Institutes at WFSG National Center.
Reminders	• WFSG are organized and meeting by October 1. • Study groups meet weekly or biweekly. • WFSG Web site is major resource. • In addition to WFSG in schools, cross-school study groups should be considered to address K–12 instructional needs. • In addition to WFSG in schools, principals and district-level administrators are in study groups. • By the end of Year Three, WFSG should be "the way we do things at this school." Continuation is not an issue. New administrators are introduced to WFSG by the faculty.

Outcomes by End of Year Three

- Student achievement has improved.
- All faculty use WFSGs to address specific instructional student needs.
- All faculty use student data to make decisions about their own professional development needs.
- All faculty see the relationship between study group work and improved classroom practice.
- All faculty see the relationship between study group work and improved student learning.
- All faculty use LASW as a strategy to reflect on instructional practice.
- School Improvement Plan is generated from recommendations from the WFSG.
- Continuation of WFSG schoolwide action research is a given.

WFSG Consultant's Toolkit

- Examples of Study Group Action Plans
- Examples of Study Group Logs from several study groups for one school year
- Worldwide Web site for posting Actions Plans and Logs
- WFSG textbook
- WFSG Institute binder
- The Video Journal of Education's WFSG Program
- Protocols/strategies for looking at an array of evidence, including LASW
- Examples of teacher work, i.e., portfolios, lessons
- NSDC Staff Development Standards
- Concerns-Based Adoption Model inventories, Stages of Concern and Levels of Use

Definitions

WFSG Consultant—an associate of Carlene Murphy with extensive experience in training and supporting WFSG faculties.

WFSG National Center—the world headquarters of WFSG. Located in Augusta, GA, in the home of Carlene Murphy.

WFSG National Conference—held in Augusta, GA, the first week in February. The Conference is preceded by stand-alone skill-building workshops.

WFSG Institutes—skill-building workshops usually held during the summer in Augusta, GA; Level I is for beginners; Level II for experienced.

LASW—Looking at Student Work.

Resource F

Support and Technical Services

National WFSG Center

The mission of the WFSG National Center is to ensure student achievement through the authentic application of the WFSG System in schools. The Center customizes services for each school, set of schools, or district.

The WFSG National Center offers a range of support and technical services to schools and districts. These services can be categorized as the following:

I. Orientations to WFSG

II. Launching WFSG

III. Support during Year 1

IV. Support during Years 2 and 3

V. Conferences and Institutes

VI. Connecting WFSG worldwide

I. Orientations to WFSG

WFSG Consultants will conduct orientations to WFSG for schools, districts, regional agencies, state organizations, and national conferences.

II. Launching WFSG

WFSG consultants work with schools and districts to determine how WFSG will be launched. The options are as follows:

A. Sending a team (4 or 5 people, including the principal) to a Level I Institute in Augusta, GA (2 ½ days) in February, June, or July. This option means that the Focus Team from a school will conduct the launch with the whole faculty.

B. Having a WFSG Consultant conduct a Level I Institute at a location within a district or the region for Focus Teams from several schools (2 days). This option means that the Focus Team from a school will conduct the launch with the whole faculty.

C. Having a WFSG Consultant lead one whole faculty through the Decision-Making Cycle, determining what study groups will do and organizing the faculty into study groups. The consultant would spend a half-day with the administrative team and a half-day with the whole faculty (1 day). This option means that a consultant will conduct the launch with the whole faculty.

III. Support During Year 1

WFSG consultants and school leaders determine the types of on-site support needed during the first year study groups are implemented. If WFSGs are launched before the end of September, three visits from the WFSG Consultant is scheduled during the school year. The visits would most likely occur in October/November, February/March, and May. During visits the consultants will conduct ongoing training and provide support to individual study groups, whole faculties, focus teams, principals, district staff, and Instructional Councils. All work is tailored to the needs of each school.

IV. Support During Years 2 and 3

WFSG consultants and school leaders determine what types of ongoing support are needed during the second and third years of implementation to ensure the institutionalization of WFSG. By the end of Year 3, it is expected that

- Student achievement has improved in the areas targeted.
- The culture of the school is more collaborative.
- All faculty use WFSGs to address specific instructional student needs.

V. Conferences and Institutes

The Center sponsors a yearly national conference for all schools currently implementing WFSG and those interested in implementing WFSG. The conference is held in Augusta, GA, the first or second week in February.

The Center also sponsors WFSG Institutes in February, June, and July in Augusta, GA, that target specific audiences. Consultants will also design Institutes for local sites. Level I Institute is to train Focus Teams to orient and lead a faculty through the WFSG Decision-Making Cycle to determine the student needs to be addressed and how the groups will be organized. Level II Institute is for schools that have started implementing WFSG and need skills to deepen the work. Other institutes can be tailored to meet specific district and school needs.

VI. Connecting WFSG Worldwide

The Center is in partnership with RubiconAtlas, the sponsor of a Web site connecting all WFSG schools. Templates for WFSG forms are on the Web site and study groups can capture its work electronically with instant connection to all other study groups in the school, district, state, and nation. It is a global Web site, so connections are worldwide.

Whole-Faculty

Study Groups™

Whole-Faculty Study Groups®
National Center

www.MurphysWFSG.org
WFSG Level I Institute

"The ABCs of Getting Started"

Participants will

- Know that the WFSG is a system that targets the instructional needs of students.
- Be able to give others the basic information about WFSG, to include definition, grounding questions, principles, guiding question, and functions.
- Know how to explain the difference in WFSG and other types of collaborative groups and the differences in WFSG meetings and other types of meetings.
- Understand how the 15 procedural or process guidelines provide a structure or vehicle for working on the work of teaching and learning.
- Understand the importance of data-based decision making.
- Be guided through the WFSG Decision-Making Cycle that identifies the student needs that will be the focus of WFSG and will determine how study groups are organized.
- Know how to write a Study Group Action Plan.
- Experience multiple uses of protocols.
- Begin developing a plan for introducing a faculty to WFSG and for leading the same faculty through the Decision-Making Cycle.

Offered in Augusta, GA, in February, June, and July. See www.MurphysWFSG.org for registration information. Also, offered at any location with a WFSG Consultant who will customize, plan, and conduct the Institute.

Whole-Faculty

WFSGs

Study Groups™

Whole-Faculty Study Groups®
National Center

www.MurphysWFSG.org
WFSG Level II Institute

"Continuing and Deepening the Work of WFSG and Focusing on Impact"

Participants will

- Focus on four questions related to continuing and deepening WFSG approach to schoolwide action research:
  - How can we design our work with faculties so teachers will transfer training in skills, content, and teaching strategies to their study group work and use these new skills, content and strategies consistently and appropriately in their classrooms?
  - How do we use our tools (forms, procedures, processes) to support and direct or redirect study groups?
  - How well do we understand the complexities of the change process and what do we need to know and understand to be able to support others as they are experiencing the anxieties, frustrations, doubts, resistance, and excitement of new materials, processes, and relationships?
  - How can we help others understand that WFSG is a bundle of innovations that include different types of, or approaches to, staff development? When should we introduce the concept of the "bundle" and, after introduction, highlight or underscore the components of the "bundle," knowing that several of the components or approaches will need to be taught? For example, we have to teach groups how to conduct action research, how to do a lesson study, and how to coach colleagues.
- Use looking at student work (LASW) protocols to collaboratively examine study group action plans, logs, and feedback from their schools and frame recommendations for improving study group work and their support for study groups.
- Review WFSG Rubrics completed collaboratively by individual study groups or a whole school and develop plans for strengthening schoolwide action research.
- Use the Descriptive Consultancy protocol to collaboratively understand, refine or resolve dilemmas that participants are experiencing in their work to deepen and continue the WFSG work in their schools or district.

Offered in Augusta, GA, in February, June, and July. See www.Murphys WFSG.org for registration information. Also, offered at any location with a WFSG Consultant who will customize, plan, and conduct the Institute.

References

Anderson, G. L., Herr, K., & Nihlen, A. S. (1994). *Studying your own school: An educator's guide to qualitative practitioner research*. Thousand Oaks, CA: Corwin.

Antosz, J., Boyd, D., & Clauset, K. (2005). Whole-faculty study groups: Qualicum Beach Middle School takes a collaborative approach to staff development and improving student learning. *Adminfo, 17*(3), 10–12.

Aronson, E., & Patnoe, S. (1997). *The jigsaw classroom: Building cooperation in the classroom* (2nd ed.). New York: Longman.

Asimov, I. (1978). My own view. In R. Holdstock (Ed.), *Encyclopedia of science fiction* (pp. xii). London: Octopus Books.

Averette, P., & Baron, D. (n.d.). *The final word protocol*. Retrieved August 30, 2006, from http://www.turningpts.org/pdf/FinalWordProtocol.pdf

Beyerlein, M. M. (1997a). Why do teams fail? Let me count the ways: The macro level. *Center for the Study of Work Teams Newsletter, 7*(2), 3–4.

Beyerlein, M. M. (1997b). Why do teams fail? Let me count the ways: The micro level. *Center for the Study of Work Teams Newsletter, 7*(2), 12–13.

Beyerlein, M. M. (2003). A tool approach to forgotten team competencies. In M. M. Beyerlein, C. McGee, G. D. Klein, J. E. Nemiro, & L. Broedling, *The collaborative work systems fieldbook: Strategies, tools, and techniques*, 581–594. San Francisco: Jossey-Bass/Pfeiffer.

Blythe, T. (1998). *The teaching for understanding guide*. San Francisco: Jossey-Bass.

Blythe, T., Allen, D., & Powell, B. S. (1999). *Looking together at student work*. New York: Teachers College Press.

Bunn Elementary School. (2005). *School Improvement Plan 2005–2008*. Retrieved August 21, 2006, from http://www.fcschools.net/SIP05/ES/BESBinder1.pdf

Bunn Elementary School. (2006a). *Year in review: A summary of whole faculty study group work 2005–2006*. Unpublished manuscript.

Bunn Elementary School. (2006b). *Radical Readers study group logs from September 11 through November 15, 2006*. Unpublished manuscript.

Calhoun, E. F. (1994). *How to use action research in the self-renewing school*. Alexandria, VA: Association for Supervision and Curriculum Development.

Calhoun, E. F. (2002). Action research for school improvement. *Education Leadership, 59*(6), 18–24.

Caro-Bruce, C. (2004). Action research. In L. B. Easton (Ed.), *Powerful designs for professional learning* (pp. 53–60). Oxford, OH: National Staff Development Council.

Centers for Quality Teaching and Learning. (2005). *Evaluation findings from 2005*. Retrieved March 26, 2008, from http://www.qtlcenters.org/qtl/evaluation/index.htm

Clauset, K., & Nelsen, J. (2004). *Improving performance in central office: The missing ingredient in NCLB*. Retrieved January 16, 2007, from http://www.focusonresults.net/newsletter/

Clauset, K. H., Parker, S. H., & Whitney, M. R. (2007). Making data-based decisions for student success. In D. W. Lick & C. U. Murphy (Eds.), *The whole-faculty study groups fieldbook: Lessons learned and best practices from classrooms, districts, and schools* (pp. 123–134). Thousand Oaks, CA: Corwin.

Cochran-Smith, M., & Lytle, S. L. (1995). *Inside/outside: Teacher research and knowledge.* New York: Teachers College Press.

Collins, J. (2001). *Good to great: Why some companies make the leap and others don't.* New York: HarperCollins.

Conner, D. (1993*). Managing at the speed of change.* New York: Villard.

Conzemius, A., & O'Neil, J. (2002). *The handbook for SMART school teams.* Bloomington, ID: National Educational Service.

Covey, S. (1990). *The 7 habits of highly effective people: Powerful lessons in personal change.* New York: Fireside.

Cronan-Hillix, T., Gensheimer, L., Cronan-Hillix, W. A., William, S., & Davidson, W. S. (1986). Students' views of mentors in psychology graduate training. *Teaching of Psychology, 13,* 123–127.

Dana, N. F., & Yendol-Silva, D. (2003). *The reflective educator's guide to classroom research: Learning to teach and teaching to learn through practitioner inquiry.* Thousand Oaks, CA: Corwin.

Drucker, P. (1985). *Innovation and entrepreneurship: Practices and principles.* New York: Harper & Row.

DuFour, R., & Eaker, R. (1998). *Professional learning at work: Best practices for enhancing student achievement.* Alexandria, VA: Association for Supervision and Curriculum Development.

Dwyer, K. M. (2004). Teacher leadership: Prevalent shared leadership practices of middle school interdisciplinary teams and whole-faculty study groups. Unpublished doctoral dissertation, Loyola University, Chicago.

Edmonds, R. (1979). Some schools work and more can. *Social Policy, 9*(5), 28–32.

Evans, R. (1996). The human side of change: Reform, resistance, and the real-life problems of innovation. San Francisco: Jossey-Bass.

Fairfax County Public Schools. (2006). *The teacher researcher network web page.* Retrieved August 24, 2006, from http://www.fcps.k12.va.us/plt/teachers/trn.html

Fullan, M. (1993). *Change forces: Probing the depths of education reform.* London: Falmer Press.

Fullan, M. (2005). *Leadership and sustainability: System thinkers in action.* Thousand Oaks, CA: Corwin.

Gansle, K. A., & Noell, G. H. (2005). *Learning Intensive Networking Communities for Success (LINCS): Outcome data 2001–2005. LINCS report 2001–2005.* Baton Rouge: Louisiana Department of Education.

Hackman, J. R. (2002). *Leading teams: Setting the stage for great performances.* Boston: Harvard Business School Press.

Hall, G. E., & Hord, S. M. (2001). *Implementing change: Patterns, principles, and potholes.* Boston: Allyn & Bacon.

Hall, G. E., Loucks, S. F., Rutherford, W. L., & Newlove, B. (1975). Levels of use of an innovation: A framework for analyzing innovation adoption. *Journal of Teacher Education, 24,* 52–56.

Hargreaves, A., & Fink, D. (2006). *Sustainable leadership.* San Francisco: John Wiley & Sons.

Hawthorn School District 73. (2004). *Hawthorn district 73 learning system.* Retrieved January 15, 2007, from http://learning.hawthorn73.org/learning_models/learning_systems

Hawthorn School District 73. (2006a). 2006–2007 *Hawthorn school district #73 curriculum guide: Curriculum maps for academic subjects.* Retrieved January 14, 2007, from http://learning .hawthorn73.org/curriculum

Hawthorn School District 73. (2006b). *Framework for excellence: Elementary & MSN/MSS framework for excellence.* Retrieved January 15, 2007, from http://learning.hawthorn73.org/ learning_models/learning_systems

Hopkins, D. (2002). *A teacher's guide to classroom research* (3rd ed.). Philadelphia: Open University Press.

Hord, S. M., Rutherford, W. L., Huling-Austin, L., & Hall, G. E. (1987). *Taking charge of change.* Alexandria, VA: Association for Supervision and Curriculum Development.

Indrisano, R., & Paratore, J. R. (Eds.). (2005). *Learning to write, writing to learn: Theory and research in practice.* Newark, DE: International Reading Association.

Joyce, B. (1992). Cooperative learning and staff development: Teaching the method with the method. *Cooperative Learning, 12*(2), 10–13.

Joyce, B., Murphy, C., Showers, B., & Murphy, J. (1989). School renewal as cultural change. *Educational Leadership, 47*(3), 70–77.

Joyce, B., & Showers, B. (1983). *Power in staff development through research on training.* Alexandria, VA: Association for Supervision and Curriculum Development.

Joyce, B., & Showers, B. (2002). *Student achievement through staff development* (3rd ed.). Alexandria, VA: Association for Supervision and Curriculum Development.

Joyce, B., Weil, M., & Showers, B. (1992). *Models of teaching* (4th ed.). New York: Allyn & Bacon.

Kirwan, B., & Ainsworth, L. K. (Eds.). (1992). *A guide to task analysis.* London: Taylor & Francis.

Kissinger, A. (2007). Strengthening school improvement plans through district sponsorship. In D. W. Lick & C. U. Murphy (Eds.), *The whole-faculty study groups fieldbook: Lessons learned and best practices from classrooms, districts, and schools* (pp. 34–39). Thousand Oaks, CA: Corwin.

Koenigs, A. E. (2004). *The affects of whole-faculty study groups on individuals and organizations.* Unpublished doctoral dissertation, Wichita State University, Kansas.

Koenigs, A. E. (2007). Answering the question: Do professional learning communities really work? In D. W. Lick & C. U. Murphy (Eds.), *The whole-faculty study groups fieldbook: Lessons learned and best practices from classrooms, districts, and schools* (pp. 51–60). Thousand Oaks, CA: Corwin.

Kotter, J. P. (1998). Winning at change. *Leader to Leader, 10,* 27–33.

Kotter, J. P., & Cohen, D. S. (2002). *The heart of change.* Boston: Harvard Business School Press.

Lasserre-Cortez, S. (2006). *A day in the PARC: An interactive qualitative analysis of school climate and teacher effectiveness through professional action research collaboratives.* Unpublished doctoral dissertation, Louisiana State University, Baton Rouge.

Learning-Focused school improvement model planning and implementation guide. (n.d.). Retrieved February 17, 2008, from http://www.learningfocused.com/files/impguide.pdf

Lewis, C. (2004). Lesson study. In L. B. Easton (Ed.), *Powerful designs for professional learning* (pp. 135–148). Oxford, OH: National Staff Development Council.

Lick, D., & Kaufman, R. (2000). Change creation: The rest of the planning story. In J. Boettcher, M. Doyle, & R. Jensen (Eds.), *Technology-driven planning: Principles to practice* (pp. 25–26). Ann Arbor, MI: Society for College and University Planning.

Lick, D. W. (1999a). Proactive co-mentoring relationships: Enhancing effectiveness through synergy. In C. A. Mullen & D. W. Lick (Eds.), *New directions in mentoring: Creating a culture of synergy* (pp. 206–207). London: Falmer Press.

Lick, D. W. (1999b). Transforming higher education: A new vision, learning paradigm, change management. *International journal of Innovative Higher Education, 13,* 75–78.

Lick, D. W. (2000). Whole-faculty study groups: Facilitating mentoring for school-wide change. *Theory Into Practice, 39*(1), 43–48.

Lick, D. W. (2006). A new perspective on organizational learning: Creating learning teams. *Journal of Evaluation and Program Planning, 29,* 88–96.

Lick, D. W., & Murphy, C. U. (2007). *The whole-faculty study groups fieldbook: Improving schools and enhancing student learning.* Thousand Oaks, CA: Corwin.

Lucas, B. A. (2000). *Whole-faculty study groups' impact on the professional community of schools.* Unpublished doctoral dissertation, University of Minnesota, Minneapolis.

Madison Metropolitan School District. (2006). *Classroom action research, 1990–2005 abstracts and selected papers.* Retrieved August 24, 2006, from http://www.madison.k12.wi.us/sod/car/carabstractintro.html

Martin-Kniep, G. O. (2004). *Developing learning communities through teacher expertise.* Thousand Oaks, CA: Corwin.

Marzano, R. J., Pickering, D. J., & Pollock, J. E. (2001). *Classroom instruction that works: Research-based strategies for increasing student achievement.* Alexandria, VA: Association for Supervision and Curriculum Development.

McDonald, J. P., Mohr, N., Dichter, A., & McDonald, E. C. (2003). *The power of protocols: An educator's guide to better practice.* New York: Teachers College Press.

McLaughlin, P. F. (1997). *The effect of a whole-faculty study group on the development of a community of learners.* Unpublished doctoral dissertation, Immaculata College, Immaculata, Pennsylvania.

MetLife Foundation. (2003). *The MetLife survey of the American teacher: An examination of school leadership.* Retrieved December 28, 2006, from http://www.metlife.com/Applications/Corporate/WPS/CDA/PageGenerator/0,4132,P2315,00.html

Mills, G. E. (2007). *Action research: A guide for the teacher researcher* (3rd ed.). Upper Saddle River, NJ: Pearson Education.

Mullen, C. A., & Lick, D. W. (Eds.). (1999). *New directions in mentoring: Creating a cultural synergy.* London: Falmer Press.

Murphy, C. U. (1992). Study groups foster school-wide learning. *Educational Leadership, 50*(3), 71–74.

Murphy, C. U. (1995). Whole-faculty study groups: Doing the seemingly undoable. *Journal of Staff Development, 16*(3), 37–44.

Murphy, C. U. (2006). *Whole-faculty study groups—Results 2005–2006, Artifacts 2005–2006, Franklin County Schools, Louisburg, NC.* Unpublished manuscript.

Murphy, C. U. (2007a). The whole-faculty study groups rubric. In D. W. Lick & C. U. Murphy (Eds.), *The whole-faculty study groups fieldbook: Lessons learned and best practices from classrooms, districts, and schools* (pp. 80–93). Thousand Oaks, CA: Corwin.

Murphy, C. U. (2007b). Establishing a support network: The national whole-faculty study groups center. In D. W. Lick & C. U. Murphy (Eds.), *The whole-faculty study groups fieldbook: Lessons learned and best practices from classrooms, districts, and schools* (pp. 261–272). Thousand Oaks, CA: Corwin.

Murphy, C. U., & Lick, D. W. (1998). *Whole-faculty study groups: A powerful way to change schools and enhance learning.* Thousand Oaks, CA: Corwin.

Murphy, C. U., & Lick, D. W. (2001). *Whole-faculty study groups: Creating student-based professional development.* Thousand Oaks, CA: Corwin.

Murphy, C. U., & Lick, D. W. (2005). *Whole-faculty study groups: Creating professional learning communities that target student learning.* Thousand Oaks, CA: Corwin.

Murphy, J. A., Murphy, C. U., Joyce, B., & Showers, B. (1988). The Richmond County school improvement program: Preparation and initial phase. *Journal of Staff Development, 9*(2), 36–41.

National Commission on Excellence in Education. (1983). *A nation at risk: The imperative for educational reform. A report to the nation and the secretary of education, United States Department of Education.* Retrieved January 17, 2007, from http://www.ed.gov/pubs/NatAtRisk/index.html

National School Reform Faculty. (n.d.). "Primer for Looking at Student Work." Retrieved February 19, 2008, from http://www.lasw.org/primer.html

National Staff Development Council. (2001). *Standards for staff development.* Oxford, OH: National Staff Development Council.

North Carolina Department of Public Instruction, Division of Accountability Services/North Carolina Testing Program. (2005). *Grade 4 reading comprehension sample selections and items, test information document.* Retrieved November 17, 2006, from http://www.ncpublicschools.org/accountability/testing/eog/reading/

Office of Technology Assessment, U.S. Congress. (1995). *Teachers and technology: Making the connection.* (OTA-EHR-616,GPO Stock No. 052–003–0149–2). Washington, DC: Author.

Preuss, P. G. (2003). *School leader's guide to root cause analysis: Using data to dissolve problems.* Larchmont, NY: Eye on Education.

Richardson, J. (2005). Springfield program nurtures leadership growth: Multifaceted approach focuses on principals. *The Learning Principal, 1*(2), 1, 6–7.

Ritchhart, R. (2002). *Intellectual character: What it is, why it matters, and how to get it.* San Francisco: Jossey-Bass.

Robinson, V., & Lai, M. K. (2006). *Practitioner research for educators: A guide to improving classrooms and schools.* Thousand Oaks, CA: Corwin.

Roth, S. E. (2005). *Principal leadership to support professional development based on the National Staff Development Council's context standards.* Unpublished doctoral dissertation, University of South Dakota, Vermillion.

Roy, P., & Hord, S. (2003). *Moving NSDC's staff development standards into practice: Innovation configurations.* Oxford, OH: National Staff Development Council.

Sagor, R. (2000). *Guiding school improvement with action research.* Alexandria, VA: Association for Supervision and Curriculum Development.

Sagor, R. (2005). *The action research guidebook: A four-step process for educators and school teams.* Thousand Oaks, CA: Corwin.

Schlechty, P. C. (1990). *Schools for the 21st century: Leadership imperatives for educational reform.* San Francisco: Jossey-Bass.

Schlechty, P. C. (2002). *Working on the work: An action plan for teachers, principals, and superintendents.* San Francisco: Jossey-Bass.

Schmuck, R. (2006). *Practical action research for change* (2nd ed.). Thousand Oaks, CA: Corwin.

Senge, P. (1990). *The fifth discipline: The art and practice of the learning organization.* New York: Currency.

Shannon, G. S., & Bylsma, P. (2004). *Characteristics of improved school districts: Themes from research.* Retrieved January 12, 2007, from http://www.k12.wa.us/research/default.aspx

Sherman, K., & Reynolds-Manglitz, K. (2007). Building commitment. In D. W. Lick & C. U. Murphy (Eds.), *The whole-faculty study groups fieldbook: Lessons learned and best practices from classrooms, districts, and schools* (pp. 94–99). Thousand Oaks, CA: Corwin.

Showers, B., Murphy, C. & Joyce, B. (1996). The river city program: Staff development becomes school improvement. In B. Joyce and E. Calhoun (Eds.), *Learning experiences in school renewal: An exploration of five successful programs.* Eugene, Oregon: ERIC Clearinghouse on Educational Management, 1995. (ERIC Document Reproduction Service No. ED401600)

Spillane, J. P. (2006). *Distributed Leadership.* San Francisco: Jossey-Bass.

Springfield Public Schools. (2002). *School report card.* Retrieved November 14, 2006, from http://www.spstoday.com/images/Links/2002/

Springfield Public Schools. (2005). *School report card.* Retrieved November 14, 2006, from http://spstoday.com/images/Links/

Springfield Public Schools. (2006). *School report card.* Retrieved January 31, 2007, from http://springfieldpublicschoolsmo.org/docs/reportcards/middleschoolreportcards/Cherokee%20Report%20Card%202005-2006.pdf

Springfield Public Schools. (2007). *Missouri Assessment Program (MAP) test results.* Retrieved August 22, 2007, from http://sps.k12.mo.us/depts/research/research%20site%20page%2014.htm

Standard & Poor's. (2005). Outperforming school districts in Missouri, 2002–03. Retrieved March 27, 2008, from http://springfieldpublicschoolsmo.org/Administration/PIO/archive/04_05/april/DistrictOutperforms4-12-05.html.

Tate, M. L. (2003). *Worksheets don't grow dendrites: 20 instructional strategies that engage the brain.* Thousand Oaks, CA: Corwin.

Turning Points. (2001) *Looking collaboratively at student and teacher work.* Retrieved December 29, 2006, from http://www.turningpts.org/pdf/LASW.pdf

Vanzant, L. (1980). *Achievement motivation, sex-role acceptance, and mentor relationships of professional females.* Unpublished doctoral dissertation, East Texas State University, Commerce.

Weick, K. E. (1976). Educational organizations as loosely coupled systems. *Administrative Science Quarterly, 21*(1), 1–19.

Weiskopf, E. (2007a). Implementing study groups for principals. In D. W. Lick & C. U. Murphy (Eds.), *The whole-faculty study groups fieldbook: Lessons learned and best practices from classrooms, districts, and schools* (pp. 34–59). Thousand Oaks, CA: Corwin.

Weiskopf, E. (2007b). Planning and implementing strategies for school improvement. In D. W. Lick & C. U. Murphy (Eds.), *The whole-faculty study groups fieldbook: Lessons learned and best practices from classrooms, districts, and schools* (pp. 208–214). Thousand Oaks, CA: Corwin.

Wiggins, G., & McTighe, J. (1998). *Understanding by design.* Alexandria, VA: Association for Supervision and Curriculum Development.

Wilm, D. C. (2006). *Whole faculty study groups: The journey of district #118 W to reform professional development practices.* Unpublished doctoral dissertation, National-Louis University, Chicago.

Wormeli, R. (2005). *Summarization in any subject: 50 techniques to improve student learning.* Alexandria, VA: Association for Supervision and Curriculum Development.

Index

CORWIN PRESS